COLT ARCHAEOLOGICAL INSTITUTE
PUBLICATIONS

The Excavation of
the Main Theater
at Petra, 1961-1962
Final Report

by

PHILIP C. HAMMOND

BERNARD QUARITCH LTD
11 GRAFTON STREET, NEW BOND STREET, LONDON

MADE AND PRINTED IN GREAT BRITAIN BY
WILLIAM CLOWES AND SONS, LIMITED, LONDON AND BECCLES

CONTENTS

INTRODUCTION

This final report on the 1961–1962 seasons of excavation by the American Expedition to Petra was prepared as soon as possible after the completion of the work in order to make the data available to those interested in the site, its history, and the provincial theater in the Near East.

Chapter I briefly describes the remains of Petra and the location of the city. It also gives a short account of the Nabataeans, their origin and place in the history of this part of the Near East.

Chapter II presents both the background of the expedition and the stratigraphic data secured in the course of its activities. Here, an attempt has been made to inc lude as much relevant data as possible—not only in support of the conclusions reached, but also in order that others may have the information to evaluate those conclusions. Photographic plates, stratigraphic sections, plans and similar visual material are included to make relationships as clear as possible.

Chapter III concerns itself with the primary period of the Theater's history, during which it was built, repaired, and served its architectural function. The separate parts of the structure are considered in detail, in order to furnish as much data as possible on this particular example of the provincial Roman theater type in the Near East. The results of the stratigraphic methods employed in the excavations, based on the techniques developed by Sir Mortimer Wheeler and Dr. K. Kenyon, are seen to have been more than justified in terms of the correlation and interrelationship of data so secured.

Chapter IV describes the Hydraulic System of the Theater and again the stratigraphic method employed permitted the isolation of the drainage system within the *auditorium* area, just outside the *postscenium* wall, as well as their relation to the main building phases of the Theater, itself. Similarly, the isolation of the two sealed pottery deposits, described in Chapter IX, provided further chronological information about the Theater's history, specially for the rebuilding phases of Period I*b* and I*c*.

The chronological conclusions of Chapter V are based on the total data secured in the course of the two seasons, in comparison with published materials, and the author's prior study of Nabataean history, culture, architecture and ceramics. Although no firm epigraphic evidence was uncovered to support those conclusions, the accumulation of their evidence, especially the architectural as seen against the history of the people, would seem to justify them.

The brief section on Miscellaneous Finds, Chapter VI, reflects the paucity of materials commonly found in Syro-Palestinian excavations, with the exception of tomb or grave finds. However, even here, some new information has been secured which may assist in filling other gaps in current knowledge concerning Petra and its monuments. Chapters VII and VIII, on the Greek and Nabataean Epigraphy, are self-explanatory and again provide further materials for research into the history and background of the site and its people. They are of known locations and are related to the over-all chronological problem of the Theater *per se*.

INTRODUCTION

The main products of the two seasons of excavation at the Theater were architectural and stratigraphic in nature with related ceramic information. The latter has been presented in as succinct a form as possible because of the preeminence, in terms of conclusions, of the former two areas. However, in critical phases, more detail on the pottery remains has been given to amplify the picture of that specific phase. Major emphasis, in any case, has been placed upon the period in which the Theater actually functioned as such (Period I), and its complexities, historical and architectural.

Especial thanks are due Dr. 'Awni Dajani, Director of Antiquities, and his department, as well as to General Kerim Ohan, then Director of Public Security (1961), to Mr. Tawfiq Nazzal, Dr. James I. McCord, Mr. James Andrews, Mr. Roy Pfautsch, Margaret L. Hammond, and to many others whose interest, encouragement and active assistance made the work of the American Expedition to Petra possible.

Thanks are also due those who assisted in the final report: Mr. S. Slaby, Chairman of the Department of Graphics, School of Engineering Sciences, Princeton University, for technical and drafting assistance, Mr. Harvey Cahn, Dr. John Hayes, Mrs. Frank Garcia, Miss Constance B. Sayre, and others who gave their time and energy in the production of drawings and final plates, typing, research assistance, and in other ways. To the staff of both seasons, appreciation must also be given for the attention to detail and meticulous care in field work which made analysis of the results possible.

This report is dedicated to Mr. H. Dunscombe Colt, whose name has long been associated with Nabataean studies and whose reputation as a connoisseur and benefactor of art and archaeology needs no further accolade than the scholarly research his philanthropy and interest have made possible through the years.

Princeton, N.J.,
1964.

SPONSORS

1961: Princeton Theological Seminary
Moravian Theological Seminary
American Philosophical Society
The American Council of Learned Societies
American Friends of The Middle East
Peter C. Cornell Trust
The Huber Foundation
The Forum of the Twelve Caesars

1962: The American Philosophical Society
American Friends of The Middle East
Peter C. Cornell Trust
The Huber Foundation
The Wrightson-Switz Foundation
Princeton Theological Seminary

PATRONS

The Reverend Mr. Earl Douglass, Princeton, N.J.
Mr. Bernth Kristian John Eenberg, Brooklyn, New York
Mrs. Virginia Cobb Moll, Jerusalem, Jordan
Mr. J. Paul Getty, Surrey, England
Mr. Warren W. McKeever, Fort Worth, Texas
Mr. Edward K. Love, Jr., St. Louis, Mo.
Mrs. H. Harden, Williamsport, Pa.
Mr. Carl Loven, St. Louis, Mo.
Mr. Tawfig Nazzal, 'Amman, Jordan
Covenant-Central Presbyterian Church, Williamsport, Pa.
Glens Falls Presbyterian Church, U.P.W.A., Glens Falls, N.Y.

STAFF

1961: Dr. Howard Cox, Moravian Theological Seminary
Dr. Jean Davison, University of Vermont
Mr. John Salmon, Princeton Theological Seminary
Mr. Mohammed Murshid, Department of Antiquities of Jordan

1962: Dr. Robert Drews, Vanderbilt University
Mr. John H. Hayes, Princeton Theological Seminary
Mr. Benjamin McLuckie, Uniontown, Pa.
Miss Constance B. Sayre, Barnard College
Mr. Mohammed Murshid, Department of Antiquities of Jordan

I

PETRA AND THE NABATAEANS

1. *The City*

Isolated by the sands of the Transjordanic desert and land-locked to the east and west by towering cliffs of Nubian sandstone, the valley site of ancient Petra has played a role in the military and commercial history of the Near East from very early times. The extent of that role has but recently been realized and appreciated.

The site is some 2700 ft. above sea level, and its bordering cliffs rise another 1000 ft. above the valley floor, which is about a mile wide. Through the valley runs a vague pass, but the main access route is a narrow, twisting cleft in the eastern ridge known as the *Siq*.

Situated at longitude 37° 37′ E. and latitude 30° 19′ N, about 95 miles south of Jerusalem and 60 miles north of Akaba, Petra controls the main north–south arterial land route passing through the area. In the days of the Edomites, as in modern times, this route was followed by caravans of travellers, merchants, and invading armies. As a consequence of the natural defensibility of the site, Petra served as an almost impregnable stronghold for a succession of civilizations. The presence of Edomite pottery, especially on the summit of Jebel Umm il-Biyara which towers over the city site, gives ample proof of the antiquity of such use. The presence of earlier lithic artifacts in and around the site, as well as the Neolithic village at El-Baidha, may even push the occupation of the site well into prehistoric times.

Sometime before the fourth century B.C., the site was occupied by an atypical Bedouin tribe, the Nabaṭu, whose activities ultimately raised the site to its greatest prominence. By 312 B.C., documentary evidence attests to both the presence of the Nabataeans at Petra and to their early commercial enterprises. This commercial interest was accelerated by the internal disorders of the Ptolemaic and Seleucid kingdoms, whose weakness permitted the isolated Nabataean kingdom to grow and consolidate with a minimum of interference. The appearance of Pompey in the Near East, about 64 B.C., in no real way threatened the Nabataeans and they appear to have resisted total Roman domination until the actual entrance of the army of Trajan into the city in A.D. 106. That some degree of Roman control was exerted, is, to be sure, clearly evidenced from a number of sources. During the Greek and Roman periods, Nabataean contact with the Jewish kingdom is recorded, as well, and provides some further data about the people, if not the site.

Following the Roman occupation of the site, Petra and Nabatene declined perceptibly, in spite of colonial honors and local beautification. The Byzantine era was similarly one of decline, with the bishop of 'Petra' seated at Kerak ('The Rock'), not Petra, to be followed by virtual obscurity. A few Byzantine remains are visible at Petra, but almost all represent only re-use of existing monuments, not new construction. Further excavation may well, however, modify that viewpoint considerably. During the early Islamic period, the strategic importance of Petra ceased, not to be revived until the days of the Crusaders. In the latter period, following Baldwin I, Petra revived as a military-commercial center, because of the ancient land routes and was re-used as a part of the great chain of feudal strong-points. The main occupation was outside the ancient city limits, at El Wuei'ra, but secondary defense outposts were established within the ancient site area, also. Following the disastrous battle of the Horns of Hattin, the area of southern Transjordania again reverted to Muslim hands and the strategic nature of the site became meaningless once more. With its importance waned its memory and the site was not rediscovered until August 22, 1812, when Johann Ludwig Burckhardt became the first westerner to enter the Siq since the Crusades.

The Siq was once guarded by a massive barrage which also diverted the flood waters of the neighborhood through a partly artificial tunnel to watercourses circling around the Kubtha range. Overhead aqueducts performed the same function, and possibly were part of a larger hydraulic system. Entering the city via the Siq, one observes a variety of hydraulic remains (including joined pressure pipes), cultic devices, and funerary monuments. It is at the interior mouth of the Siq, however, that the rose-red stone and Nabataean architectural ability are suddenly joined in the magnificent tomb façade known as Khazna Far'un. From that point onward, Nabataean funerary and cultic art abound on every side. The cliffs are dotted with tomb façades from the classical period of Nabataean stone carving. The Theater alone forms the single exception to this rule, just outside the city area, along the main road into the valley site. In the valley area, the remains of a Roman period paved street, with colonnade, side buildings, triumphal gateway, and Roman temple, declare the foreign occupation. At the same time, Nabataean work is apparent and the cliffs, clefts, and side avenues are choked with further Nabataean funerary and cultic specimens. The western face of the Khubtha ridge, bordering the eastern edge of the city area, is filled with a group of tomb façades, known today as the 'Royal Tombs'. Neighboring mountains shelter one of the finest examples of the open-air high place ever discovered, along with numerous specimens, of similar cultic installations of lesser importance. Jebel Ed-Deir, to the north-west, boasts of still another 'royal' type tomb façade, modelled on the Khazna, but less complex. Triclinia and other installations may also be found. Inscriptions are rare, petroglyphs infrequent, but both exist. Hydraulic installations are scattered throughout the valley area, some still functioning today. Aerial stairways, carved into the cliff faces, invite exploration to forgotten monuments. On the valley floor, the tumble of ruins is likewise impressive. Many periods must be represented in these ruins, but the overwhelming presence of the characteristic diagonal dressing of the Nabataean stone-mason is expressive.

Scientific archaeological investigation of Petra has proved to be an arduous task, simply because of the proliferation of ruins and the vast expanse of the area itself. The reports of a series of 'learned travellers' long supplied the only information available about the site. Learning and opinion were inextricably mixed in these reports, and this quasi-factual information still haunts the scientific investigator. Actual excavation on the site only began in 1929. In that year George Horsfield began a series of cuts at various points along the southern area of the ancient city. Following that work, further investigations were conducted, including the excavation of the tomb of the Roman Legate Sextus Florintinus. In 1934 the 'Conway High Place' was excavated, and, in 1936, the Khazna, the Urn-Tomb (Ed-Deir) and the Tomb of the Roman Soldier. Margaret A. Murray and J. C. Ellis conducted a short excavation in 1937.

With the removal of the Mandate Government and the consolidation of the Hashemite Kingdom of the Jordan, a new era of archaeological research began at Petra. In 1954, the Department of Antiquities began restoration and clearing activities which have continued to the present time. Under the supervision of P. J. Parr, Diana Kirkebride, G. Wright, and others, portions of the Roman Street were cleared, part of the colonnade restored, and the Triumphal Gate repaired. In 1955, a party from the American School of Oriental Research in Jerusalem undertook various surface projects on the site. The British School of Archaeology in Jerusalem then began a series of limited excavations from 1958 onward, under the direction of P. J. Parr. This group was joined, for part of a season, by an American group under P. C. Hammond. This was the first stratigraphic work of significance to be conducted in modern times. During two seasons of 1961 and 1962, the American Expedition to Petra cooperated with the Department of Antiquities in the excavation of the Main Theater (see below). From 1963 on, clearance activities have been conducted in various parts of the ancient city site. Throughout the whole period, epigraphic and photographic surveys have been made in and around Petra.

2. The People

The pre-Nabataean inhabitants of Petra—Edomite and others—remain uninvestigated up to the present time. The presence of lithics from Upper Paleolithic and Neolithic times in and around the site, and especially the developed Neolithic village at nearby El-Baidha, indicate further study of this early period is needed. The quantities of Edomite pottery fragments, as well as occasional pieces of complete Iron Age pottery found in the area, fully attest to the presence of occupation of the site during the Iron Age. Again, however, little critical research has been done on this material.

The Nabataeans brought Petra to the height of its prominence, and concerning them a great deal can be gleaned, from Petra, from Coele-Syria and elsewhere.

The precise time of the appearance of this people is lost, but by the end of the fourth century they are fully documented and already in commercial residence at Petra. Sometime in that vague period of Transjordanic unrest and migration which followed the Neo-Babylonian rise to power at the end of the sixth century B.C., a tribal group known as the Nabaṭu came out of the desert. The exact origin of this group is vague, but evidence would seem to point to a southern point of departure. Reputed to have been Red Sea pirates for a brief time, the Nabaṭu turned first to the life of land brigandage and then to that of the caravaner. In the latter role they functioned admirably and by it the commercial kingdom of Nabatene soon flourished.

The first historical note of these people is that of Diodorus Siculus.[1] In it he describes abortive attempts by Antigonus, in 312 B.C., to absorb the Nabataeans fully into the Greek state. Although the 'Rock' was looted by the general, Athenaeus, while the Nabataean males were attending a market, a reprisal ambush virtually wiped out the Greeks departing with their spoil. After a truce was arranged, via a letter 'written in Syrian (Aramaic) letters', Antigonus later sent a second force against Petra under the command of his son, Demetrius Poliorcetes, in the same year. On this occasion, the Nabataeans set their goods 'in the Rock' (presumably Umm il-Biyara, since there was 'only one way up') and the majority sought refuge in the desert. The defenses proving strong—and the chance for loot poor—agreement was reached and the Greeks withdrew. This was the last attempt made to storm the site until the Roman occupation in A.D. 106. More important in the account of Diodorus, however, is the mention of spices, frankincense, and myrrh, as well as the discussion of the Nabataean bitumen industry at the Dead Sea.[2]

To this notice of early commercial importance must also be added Strabo's[3] description of the Nabataeans, said to have been based on the information supplied by one Athenodorus, a philosopher 'who was born among the Petraeans'. In this account the description of the people, as a sedentary commercial nation, differs widely from that of Diodorus, who pictures a semi-nomadic one. Yet Strabo, probably with a bit of hyperbole on the part of Athenodorus, writes glowingly of the riches of the people, locally produced, or imported: gold, silver, spices, copper, iron, purple raiment, storax gum, embossed work, paintings, and molded images.[4]

Side by side with commercial interests, must also be set the agricultural acumen of the Nabataeans, as witnessed by their hydraulic installations. In this latter area, the Nabataeans reached heights only matched by the Romans outside the Near East, and not again reached in the Near East until modern times. The extent of these installations, and hence the agriculture which must have been served by them, has only recently been realized and examined.

Earlier references to the Nabataeans, especially the Targumic identification with Nebayoth (Gen. 25:12, I Chron. 1:29, etc.) can no longer be supported, as the study of Jean Starcky[5] indicates. The same may be said for the alleged 'reference' in the Assurbanipal list of the seventh century B.C.[6]

The next clear references to the Nabataeans (as 'Arabs') comes from a much later time. Nabataean commercial strength had brought with it expansion, and subsequent contact with the Jewish state,[7] the Idumeans,[8] and eventually, the Romans[9] following 64 B.C. Less informative, concerning details, but equally valuable for the historical scene, are the series of inscriptions and other epigraphic materials which stem from about the same period and proliferate from that time on.[10] From about 150 B.C. on, in any case, the Nabataeans were ruled by a king and greatly extended their boundaries, both north and south. Their precise relation to the Romans, in terms of degree of dependency, raises a number of questions, as does the extent of their territory in the north, during the Roman period. Starcky[11] has discussed certain critical developments in the historical picture at some length, and further discussion of it need not be done here.

The high point of Nabataean life, and the real prominence of Petra, seems to lie in the period of Aretas IV (9 B.C.–A.D. 40). This was partly in the period of Herod the Great and Augustus and was a period of great cultural achievement in the ancient world, as well as a period in which the commercial enterprise of the Nabataeans brought them to a peak never achieved before and never to be reached again. As dealers in luxury items along the great land routes, the appetite of Rome provided a ready market, even though certain trade routes had been shifted to lanes between Egypt and Rome.[12] Relations with Rome were more than cordial, even if Aretas seemingly encountered some difficulty concerning his succession. Relations with the Herodian kingdom continued strained on both sides, being only mollified by the establishment of a marriage connection between the royal houses in the days of Herod Antipas. This arrangement fell apart with the disruption of that marriage, in about A.D. 27, with a subsequent renewal of hostilities.[13] Aretas IV was able to keep Roman favor throughout his reign, however. Even an attempt to re-establish Nabataean control over the area beyond the Sea of Tiberias, did not seem to have affected the Nabataean position adversely. Whether Damascus was controlled by Aretas IV after the death of Tiberius (cf. II Cor. 11:32), is, however, a moot question.[14]

Following Aretas IV, the people and the city fell into decline, as noted above. Although documentation is meagre, little is reported of major contributions made even by Rabbel II, whose thirty-six-year reign pales into insignificance beside that of his predecessor of like years. Starcky suggests the effects of Roman economic policy as a possible source for this situation, although capitulation to Roman culture, in general, may also be seen: e.g. the new capital at Boṣra, where both Malichus II (A.D. 40–70) and Rabbel II (A.D. 70–106) luxuriated.[15]

Thus it was that A. Cornelius Palma, Syrian legate of Trajan, occupied Petra in A.D. 106, bringing to an end, for all practical purposes, Nabataean history and culture, and whatever quasi-independence the Kingdom of Nabatene had enjoyed up to that point.[16] Boṣra became the capital of the new province of Arabia, and, before long, Petra was no longer of any great significance. Elevated to the rank of *colonia*, graced by the tomb of Sextus, and refurbished in Roman fashion, the city soon was but a hollow shell of its former prominence. Palmyra became the trade center of the Roman world in the near East, military strategy no longer demanded Petra's command of the trade routes, so the city lost the two major reasons for its earlier existence.

This is not to say that Nabataeans, or Nabatene, simply ceased to exist in A.D. 106 but rather that both were absorbed in the greater sphere of the Empire and lost their special identity. Nabataean inscriptions continue to be found, dating as late as the early fourth century A.D., but even the characteristic language underlying the Nabataean script is lost.[17] Nabataean cult festivals are reported as late as the third century A.D., as well. In point of fact, part, at least, of the Nabataeans, as a specific group, probably melted back into the great tribal bodies of Arabs, wherein their characteristic accomplishments were reemployed, but became anonymous. Others readjusted themselves to the Empire and found their places among its other people, likewise anonymously.

That the over all foreign artistic culturization of Nabatene was Hellenistic can be seen from a number of directions: numismatically, architecturally, and ceramically. That this cultural influence should have been the most coercive is evident from the remains. That this foreign artistic influence was strongly modified by a vital indigenous culture is also evident. That truly Roman influence also entered the picture, especially in the Augustan era (i.e. the time of Aretas IV) is also definite. That other influences, (e.g. Parthian) a bit less strongly marked, were also at work may be seen in the eclectic nature of all phases of Nabataean life and artifacts, as well.[18]

II

THE MAIN THEATER AT PETRA

A. EARLIER REPORTS

Certain reports of earlier visitors to Petra note the presence of two theaters on the site. The remains of one are indicated as having been seen along the bank of Wadi Musa, close to the main site of the ancient city. These remains, if they indeed were of a theater, have virtually disappeared and little interest has ever been paid to them architecturally. The remains of the other theater, variously referred to as the 'Roman' or 'Main' Theater, however, have always elicited a great deal more attention, because of their state of preservation and size. The designation 'Main Theater', therefore, is used herein simply to avoid confusion with earlier studies referring to the remains which have disappeared and also to relieve the main theater site of its previously acquired designations of 'Greek amphitheater' or 'Roman Theater', which are misnomers in the strictest sense.

The Main Theater lies just inside the 'Outer Siq' of Petra, on the left as one enters the principal approach to the actual city site. At this point the Wadi broadens into a small valley, with the El-Khubtha ridge, through which the Siq makes its entrance, on the east, and the lesser height of El-Madhbaḥ on the west. The Main Theater has been carved and built into the western cliffs, which provided not only the locus, but a backdrop of unsurpassed magnificence.

The exact location of the Main Theater can be specified, geographically, since its *orchestra* marks the juncture of 30° 19′ N latitude and 35° 20′ E longitude. The elevation of the general area, as shown on Musil's plan of the city, is 955 m. (see Plate I).[1]

The Main Theater at Petra was noted by Johan Burckhardt[2] in his journal entry marking the rediscovery of the site on August 22, 1812: 'to the left is a theatre cut entirely out of the rock, with all its benches. It may be capable of containing about three thousand spectators: its area is now filled up with gravel, which the winter torrent brings down . . . there are no remains of columns near the theatre.'

To this account, Irby[3] contributed the information that the diameter of the podium was 120 ft., the number of seat rows thirty-three, and that no *vomitoria* existed, as well as noting four column bases in the area. Robinson[4] ventured to raise the seating capacity of the visible *cavea* above the estimate of Burckhardt, and also commented on the 'row of small chambers' excavated above the *cavea* 'looking down upon the scene below'. Kinnear[5] related these to the upper gallery and added that 'several doors' led into them. These 'chambers' continued to draw attention, as 'loges reservées pour des personnages distingués',[6] or as 'private boxes' for royalty and for the guests of the city',[7] even after Lenoire,[8] among others, called attention to their relation to other tombs in the area. Bertou[9] took issue with Burckhardt's seating estimate, accused him of exaggeration, and revised the number of possible spectators down to only 1200! This revision Kinnear[10] ignored, and suggested, in turn, room for between three and four thousand. Perhaps Morris[11] is responsible for the initial reference of the Theater to the Greek amphitheater type, as it sometimes is called, even today, for he speaks of it rising, 'like the Greek theaters', in 'amphitheatrical form'. Wilson[12] continued this mistake by his reference to 'the great open amphi-theatre'—and extravagantly described its wonders, concluding that it was 'reckoned that the theater could easily accommodate, at one time, five thousand of the votaries of pleasure, who might make it their resort'. Visconti[13] hurled more confusion into the picture by suggesting that the use of the installation included its being a *naumachia*—filled by water led through the Siq.

To the mass of interesting, but often confusing, verbal description of the Theater at Petra, was added an equally interesting collection of sketches and detailed drawings of the visible (and invisible) plan. These range from hasty jottings to involved architectural plates. Perhaps the most artistic of these was the drawing of Leon de Laborde (*Journey Through Arabia Petraea*, French Edition, Paris, 1830, (Plate II, 1), the first published drawing known. David Roberts also included one in his famous portfolio of Near Eastern sketches.[14] The plan of Alois Musil[15] presents a Greek auditorium, with four *cunei* in the *cavea*. The plan of Wiegand[16] was the most accurate published up to the present time, however (Plate II). Using surface indications, Wiegand was able to reconstruct most of the *scaena* and *postscenium* features.

With the advent of photographic surveys, Petra and its monuments were subjected to close scrutiny because of the architectural interest, soon to be followed by photographic coverage elicited by the natural beauty of the site *per se*. As a result of the accuracy achieved in this manner, the misapprehensions concerning the Theater, created by much of the earlier descriptive reports, have been reduced. However, it was not until actual excavation was possible on the site that a complete and accurate survey, architecturally and historically, could be achieved. It was to this task that the work of the American Expedition to Petra was committed.

B. THE AMERICAN EXPEDITION TO PETRA

The American Expedition spent two seasons, during the summers of 1961 and 1962, working at the Main Theater for a total of 134 days.[17] Although the Expedition was an independent body, the work was done in close cooperation with the Department of Antiquities of the Hashemite Kingdom of Jordan.[18] The staff was housed, during both seasons, in the tomb-caves in Jebel El-Habis, inside the ancient city site. Labor was recruited from the local Bedouin tribe, the Bedul, with the assistance of the tribal sheikh, Selim es-Salami.

Prior to the beginning of work on the Theater itself, excavations were undertaken at the tomb-cave site called El-Khan between Petra and El-Ji. This installation was to be cleared for tourism purposes and the request was made by the Department of Antiquities that a scientific sounding be made in the courtyard prior to the clearance operations. It was felt that this could provide valuable training for both staff and labor before work began on the Theater area proper. A 5-m. square was therefore opened in the forecourt of the site and carried to bedrock. The stratigraphy dated the area to re-use during the Medieval Arabic period, following primary Nabataean use and subsequent disuse. The façade of the cave was also planned, as a field exercise.

During the excavation of El-Khan, a preliminary photographic survey was made of the Theater site, both as a record of the state of the installation before excavation, and as a guide to the strategy of the excavation (Plate XIII. 1, 2, 3—stages in excavation). Upon completion of the work at El-Khan, operations were shifted to the Theater, on the basis of the surveys conducted. It was noted, in the preliminary surveys, that many discrepancies existed in the published literature concerning the site. Because of the ruined condition of the *scaena*, and the depth of debris over most of it, previously published plans were misleading. The *vomitoria* were almost completely sub-surface and were generally overlooked. Ruins of the *tribunalia(e)* and related features were also not previously noted, along with the remains of passage blockades high on the cliffs at each side of the *auditorium*. The drainage systems of the installation also had escaped the notice of previous visitors, in spite of the obvious presence of remains along the *praecinctio* of the *media cavea*, along the upper gallery of the *summa cavea*, less obviously along the topmost gallery above the latter, and along the line of the *postscenium* wall in front of the installation.

Prior to the arrival of the American Expedition, the Department of Antiquities began a preliminary clearing of the *orchestra*. This assisted the work, in terms of the removal of surface debris, although it introduced some minor problems of stratigraphic control. These latter were resolved by the interlocking of trenches, and by the careful correlation of strata so that complete section drawings were possible, from modern surface to the bedrock floor of the *orchestra* extending from the *frons scaenae* to the seats of the *ima cavea* and ultimately through the entire *postscenium* complex.

The primary aim of the 1961 season was the determination of the stratigraphic history of the Theater proper. The approximate diameter of the *orchestra* was calculated as the basis for trench lines across the *auditorium*-stage areas. Trench lines, 3 m. wide, were laid out perpendicular to the diameter of the *orchestra*, from the center *itinera* of the *cavea*, to the intersection with the probable diameter of the *orchestra* at the face of the *finitio proscenii*. This trench was then continued eastward until the surface remains of the main doorway of the *scaenae frons* was reached. A third trench was laid out 1.50 m. wide on each side of the probable *orchestra* diameter previously determined, at right angle to the two above. These three trenches constituted the main exploration areas in the initial phase of the excavation, and were designated I.1 (from the *scaena frons* to the N–S intersection with the *orchestra* diameter), I.2 (from that juncture to the *cavea*, westward along the same line), and I.3 (the N–S trench along the line of the *orchestra* diameter). Each trench had a definite objective: I.1 was designed to determine and clarify the stage-depth area from the *scaena frons* to the *finitio proscenii;* I.2 was to establish the extent of the *ima cavea* and the stratigraphy of the *orchestra* debris; and I.3 was the control trench for both plan and stratigraphy, as well as the one which was ultimately to relate all other stratigraphy to the *vomitorium sinistrum*, the face of which it bisected (see Plan—Plate Folder C).

In order to correlate all strata to the modern surface level, and to the eventual stratigraphy related to the *postscenium* complex, one further extension was necessitated. The previous clearance by the Department of Antiquities had stripped the surface level from the *orchestra*-stage area, reaching the stage pavement in the southern section, clearing the *vomitorium dextrum* completely, but leaving stratigraphic connection with modern surface to be made at the northern side, beyond the *vomitorium sinistrum*. As a consequence, therefore, Trench I.4 was opened, extending from the northern end of I.3 across the face of the *vomitorium sinistrum*, eastward to the north door of the *scaenae frons*. This also helped to verify the stratigraphy of I.1 as well but, more importantly, carried the entire stratigraphic relation up to modern surface, thus linking and correlating all the other levels to bedrock and providing a relational point for subsequent excavation through the *postscenium* complex (Plates Folder, A1, A2, B1. Section Drawings).

Following the excavation in these trenches, the entire northern sector of the stage was cleared stratigraphically in order to secure a complete picture of the paving, sub-paving, and the details of the *hyposcenium*. This clearance was done in a series of area trenches designated I.5, I.6, and I.7, extending in that order, from the side of I.4 to I.1. After the section drawings of all levels in the main trenches had been made, the stage and *scaenae frons* were planned, in a preliminary way, along with visible lines of the still unexcavated *postscenium*. This preliminary planning permitted analysis—mathematically, stylistically, and architecturally—of those areas, pending final clearance.

The 1962 season had a dual objective: the completion of the entire stratigraphic analysis, via excavation; and, of equal importance, the complete planning of the structure and its related features. The planning operation was begun first and started with the southern sector, working northward. The upper complexes of the outer barrier walls were planned, along with a reasonable section of the *cavea*. The *vomitorium dextrum* was completely planned, as well as a section drawing made of its passageways. The *scaena*-stage area was planned in detail, along with necessary parts of the *orchestra* floor. The northern sector of extra-*auditorium* walls was planned, again with necessary parts of the *cavea* at that end. The interior of the *vomitorium sinistrum* was not planned, in view of its incompleted (anciently) nature, and the data recovered from the *vomitorium dextrum*. Finally, a section was made of the *cavea* and upper galleries in order to present a complete section through the entire theater.

Upon completion of the planning, excavation was resumed. A series of related trenches were laid out against the cliff side in the northern sector, proceeding eastward through the *postscenium* complex to just beyond the remains of a canal drain partly visible on the surface. Because of visible and assumed wall lines, these trenches were designated I.21, I.21A, I.22A, I.22B. I.21A was directly against the cliff face at a point calculated to bisect the outer exit of the *vomitorium sinistrum*. I.22A/B led across the probable *postscenium* walls, bisecting probable exit doors, and through the drainage system noted above. Excavation subsequently justified the positioning of the trenches, as anticipated features appeared at or near the locations calculated. The stratigraphic work was seriously hampered, however, by the presence of heavy fall from the upper (extra-*auditorium*) complexes from the cliffs above. Heavy blocks protruded from the trench sides, especially near the mouth of the *vomitorium*, causing considerable difficulty, from the standpoint of safety, as work, progressed in depth (see Plan, Plate Folder C.).

Stratigraphic discontinuity was also a troublesome factor (see below), since this area of the Theater had not lent itself so readily to subsequent re-use, and gaps therefore existed. The stratigraphy of the 1961 season furnished guidance at this point, and reconciliation of total stratigraphy was made possible (Plate Folder B2. Section Drawing).

At the same time, further work was undertaken on the stage area, in order to complete the stratigraphy there, especially in regard to the Period of Main Use (see below) of the Theater, as such. The *auleum* slot on the northern end of the stage was excavated (I.23), in order to secure a complete picture of the method by which the curtain was lowered, and to investigate

2

the possibility of remains of its machinery. The first objective was gained, but no machinery remains were recovered. Next, excavation was continued behind the central niche of the *finitio proscenii* to unravel the periods of rebuilding obvious there from the 1961 season (I.25). As a result of this operation, further details of the *hyposcenium* were uncovered, as well as indubitable evidence concerning the periods of Phase I (see below). Finally, excavation was conducted at the northernmost edge of the *finitio proscenii*, (I.24), beneath the pavement, to investigate the *hyposcenium* at that point. This excavation produced no evidence concerning the *hyposcenium*, but did produce startling data relating to an unanticipated modification of the *finitio proscenii* completely masked by subsequent rebuilding in the orthostat-facing period. A sealed deposit at that point also provided further data relating to the chronological relationships of the rebuildings of Phase I. As a result of the two seasons of stratigraphic excavation, a total of some 269 main strata were isolated. These were then phased into eight clearly defined periods, from ancient to most recent (for all periods, refer to Plates III–IV. Schematic Analysis):

I. Period of Main Use—the period in which the Theater was put to its designated use as a place of entertainment.

II. Period of Early Re-use—this period may be divided into two parts (a) and (b). It is characterized by a triple rebuild wall over the lower parts of the *ima cavea* and an intrusive drain canal cut into the stage pavement, with some of the pavement, especially over the rear area of the center niche, removed. The Theater was now no longer used, as such, and the installation was put to another purpose.

III. Period of Dis-use, Pre-Fall—this period may also be subdivided into parts (a) and (b) on the basis of pottery sterility in the lower levels.

IV. Main Destruction Period—the cataclysmic fall of the Theater *scaena* took place at this time, along with the destruction of related (main) complexes and parts of the rebuildings of Period II above. Destruction was complete, even though the lowest *podia* and wall levels of the *scaenae frons* remained standing. The *episcenium* was completely destroyed, and the fall of all parts destroyed at this time appears simultaneous.

V. First Period of Dis-use, Post-Fall—this period is that in which the destruction debris of Period IV was covered by obvious and characteristic alternating levels of water-laid and wind-drifted soil.

VI. First Period of Re-use, Post-Fall—this period may be subdivided, (a) and (b), on the basis of internal and ceramic evidences. It is chiefly characterized by the building of a massive robbery wall, followed by the successive addition of less sturdy extensions, roughly along the line of the *finitio proscenii*, parallel to the *scaenae frons*.

VII. Second Period of Re-use, Post-Fall—this period represents occupation subsequent to the robbery wall phase (Period VI), but appears to represent only chance, casual, and occasional re-use, without definite purpose. A destruction of previously untoppled wall lines appears to have taken place at the end of this period.

VIII. Second Period of Dis-use, Post-Fall—this final period in the history of the Theater area goes to modern surface and generally shows neglect of the site, except for transit and other purposes.

Period I will be considered in detail in the following chapter, therefore analysis of the phases will begin with Period II. The levels noted for each phase are numbered upon the section drawings (Plates Folder A1, 2, B1.), with the appropriate trench designations as noted above. Schematic Tables of phased levels, by Period, will also be found for reference purposes in relation to the section drawings and text (Plates, III, IV). Pottery and other finds noted in the discussion will be found on the Plates, as specified.

C. STRATIGRAPHY OF THE MAIN THEATER: PERIODS II–VIII.

Period II: Period of Early Re-use

This period seems to have followed immediately upon the disuse of the Theater as a place of public entertainment, but well before extensive deterioration took place, especially in the case of the *scaenae frons*. Essentially the period is a building phase (IIb), but this building phase rests, in part, on the brief succession of wash-drift debris (IIa). This part of the general period ought, ordinarily, to be considered separately as a non-occupational period in itself. However, its apparent brevity, as indicated by accumulation, and its indistinctness over the entire area, permit its consideration with the higher levels, as a composite sub-phase.

It is only over the stage area (I.1 (18)), between walls 1–2 (I.2) and in I.22a (22), that definite tracing of the drift-wash prebuilding part of the general period can be achieved. On the stage, the single level assigned to this phase is sandy to muddy in constitution and was conspicuous for its heavy concentration of Roman, Nabataean-Roman sherds. Between walls 1–2 (I.2) no characteristic sherds appear. Further, the lower of the two levels at this point (I.2 (23)) seems more like an actual plastering over the lower *ima cavea* (grey, thick, mortar consistency, with charcoal grits and some stones) and may actually represent the foundation preparation for IIb, itself. In I.21 (27) a thin red sandy (drift ?) level appears assignable to this part of the phase, along with some lower parts of level (20). In I.22A, level (22), a brown, hard-packed level also is assignable here.

Period IIb is the more important division of the Period, and represents a firm building phase. This building phase is particularly evident in eight contemporary levels (I.2 (24/28), (25), (26), (27), (8/6/5)) which form a triple-faced filled rubble wall over the lowest part of the *ima cavea* and its junction with the *orchestra* floor (Plate V, 1, 2, 3, 4, Plate VI, 1). This triple wall (I.2, Wall 2A-B-C) is roughly 2 m. in total thickness, with its faces filled behind with debris (Plate VII, 1). The eastern face is semi-dressed and battered. The building of this wall over the *ima cavea*, along with the fill of the build (i.e. small column drums, building blocks, and small architectural debris), clearly indicates a robbing phase post-dating the actual use of the Theater, but at the same time clearly pre-dating any extensive fall. The soil filling of the faces is generally all red sandy soil containing some Nabataean/Roman thin ware sherds. In addition to the triple-faced wall, however, other features of this part of the building period are also significantly evident. When the *postscenium* outer doorway was excavated, it was found to have been blocked by a poorly laid rubble fill (I.22B (2)), which can only belong to this period (Plate VI, 3, 4). This fact gives further evidence that no great deterioration of the Theater had occurred during the time between Period I and Period IIa.

On the stage, as well, other features of this period are obvious. The *scaenae frons* Main Door showed blocking (Plate VI, 1), in the same manner as had the *postscenium* exit noted above. This blocking was elusive, because of proximity to the eroded and robbed modern surface, which may also explain why the blocking was not detected in the other *scaena* door excavated. Still another feature of the period is an intrusive drain (?) canal crossing the lowest step of the Main Door of the *scaenae frons* and cut into the pavement of the stage, itself (Plate VI, 1, 2, Plate VII, 2). It is shallow, slightly curved in line, about 7 cm. wide and extends about 3.90 m. west of the stair over which it emerges. Flat edging slabs mark its course. Whether or not this canal was plastered could not be determined because of the presence of fall debris within it. The precise use of this canal also could not be determined, but appears to have served as a drain (into the *hyposcenium*?) during the re-use of the complex represented by the rubble walls.

The fall of the upper courses of the triple-faced wall coincides with the main fall of the Theater (Period IV), as the section drawings clearly indicate (Plate Folder A1).

In the stage trenches (I. 4, 5, 6, 7, 23B, and 25), no clear distinction between Periods II and V could be determined because of the force and impact of the fall debris which also filled the rear of the central niche of the *finitio proscenii* (I.23-B) and the *auleum* slot, as well as other factors. As a result the levels of these trenches can only be considered with Period V. In I.21-A, Period IIb was absent, because of location.

Sherds from this dual period were particularly rich, in both IIa and IIb, in terms of thin ribbed wares. In IIa, thin common ribbed wares were in high concentration. In the building fill, the thin wares again predominated, all of Nabataean/Roman types. The *postscenium* wall filling (I.22b (2)) also produced similar sherds. Fine thin red ware fragments, a few Nabataean painted ware fragments, one fine thin Nabataean red ware fragment with impressed design, and a few bits of ribbed cooking pot types emerged, along with a piece of drain tile (rounded).

Period III: Period of Dis-use

With the discontinuance of the re-use complex noted in Period II, there followed a period of architectural disuse, although the presence of ceramic materials in the upper half of the period (IIIb) indicates that the area was not ignored in the general traffic of the site.

Period IIIa is composed of a series of ceramically sterile, generally wash-drift levels, whose presence can be detected over most of the entire area. The sterility of these levels is a point in fact against extensive wash-in of sherds, hence suggesting that the presence of sherds in other levels indicates occupational traffic, if not functional use. The alternation of sandy and muddy levels show the clear alternation of seasonal climatic change in the area. It is not considered probable, however, that chronological conclusions may be drawn on the basis of any level count, because of the penetration of drift by wash waters and the drying of wash levels.

The apparent absence of Period IIIa indications in I.2, 3 and the impossibility of differentiating between Periods II and III in I.22A, B, 23B, and 25 may be explained by location. In I.2, 3 the open basin of the *orchestra* could not be expected to accumulate as much of either wash spill (over the edge of the stage, from the *wadi* to the east) nor of the wind-borne drift (which scattered itself, instead of piling against wall lines). In I.2, however, both spill-wash and wind-borne fill could be checked against the stage front and accumulate. In I.23B and 25, the presence of heavy accumulations of wash-drift levels would tend to place them in IIIa, with no place for rebuild indications (IIb), and no sure way to differentiate them from similar preceding levels (IIa), but the intrusion of heavy fall forces the assignment of all levels there to Period V. As a consequence, these eleven levels must be labelled as Periods IIa–V, but the strong probability is that they do represent IIIa/b (?) to V accumulations.

The case of Period IIIb levels is quite different, however. Heavy sherd concentrations appear in levels which are also wash-drift in nature, but whose surface strata appear to have been a floor level, from which penetration of sherds originated. In no case are the levels particularly deep except against wall lines, where accumulation is again to be expected. This floor level may be traced over the entire area because upon it rested the debris from the main destruction (Period IV) and by which identification and reconciliation of related levels is possible.

The comparative sameness of ceramic fragments between Periods IIb and IIIb would suggest that no great chronological span intervened between the re-use period, the accumulations of drift and wash, and the floor level aspect of Period IIIb.

In Period IIIb, thin, fine, and coarse-ribbed ware sherds appeared in great abundance, as did heavy common ware sherds, and a high concentration of fine, thin, Nabataean plain ware fragments. Extremely rare were fine Nabataean painted ware pieces (2 in I.1 (13)–(12)). Yellow-beige slipped fragments of heavy common ware, with combed decoration (as in Period I, b–c) were likewise found, but were uncommon (see Plate LII, 2). The horizontal loop handle (Plate LV, 2) is seen by Kelso (*AASOR* XXIX–XXX, p. 30, type 'c') as Late Roman; cf. also James Pritchard (*AASOR* XXXII–XXXIII, Plate 41, #6); the Period IIIb rims appear to be continuing forms and are all sharply defined.

The presence of plaster debris in I.1 (20), at the bottom of Period IIIb, would indicate that weathering deterioration had begun to take its toll of the *scaenae frons*, even prior to the fall of Period IV.

Reference to the section drawings will show the relation of the various levels of this Period as shown on the Schematic Table of Phases (Plate Folder A1. Plate III).

Period IV: Period of Main Destruction

The main destruction level of the Theater was quite obvious, stratigraphically, once it had been reached. A great deal of care was therefore given to its removal in order to provide data concerning the original build of the *scaenae frons*, and particularly in regard to the detail of the *episcenium*. The lines of the fall, the extent of the fall, and the makeup of the fall were therefore carefully isolated in order to recover the maximum amount of architectural data (Plate IV).

There can be no doubt about the fact that the entire *scaena* was cataclysmically destroyed at one time, and hence that the Theater as a whole suffered that fate. The depth and superimposition of the fall, the rigidity of the architectural makeup, along with its extent along the entire *scaenae frons* line, as well as its subsequent stratigraphic relations, make this conclusion unquestionable (Plates Folder A1, A2–B1.).

The contents of the destruction period levels (see Table and Plate IV) was composed of expected debris: building blocks, fill rubble, cement, cement fill (e.g. sherds with cement adhering, indicating use), architectural blocks (frieze and cornice pieces), inscriptional material, bronze pins and iron nails used in facing, marble and breccia facings (*crustae*), moldings, column bases, column drums, capitals, tile (*tegulae*), and similar materials.

Materials tended to group themselves in the fall debris by original function, as well. Thus rows of column drums, with bases and capitals, some in numbered and lettered order, could be isolated in certain areas; marble facings tended to group near the *scaenae frons* and especially the niches; inscriptions, cornice and frieze pieces grouped both horizontally and in terms of fall height distances.

SCHEMATIC DISTRIBUTION TABLE

PERIOD IV—PERIOD OF MAIN DESTRUCTION

Distribution lines at approximate distances from *scaenae frons*.
b = bases; cd = column drums; cap = capitals; c = cornice blocks; (c = cornice corners; f = frieze blocks; insc = inscription fragments: general building blocks not indicated

```
                                    scaenae frons
                          _____            _____

            b insc   cd                6 m.
                     cd                         b c f    cd
    1 m.             cd                                  cd
                     cd                7 m.              cd
                     cd                        cap       cd
    2 m.   (c        cd                                  cd
                     cd cd             8 m.              cd
                     cd cd                      b        cd
    3 m.   insc cap cd cd (c f c                b        cd
            insc     cd                9 m.              cd
                     cd                         cap b    cd
    4 m.   b c f     cd insc                             cd
                     cd               10 m.              cd
                     cd                                  cd
    5 m.   (c f c    cd                                  cd
                     cd               11 m.              cd
```

Thus composition, in general, and in terms of parts of the order, could be analyzed. Specific detail concerning these materials, as they pertain to the order involved, will be discussed under Period I, but certain general details of fall distribution may be noted here.

Fall Distribution Ranges

Building blocks: heavy over entire range of stage area excavated, extending to c. 12.8 m. from *scaenae frons*, but slanting down and decreasing from *scaenae frons*.

Marble facings and moldings: over entire range excavated, very heavy near niches; breccia especially in niche areas.

Columns (bases, drums, capitals): heavy over entire stage area excavated; column lines, in order (up to six) numbered (marl) or unnumbered (hard grey stone) isolated: extended from *scaenae frons* 0–3.1 m., 2–5.1 m., and 6.5–10.8 m.; drum marked '2' and drums marked '5' and '6', c. 10.8 m. from *scaenae frons* would seem to indicate extent of fall of columns at extreme distance; related bases at 0, 3.8, 6.5, 8.5–9.5 m.; related capitals at c. 5 m., 3 m., 7.5 m., and 8.9 m.; two plastered drums, smaller diameter at 6.4 and 6.9 m.; 'Ionic' type capital at 1.8 m.; bases at c. 8.15–9.5 m.

Cornice pieces: heavy concentration over range of stage area excavated; horizontal extension, peaks at 2 m., 3 m., 4 m., 5 m., and 6.5–7.0 m. from *scaenae frons*; with possible peaks at 5 m. and 6.5 m.

Frieze (plain) blocks: concentration over entire range of stage excavated; peaks at 3 m. and 4 m. from *scaenae frons*, with possible peaks at 5 m. and 6.5 m.

Inscribed blocks: concentration spread over range of area, but grouped concentrations at 0–0.5 m. near the first northern niche and Main Door areas; in heavy concentration at 3 m. and 3.5 m. opposite first northern side door, and Main Door northern outset, these showing red paint in lines; again heavy concentration at c. 4.5 m. opposite Main Door.

Bronze pins: especially frequent near edge of *scaenae frons*, as would be expected from use with lower facings.

Iron Nails and brackets: brackets rare, at c. 0.5 m., and 5 m., only; nails near *scaenae frons*.

Thus certain relationships may be seen emerging from the fall material, which are relevant to the order and arrangement of the *episcenium* (see Period I).

The fall debris is so positioned that a simultaneous destruction of all parts must be postulated, as was noted above. This general destruction can only be attributed to natural causes. Hence it must be seen as the result of one of the earthquakes which periodically rock the Near East. The magnitude of the fall must necessitate narrowing down the destruction to one of the *major* earth tremors, as well. In addition, the chronological search among major earthquakes must also consider the relationship of ceramic remains associated with the fall and the strata overlaying it. In this regard, it is to be noted that much thin ribbed ware was used as cement filler, along with coarser wares and some Nabataean fine, thin, painted (red) wares, along with occasional Nabataean (rosette and slash) lamp fragments. Little, if any, Nabataean fine, thin, *black* painted ware was so used. In the cover levels (Period V) especially, Nabataean fine, thin, painted *and* black-painted wares appear, along with Nabataean lamp fragments of the same type noted above, and rare *terra sigillata* sherds (see Plates LIII, 1. LIV, 1).

Hence there is some indication of chronological proximity between the original building period (Period I) and the immediate post-fall period (Period V)—and hence the destruction period.

The range of possible earthquakes to which this destruction might be assigned does, of course, extend over a considerable chronological span. In terms of severity, however, the number of possible tremors sufficiently intense to cause such widespread destruction is considerably narrowed.[19] In view of the numismatic evidence of Period V, the cover of the fall, and the stratigraphy of Periods VII–VIII, where destruction is also evident, the earlier part of the possible dating range, on the basis of earth tremor, would seem indicated. Of the possible earthquakes, therefore, those of A.D. 130, 365, 419, 447, 551, 631–2, 658, 672 and 746/48 would be the only ones probably severe enough to have caused the destruction. Chronologically, the earthquake of A.D. 130 would seem too early, in view of the span indicated by Periods II–III. The numismatic evidence of Period V, although admittedly scant, would seem to be contemporary with the immediate fall cover—hence the closest earthquake would be that of A.D. 365. The debris accumulation of Periods V, VI and VII would then be sufficient to explain the chronological span necessary to meet the requirements for the destruction of remaining wall lines seen between Periods VII–VIII (below). Likewise, this date would not be out of line with the (scant) evidence of Period VI (see below).

As was noted previously, the destruction of the Period I remains of the Theater was also accompanied by the partial dislocation of the upper parts of the triple-faced robbery wall of Period II (Wall 2A-B-C, in Trench I.2), as will be seen on the section drawings (Plate Folder A1).

Period V: Period of Dis-use, Post-fall

This period is composed of some 112 strata, and represents a fairly long period of general disuse. Characteristic of the period are the alternate levels of wash and drift, most obvious in the more open areas (e.g. I.1, 2, 3, I.21/A, 22A, and even in I.25, I.23/B). These strata are quite distinct in excavation and section because of the hardness of the wash levels and the sandy nature of the drift accumulations (Plates Folder A1, 2, B1, IV).

The difference to be seen in the number of strata discernible in the different parts of the complex that have been related to this period lies in the fact that the basin-like *orchestra* and the narrowness of the *aulium* slot and related sub-stage openings trapped enough deposit each time to produce a traceable level, while the stage pavement area, being both elevated and open, failed to retain traceable indications of actual count. The stage area, in particular, is further complicated by the presence of the fall debris (Period IV) of the main destruction. The strata of the period as a whole form the direct cover of the Period IV debris, and of the minor fall dislocations of the triple-faced wall of Period II, and effectively seal the single phase of total destruction over the site.

The period is itself capped by a hard-packed floor, resulting from the use of the entire area in the next phase.

The pottery of this period is homogeneous in make-up over all parts of the complex (Plates LIII, 1, 2; LIV, 1, 2). In virtually every excavated area, a heavy concentration of thin ribbed fragments of typical Roman/Nabataean type appeared, in association with plain Nabataean thin wares, thin coarse wares, and lesser quantities of heavier, coarse, common wares. Significant also is the presence of black-painted later Nabataean sherds, a few *terra sigillata* fragments (I.2 (11), I.23B (3), I.22B (4)), glass fragments (I.3 (7A), I.25 (3), (5)) and Nabataean lamp fragments of the rosette and and slash pattern (I.2 (11), I.3 (6) (7A). I.4 (2)). Equally significant is the fact that many fragments were coated with mortar, indicating that they belong with Period IV as part of the mortar binding of Period I. That similar fragments appear both *with* and *without* mortar traces thus indicates that the upper levels of this period (i.e. above the wash-drift sequences) were not chronologically far apart, in spite of the duration of the period as a whole. Hence, the period spans a time sequence during which wares continued to be used similar, but later than, the wares used to fill the mortar of Period I. This would therefore seem to indicate that Periods II–III were still periods of the use of Nabataean pottery types, even if in a decline period as evidenced by the disuse and re-use noted above, and that the destruction occurred *before* those types, and particularly related Roman types, completely disappeared from use. Hence, after the Roman occupation in A.D. 106 and following, the local factories continued at least the fine, thin, ribbed wares known earlier and related, ultimately to Roman common thin wares. The complete absence of distinctly Byzantine or Arabic wares seems to further support this indication. Handles from this period range from Early to Late Roman, with some probably to be placed at the latter end of that range. The later appearing examples show no traces of cement, and hence probably must belong to Period V, proper. The ridged elliptical handles Kelso, (*op. cit.*, p. 30) sees as Early Roman, but these may have continued, especially in outlying areas. The same forms appeared in Period I (b) as well. Thus some of the materials from the fall cover represent either continuing forms (i.e. into Period V use), or Period I (a) fall debris. The number of other sherds which strongly resemble Period I (including I (c)) examples would tend to suggest this (e.g. the black painted, fine, thin Nabataean pieces identified with I (c), especially the 'marl' combed ware, *terra sigillata*, and especially the Nabataean lamp fragments whose first century A.D. range is definite). Where cement is present on such sherds their assignment to Period I is unquestionable. However, weathering, as well as the processing of excavated sherds, may, in some cases, have removed cement traces, placing Period I sherds in doubt.

On the other hand, the fact of wash levels suggests the possibility of earlier sherds being brought into the area during the high-water levels of the rainy periods, as any analysis of a *wadi* bed at Petra will show. Hence, in the wash levels, in the cover levels directly over the fall, no chronological significance can be assigned, *per se*, to the sherds recovered. However, that *all* such sherds resulted from such action cannot be maintained either. The fact that specifically Nabataean sherds of the fine, thin ware variety, along with probably Nabataean, or Roman-Nabataean, sherds of the thin, common, ribbed types, in company with voluted lamp fragments, occur in heavy concentration in the generally dense sandy and rocky upper levels over the entire area (e.g. I.1 (4), I.2 (7A/9), I.3 (6/6 A/1D, I.4 (1), I.6 (8), I.7 (6/7), I.25 (2), I 23/B (3), (6)) as well as below the drift-wash levels in the north (I.21 (15/5Q), (22), I.22A (4), (7), (8), as well as (11/10), and I.22 B (3A/B/C), (4) upper levels) would seem to stand against *all* such materials being intrusively water laid. The same factors must be considered in relation to those sherds appearing below the drift-wash strata of this phase. The importance of these sherds in the topmost levels is also strengthened by the fact that those levels subsequently served as the floor level for the re-use period following.

That these levels, and hence this identifiable phase, have been absent, or undetected, in other areas of fall at Petra is to be expected from the particular nature of the site, where the most open areas (e.g. along the Street, near the Triumphal Gate, etc.) are not ones apt to retain the water-laid/wind-borne alternate strata as clearly discernible levels as did the protected and basin-like *orchestra* and related parts of the Theater. It is suggested that the characteristically first-century sherds from this phase may be assigned to the mortar fill of Period I, with the mass of thin and heavier common wares to be related to Period V proper and later. The partially complete red-ware plate (Plate LIII, 3a, 36) from Trench I.21/A (2p), with incised (*sic.*) decoration on the interior bottom, appears to be an example of Late Roman 'A' ware, or its imitation. The piece is skilfully turned, well levigated, and evenly fired. It was decorated with a burnished slip, resulting in a shiny finish (as against the matte wash of Late Roman 'B' wares—cf. R. J. Charleston, *Roman Pottery*, p. 23). Since the terminal date of the 'A' ware is not later than the first quarter of the fifth century A.D. (*Idem.*, p. 22) the Petra piece easily fits the chronology of the period, as suggested above. This further strengthens the suggested date of the Period IV destruction, as well, in contrast to a later date (cf. also, *PEF Annual*, 5, Plate XII, 'sealing wax' type ware, p. 73; Kelso, *AASOR, XXIX–XXX*, p. 35 shows everted rim bowls from En-Nitla, but of different ware types, from the later period).

In addition three coins were recovered in two separate *loci* in strata assignable, stratigraphically, to this phase. While the number is not sufficiently great enough to permit unquestionable dating, the presence of datable coins in related stratigraphical contexts, tends to support the other data. Two of the coins (#2075, in I.21 (23) and #2069 in I.25 (9) are of Constantine the Great (following his receiving the title of 'Augustus' in A.D. 308). The third coin (#2067 also in I.21) is of Constantine II (A.D. 337–40). While these coins only indicate they could not have been present *before* A.D. 308, and give no indication of how long *after* that date they were deposited, their presence does coincide with the other indications, especially with the earthquake possibility suggested above in the discussion of Period IV.

Period VI. Period of Re-use, Post-fall

During this period the Theater area was again put to use for some temporary and obscure purpose. Wall lines became quite obvious in excavating the levels at related points and three distinct wall phases were isolated. Stratigraphically these may be divided (and the period, as well) into two main building phases. The early part of the Period (VIb) is characterized by a massive robbery wall, I.21, Wall 1, with repair wall 1B) and related blocking wall (I.22A Wall 2 (5) (Plate X, 1, 2, and Plates XI and XII. Wall 1 (Tr. I.1) is about 1 m. wide, extending some 21.4 m. along, but east of, the line of the *finitio proscenii* (i.e. roughly along the diameter of the *orchestra*). This line turned at right angles toward the east for about 4.20 m. at its northern end, toward the *scaena*. At the far northern end of the Theater complex, the line of the main robbery wall (I.21, Wall 1B/C) appears to seal the *vomitorium sinistrum* exit, probably against the side of the *scaenae frons*, with the additional wall (I.22A, Wall 2, level (5)) concluding the sealing (Plate X, Plate XI, Plate XII).

That the main robbery wall in Trench I.1 was designed to enclose the stage area, alone, is indicated by the semi-dressed appearance of its western (hence, outer) face (Plate X, 1, Plate XII) and the careful alignment of the robbed column drums, which were used as the foundation course on that side, in marked contrast to the rather poor build line of the eastern (hence, interior) face. Large building blocks from the *scaena*-stories, orthostats from the stage front, fragments of entablature, and other fall rubble were incorporated into the total build of this wall. It was set into its floor level, but ditched, not built into a foundation trench. This was of course possible because of the use of the column drums on the west side. The robbery walls in the north (I.21) likewise show a roughly dressed western face, c. 1 m. wide, composed of the same general debris makeup, and also show no foundation trench.

Wall 1B (I.21) appears to be a rebuild or repair addition to Wall 1C, extending slightly beyond its western line, and resting directly on Wall 1C. This apparent differentiation may be merely a difference in a single build, however. Wall 2 (I.22A (5)) is similarly rubble built of robbed materials, and without a foundation trench (Plate X, 3). All the walls of this part of the period are built on (or in) definite floor levels which seal the preceding period (see Analysis, Plate IV).

The second part of the period (VIa) is related to the earlier part by continuation of the robbery walls over the entire complex. In the area of the main robbery wall in the stage-*orchestra* sector, two smaller extensions are to be noted. One is simply a curved, single course extension to the north-west, c. 5.35 m. long (in I.3) (Plate X, Plate XI, 1, 2, Plate XII). The other extension is a semicircular rebuild of rubble c. 4.5 m. in extent (in I.4) (Plate XI, 3). The first of these rests on floor levels raised above those of the first stage of robbery walls (i.e. floor levels I.3, 5–5A).

In Trench I.21, Wall 1A (level (9)) is likewise composed of a single course width of poorly stacked rubble, resting on Wall 1B–C, but set back to the east c. 50 cm. (Plate X, 2). Below this wall are drift-wash levels (I.21A (5a) and below, to floor level of Wall 1B–C, (17)) corresponding to the situation in I.3, and to the drift-wash levels of I.22A (2C–D)), whose upper continuations have been eroded away. None of the extensions have been bonded into the walls of the earlier part of the periods. Further building on Wall 2 (I.22A (5)) could not be detected because of surface erosion at that point.

The rubble fill of all of these walls included a miscellany of red ribbed wares, some Nabataean fine, plain, and painted wares, heavy, coarse, and ribbed wares, a few yellow combed sherds, a few figurine and lamp fragments, tile fragments, cement-coated sherds, and similar pieces, as would be expected from excavation into the previous periods (V–IV) for the robbery masonry of the builds. No definite material could be isolated to aid in dating the rebuild phases as a result. Tentatively, it might be suggested, even without ceramic support, that these rebuilds may possibly reflect the rather sparse Byzantine occupation of the site, for which documentary evidence, along with the re-use of certain other monuments, clearly exists. This would then extend the disuse period preceding (period V) over the later Roman period, as has already been suggested above. The upper part of the phase may also represent early Islamic re-use, because of the nature of the rebuild extensions, which do little more than fence for casual use.

The function of either wall series is also not able to be determined, since no distinctive artifacts, animal bones, or other definitive occupational debris was associated with the phase. Housing, industry, or herding facilities of a temporary nature, could all be the possible uses to which the wall lines served as boundaries.

Period VII. Second Period of Re-use, Post-fall

This period is represented by only six clearly isolated strata, with at least two divisions evident (at I.3, (4)–(4A)), but only in Trench I.3, where pottery fragments *in situ* (see Plates LV, 3, LVI, 2, 3) on a floor level differentiated the period from the next following (see Section Drawings and Schematic Analysis) and in I.1, I.2, and I.7 where fall debris was such as to permit definitive isolation. In I.4 and I.6 that debris was of such a nature as to preclude the differentiation, and no clear relation could be determined in the northern sector (I.21–I.22B) as a result. In any case, the levels isolated constitute a period of re-use, apparently as the floor level of a period unrelated to the walls of the preceding period (VI). Hence a disuse period is also involved, up to the floor level, itself. The re-use involved was apparently of little consequence, but is to be noted, stratigraphically. In the accumulation in the immediate vicinity of the *scaenae frons*, architectural debris marks the final deterioration of the still-exposed face of those parts still standing after the main destruction and subsequent periods.

Still further, the ceramic and architectural debris covered by Period VIII indicates the violent fall of previously undestroyed wall lines, both original and robbery. Such a destruction would seem to be of chronological significance for the end of Period VII, but is discussed with Period VIII because of the stratigraphic difficulties noted concerning the isolation of Period VII, itself.

The recovered fragments noted above resemble Roman-Byzantine ribbed types, but the quality of the ware is grossly different. This and other facts about the pieces suggest Arabic manufacture (or degenerate later Byzantine?). The heavy jar handles also found in this period (Plate LV, 3) appear to be Byzantine types, and thus accord with the date suggested below for the end of Period VII and the beginning of Period VIII. Trench I.6 (1) also produced an Arabic sherd (Period VIII), which relates stratigraphically here.

Period VIII: Second Period of Dis-use, Post-fall to Modern Surface

As was noted above, differentiation between Periods VII–VIII was not possible except in those areas where equivalence of levels assignable to the periods was possible.

As a result most of the northern sector of the Theater complex must be considered as spanning the two periods involved. However, on the basis of the stratigraphy, it is possible to assign certain levels to tentative position within the two periods. As the Schematic Analysis indicates, I.21 (10), related to I.1 (3), especially, would suggest the placing of that level, plus I.21 (5), I.21A (5) and I.22A (2A), (2B), within Period VII.

These levels are all soft, sandy drift (except a wash level, I.22A (2B)), and contain fall materials. Since these materials are also present in both upper and lower portions of I.1 (3) and related context, some question may be raised as to the assignment to Period VII. However, the fall debris present would seem to indicate that it came from robbery walls, or, and most probably, in this area, from the upper levels of the Theater complex, built on the cliffs above the northern sector. This is particularly obvious because of the presence of cement on sherd fragments. Since, stratigraphically, such debris could not be from Period IV, the main destruction, but resembles it in specific complexion, fall from the same and related build, at a later period (see below), is indicated. As the upper complex toppled, from earthquake and decay, this material was mingled with strata of the Period VII drift-wash levels. The sherd debris from these levels is parallel to that of Period IV/V material and must come originally from Period I build (Plates LIII, 1, 2; LIV, 1, 2.). Penetration of these levels by fall in Period VIII seems indicated and may explain the specific debris content. To Period VIII, which represents the final stratigraphic phase of the Theater, belong some forty-six individual excavated strata, or partial strata, which represent eleven actual levels over the entire complex and are separated from Period VII by a further destruction level, apparently resting on and penetrating into the Period VII levels which formed the floor at the end of the period.

In the *orchestra*-stage area, the difficulty of isolating Periods VI–VII and hence VI–VIII, is again reflected in those strata which dip into the heavy fall debris of Period V. The lowest levels (I.1 (3), I.2 (3), I.3 (3), I.6 (6), and I.7 (3)) are drift levels, blending with Periods V–VI sandy drifts, and covering similar fall as was found in Period V, probably related to the fall debris from both Period V and Periods VI–VII. The presence of fall debris in I.1 (3), especially, may represent the decay of the exposed parts of the *scaena*. The sherd content of all related levels in homogenous, and related to Periods V–VI–VII, as would be anticipated. Above these levels, over the area, hard-packed wash levels appeared, but do not represent a single chronological succession, on the basis of their depth. The next drift levels, (I.1 (1), (1A), I.2 (1), I.3 (1), (1B), I.4 (1 +), a composite level, I.5 (1), a composite level, I.6 (1), and I.7 (1)) now form the stratigraphic link with the northern sector (I.21 (7), I.21A (4), (4B), I.22 A(3)) and the later levels removed by the *orchestra*-stage area clearing prior to excavation in that area.

Over the entire Theater complex the drift levels which make up this stratum, continue to show homogeneous sherd composition, resulting from further decay of the *scaena*, robbery walls, and tumble from the upper northern complex. The fall of the robbery walls (Period VI), because of the origin of its fill, gives the appearance of Period IV fall, exactly paralleling the fall content from original Period I builds. It is not probable that much of the sherd content is merely wash deposit, because of its nature, but at least some of the high concentration of fine and common thin wares may be so explained at this height, along with a more considerable amount deposited from fall content, *per se*. The quantity of Nabataean dressed blocks, cement, and cement-coated sherds, especially in the northern sector, points to a rather heavy fall of previously undisturbed wall lines.

That such extensive destruction occurred to wall lines previously *not* toppled, would point to an especially severe earthquake. When the earthquake calendar is again consulted[20] a series of later strong to severe earthquakes may be suggested for possible dating of this later destruction. The most severe, after a series of chronologically separated shocks, appears to have been the earthquake of A.D. 746/48. This quake had an intensity of 18.1 and was the one in which Jerash was destroyed. Chronologically, it is felt that no objection, stratigraphically or otherwise, would preclude assignment of the destruction represented by the fall debris in the levels in question, even though ceramic or other data is lacking to confirm this conjecture.[21] This would then provide a terminal date for Period VII, or at least, for the beginning of Period VIII. This possibility is made even more probable in view of the pottery remains found on the surface of Period VII, which appear to be Arabic.

The clearance of the *orchestra*-stage areas removed any higher stratigraphic levels from that area, as has been noted above, but these levels are represented, and related, by Trench I.4 and the northern sector. I.4 (1+) and (1++), the surface levels at that point, may be tied in with I.21 (4) and its related strata, I.21 (4B), I.21A (3), and the lower part of I.22A (2) (see Schematic Analysis Plates IV, V). Again the sherd content of this over-all level, as well as those directly above (I.21 (6–8), (3), and the harder-packed following levels, I.21 (2), and I.21A (2)) reflects fall cover and wash, peaking toward the center of the excavated length. This appears heaviest near the western and north-western parts of the area, as might be expected for fall from the upper complex. Probably some further dislocation of weakened wall lines continued to fall over the cliff edge, and new areas of erosion brought debris from chronologically earlier periods over the cliff side as winter rains found new channels and eroded deeper. The surface level of the northern sector resembles the soft, sandy, wind- and water-eroded surface of Petra as a whole. The extent of erosion may be seen in both the slope southward toward the *orchestra*-stage, and, more especially, in the steep slope toward the east.

III

PERIOD I—THE PERIOD OF MAIN USE

A. GENERAL DESCRIPTION

Period I is the period in which the Theater was actually put to use, as a place of public assembly, for entertainment, and other purposes. As such, it is represented by the remains which constituted its form in the various phases of its use. These remains are virtually all architectural in nature, with the exception of a few stratigraphic levels which constitute specific inter-phase accumulation, and scant, but possibly significant, numismatic finds.

The significance of the architectural data is major, however, both as general information concerning the architecture of the eastern provincial theater type—of which very little is to be found in publication—and in terms of establishing the chronological setting of the structure.

As it stood in Period I, the main Theater at Petra was a combination of rock-cut and built masonry. The site chosen was a high sandstone cliff face, facing SE by S (E by 33° 30′ S), along the direct *wadi* bed route leading from the Siq into the actual valley site of the ancient city (see Plate I and Plate XIII). The significance of this site choice, and other factors emerging from it, will be discussed in the conclusion.

Into the cliff-face were cut the *auditorium* and the *orchestra* of the theater, with the *scaena* and its parts, including the *proscenium*, erected on the bedrock floor of the complex. The *hyposcenium* was partly built up of masonry and partly composed of bedrock piers left free standing when the *orchestra* was excavated. The *tribunaliae* and associated upper barricade walls adjoining the *auditorium* were of built masonry with bedrock cuts. The *vomitoria*, both dextrum and sinistrum, were rock-cut, with masonry arching consolidated with concrete.

The *auditorium* consisted of an upper drainage gallery, an upper gallery, and a three-fold *cavea* (*summa*, *media*, and *ima*), divided into six *cuneii*, with a *praecinctio* between the *summa cavea* and *media cavea* and between the *media cavea* and the *ima cavea*. A *bisellium* seems probable at the foot of the *ima cavea*, with steps or seats leading from it to the *orchestra* floor. Straight stairways led from the *orchestra* to the upper gallery.

The *orchestra* was excavated more or less level into bedrock and finished with a cement-like plaster, covering tie davits cut into the bedrock during construction of the *scaena*. Two *vomitoria* and one completed *aditus* (*dextrus*) led into the Theater and to the first *praecinctio* of the *cavea*. The remains of the southern *tribunalium* (*dextrum*) are quite clear, but no comparable remains could be seen on the northern end. Surface erosion (and robbery accessibility) may possibly explain the absence of such indications. However, since the northern *aditus* was never completed, although the quarry marks for its cutting are evident in the wall of the *vomitorium sinistrum*, it may be that the *tribunalium* was never completed at that point either. In the north-west, a rather complex feature is evident, which may have functioned similarly. A masonry wall was built continuing the cliff face toward the east, with an entry parallel to the entry between the *scaena-postscenium* walls, with a stair system providing access to its top. Access to the *auditorium*, as a whole, was blocked on both sides of the upper cliff areas by barricade walls, with internal rooms evident on

Plate Folder A1

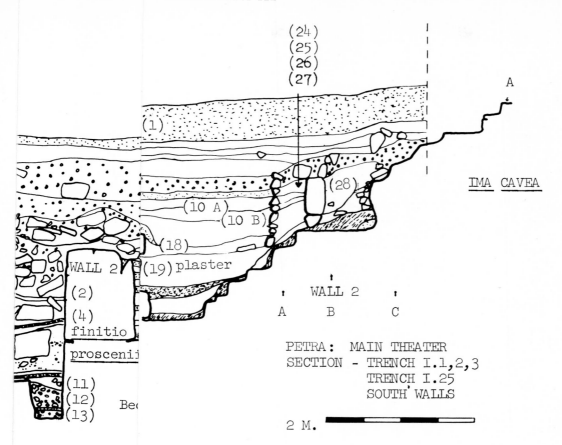

(24)
(25)
(26)
(27)

A

IMA CAVEA

(1)

(10 A)
(10 B)

(18)
(19) plaster

WALL 2
(2)
(4)
finitio

proscenii

(11)
(12)   Be
(13)

WALL 2
A   B   C

(28)

PETRA: MAIN THEATER
SECTION – TRENCH I.1,2,3
TRENCH I.25
SOUTH WALLS

2 M.

Plate Folder A2

CL

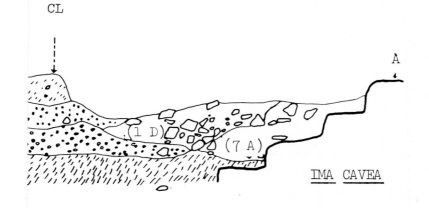

A

(1 D)
(7 A)

IMA CAVEA

PETRA: MAIN THEATER
TRENCH I.3 WEST WALL

2 M.

the northern side. The *orchestra* plan is roughly semi-circular, establishing the plan as unquestionably Roman, even though the use of a cliff-side for the *auditorium* has led to identification of the complex as Greek or Hellenistic.

The *scaena* complex was built on the bedrock and built foundations noted above, with its main walls firmly laid on outset foundation lines. The *finitio proscenii* was built parallel to the *orchestra* diameter line (set back 3.10 m.), again in Roman style. The *hyposcenium* was arched over and sub-paving laid on the arches and foundation piers. Over this a fine pavement was laid. In the earliest phase, at least, stairs rose directly from the *orchestra* floor to the stage level, in the direction of the *scaenae frons*. The *scaenae frons* was of the niche type, with *podia* for columnation effect. Hence this is the 'western' style. The *scaena* wall lines continued on each side to bond into the projecting cliffs. This is especially evident in the northwest, where tremendous squared and staggered recesses were obviously cut to receive the wall bonds. On the southeastern side, the cliff ends were lower, and the exaggerated rock-cutting unnecessary, although some was done.

Published plans of the main Theater generally go back to three basic versions, some of which have already been noted: that of Brünnow, that of Musil, and that of Wiegand.[1] Of these, that of Wiegand alone shows some remarkable degree of accuracy, in the light of the present excavations, in spite of the fact that most of the necessary data for determining such a plan was buried at the time the plan was drawn! Obviously, Wiegand constructed a theoretical plan on the basis of the *orchestra* depth, even though the final form of the reconstruction was misconstrued because of the depth of debris over the *finitio proscenii* which could alone furnish data concerning the diameter of the *orchestra*. The plans of Brünnow and Musil are simply schematic representations which would fit virtually any Roman structure. Since a considerable amount of debris covered the necessary reference points, no accurate plan has actually been possible up to the present excavations. Emphasis was therefore placed on survey during the course of the work, in order that a plan might be secured. As a result of this survey and the excavations, it is quite clear that the plan of the Main Theater was definitely, and often slavishly, Vitruvian. Site selection, plan detail, and general layout, mathematically, are all quite in order. Consideration of these aspects will be made in detail below.

I. *CAVEA*

Since the *cavea*, and its related galleries, were cut into the bedrock of the cliff-face, the rows of seats, the passages, and the stairways are all of solid rock, except for the addition of masonry stairs and drain covers over the *praecinctio* between the *media cavea* and *ima cavea*.

The top-most gallery of the *cavea* rises some 15 m. above the floor of the gallery of the *summa cavea* (see Plate XIV, 1). This upper gallery is part of the hydraulic system of the Theater as a whole, and contained a channel for diverting rain and spill waters around the complex (see section B of this chapter). The 15 m. back wall of the *summa cavea* below this gallery (see Plate XIV, 2) provided splendid acoustical advantage to the Theater, as well as keeping the hydraulic system well above the entire installation, thus precluding additional drainage protection at lower levels. At its top this wall is roughly stepped back and rises another 80 cm. This wall is well cut, although a few degrees from plumb. It was the construction of this part of the Theater which penetrated into ancient tombs and provided the box-like chambers which appear in the wall. The presence of similar, untouched tombs, with rock-cut façades, in the immediate area indicates that the destruction of the tombs was done knowingly.

The line of the gallery wall is broken, toward the NW, by a deep natural cleft which also contains (untouched) tombs of the façade type. Miscellaneous aberations of true face also occur here and there in the cutting, but seem to have no real architectural significance, as far as the *cavea* is concerned. A few indentations, natural or carved, in the wall, especially at the level of the *summa cavea* gallery floor proper might have been attempts at decorative niches, but appear never to have been completed, if they were indeed artificial and purposive. Some set-back may be seen in the NE line of the *summa cavea*, where the natural rock of the cliff face is less in extent than further down the cliff side.

The floor of the upper gallery of the *summa cavea* (perhaps a true *praecinctio*) is about 3.55 m. wide and is carried around most of the upper line of the *summa cavea*. Into the floor are cut runnels and drains, permitting water to be channelled down to lower areas in a regulated fashion (see Plate XIV, 3). The drains are simply excavated holes, wider at the top than at the bottom, diagonally piercing the top edge of the uppermost seat of the *summa cavea*. The lower gallery does not seem to have had any awning slots, or other features seen elsewhere for supporting temporary covering over the *cavea*.[2] The answer to this lack is quite obvious, however, on the basis of local climate. In the area of Petra no rain falls for almost nine months of the year, and during the rainy season out-door performances would have been exceedingly uncomfortable, regardless of covering. In addition, the orientation of the Theater is such that the sun is off the *cavea* area soon after mid-day,[3] (although the stage area would have needed some protection, and may have had a roof or other covering), because of the height of the cliff into which it was cut. The upper drainage gallery thus served a protective role during the rainy season, supplemented by the drains in the floor of the lower gallery directly above the seats of the *summa cavea*, noted above. To the failure of the upper gallery system, after the Theater had fallen into disuse and the upper gallery channel silted in, may be traced much of the modern appearance of the *cavea* seats. Erosion has, in some areas, completely effaced the seat and stair lines, or has eaten away the softer sandstone, leaving blackish knobs of harder stone exposed ('differential weathering'—see Plate XIV, 4).

Nor does the upper gallery show any indication of any provision for a colonnade, as the Vitruvian plan suggests. However, since such a colonnade was for acoustical purposes, the massive bedrock back wall took its place and precluded functional necessity for it. The *summa cavea* is composed of a varying number of seat rows, depending upon the location in which they are counted. This factor arises from both erosion and a rather disordered original cutting at this level. Apparently the rock quality was involved, even in antiquity, and the opportunity of cutting even rows across the entire area was lacking, hence the rows vary as rock stability or presence afforded the possibility. Thus the count varies from fourteen rows at the SE end to twelve rows at the NE end, and about nine rows in the center. In addition, vaguely across the length of the *summa cavea*, below the lowest row, was a wider row, with a curb appearing sporadically, indicating a *praecinctio* between the *summa cavea* and the *media cavea*. Stairway variation also occurs in the *summa cavea*, with the exact lines vague, probably because of erosion and original cutting difficulties noted above.

Seat widths in the *summa cavea* vary from c. 1 m. to as narrow as c. 65 cm., with the *praecinctio* measuring c. 80 cm. Seat backs also vary in height from c. 30 cm. to c. 55 cm. The *praecinctio* wall rises to only c. 75 cm.

The *media cavea* was composed of a varying number of seat rows as well. On the SE side twenty-five rows could be counted; on the NE side there were twenty rows, and in the center twenty-three rows: for the same reasons cited above. Seat widths are a bit more uniform in this area, however, being generally c. 70 cm. wide, although a few variations up to c. 80 cm. and down to 55 cm. occur. Erosion might well explain the latter decrease. Seat heights are generally about 40–48 cm. with inset stair treads matching seat heights and with intermediate rises of about 20–30 cm. Some offsetting of the lines of the stairway is also to be seen here, and stairway width goes as high as 1.2 m.

Below the *media cavea* and separating it from the *ima cavea* appears a well-defined *praecinctio* (see Plate XV, 1), with a wide floor and high back. Four steps lead from the *praecinctio* floor to the next seating row, and some degree of stair decoration may be seen, where offsets are cut into the stair openings through the *praecinctio* back wall. The passage floor measures about 2.1 m., with a back wall about 1.8 m. high and c. 58 cm. wide.[4] An additional front curbing and a drain went along the passage floor, built up and covered where the stairs rise to the next level through the *praecinctio* wall. The drain covers were incorporated in the stair system, with a drain canal some 20 cm. wide and 25 cm. deep below (see Plate XV, 2, 3).

The *ima cavea* was composed of a uniform ten rows of seats. This uniformity was probably the result of both the better quality of rock at that depth and the importance of the *cavea*, socially. The stair widths at this level are between 50 cm. and 80 cm., with backs rising between 30 cm. and 40 cm. The stairs again roughly reduce the rise to half that of the seat rows. The third seating row from the *orchestra* floor is about 95 cm. wide and may have been intended as a *bisellium*, since it does exceed the width of any other row in the *ima cavea*. Below it are two further rows of seats of c. 30 cm. and 70 cm. width, respectively. Stairway width in the *ima cavea* varies between c. 70 cm. and 88 cm., with the average width at about 76 cm.

Both the *media cavea* and the *ima cavea* suffer from the presence of a natural fissure at the NE edge, with the stair line of the *media cavea* almost totally destroyed above the *praecinctio* at that point. The presence of considerable masonry fall would seem to indicate that a masonry stair may have been necessitated by the natural rock fault (see Plate XIV, 2, 4).

The variations in seat measurements shown in the various parts of the *cavea*, as a whole, may be attributed to original variations in cutting, to wear, and more particularly, to the effects of weathering. These variations, as noted above, ranged from about 50 cm. to 1 m. (c. 19¾ in. to 39¼ in.) in width, and from about 30 cm. to 48 cm. (c. 11¾ in. to 17⅞ in.) in height. Although these dimensions are not exactly according to Vitruvius' standard limits (i.e. '*pedes duo semis*' by '*pedes duo*' for width, or roughly 2½ ft. to 2 ft.; and '*palmopede*' by '*pedem et digito sex*' for height, or roughly 16 in. to 18 in.),[5] the variation is not too great and probably represents factors mentioned above working in concert.

The entire *cavea* is divided into six *cunei* by seven *itinerae* rising straight to the gallery of the *summa cavea* from the *orchestra* floor, along the general lines of the model Vitruvian plan.[6]

The standard Vitruvian plan laid out the *orchestra* circle with five equilateral triangles in-

3

scribed within it. The apex of the triangle whose base was parallel to the line of the *finitio proscenii* marked the line of the center stairway of the *cavea*, with the apexes of the remaining triangle in the *orchestra* area marking the lines of the other six stairways. These seven points would, theoretically, be 30° apart from each other around the *orchestra* curve. This model plan had to be modified, however, when the *vomitoria* passages were introduced next to the line of the *finitio proscenii*, thus requiring the adjustment of the stairway lines immediately at each side of the *finitio proscenii* itself. This modified plan became the usual one followed.[7]

At Petra the stairway displacement was 3.5° on the southern end and 4.5° on the northern end, calculated from the banisters of the stair, not the stair centers. The stair lines, numbered in order from the *vomitorium dextrum*, were separated by the following angular measurements:

#3–#4:	30.5°	#4–#5:	30.5°
#3–#2:	30.5°	#5–#6:	30.0°
#2–#1: (banister line	25.5°	#6–#7: (banister line	26.5°

These figures, based on line and instrument measurements, indicate the degree of accuracy in layout achieved by the original builders. It is possible that wear and deterioration, which made it difficult to determine exact center points, may be responsible for some degree of apparent error in the figures noted, and the accuracy of original layout measurement was even more exact than the present survey was able to determine.

In the present condition of the Theater, an apparent error of original layout does seem to be made, however, especially on the NE end. On the assumption that *itinera* #4 (center) was the first point set, and subsequent points swung from it, the points show variations from 0.5 to 1.0°. These are cumulative, and may explain certain minor variations observable in the plan, especially on the NE (*sinister*) side of the complex.

The Vitruvian canon also results in certain equations of other parts of the plan, on the basis of the equilateral sides of the inscribed triangles. Thus distances measured from #1–#5 = #2–#6 = #3–#7.

At Petra these distances were as follows:

#1 (banister line)–#5:	21.3 m.
#1–#5 (centers):	20.9 m.
#2–#6:	21.35 m.
#3–#7 (banister line):	21.3 m.
#3–#7 (centers):	20.9 m.

Thus, with the assumption that wear and erosion may have disturbed center determination, in terms of the ancient points, the triangle sides are seen to have been roughly 21.35 m., with adjustment for cumulative variations affecting the position of #7, as well as #6. This slightly modifies the linear relationships across the *orchestra*, as well.

The inscribed triangles also determine, in the 'usual' as well as the 'model' plan, the location of other features of the theater. The two sides of the triangle, whose apex determines the center *itinera* (#4), determine also the side exits of the *scaenae frons*. At Petra, as elsewhere, this was accomplished by projecting these sides beyond their base, to the point of intersection, with the

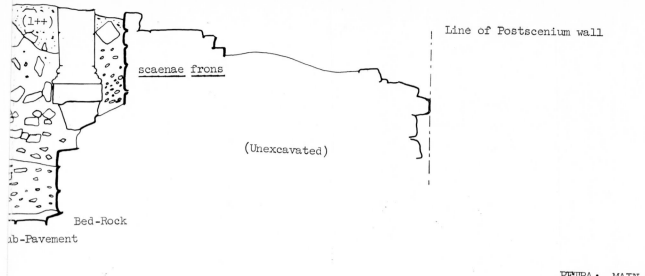

Line of Postscenium wall

scaenae frons

(Unexcavated)

Bed-Rock

b-Pavement

2 M.

SCAENA   POSTSCENIUM

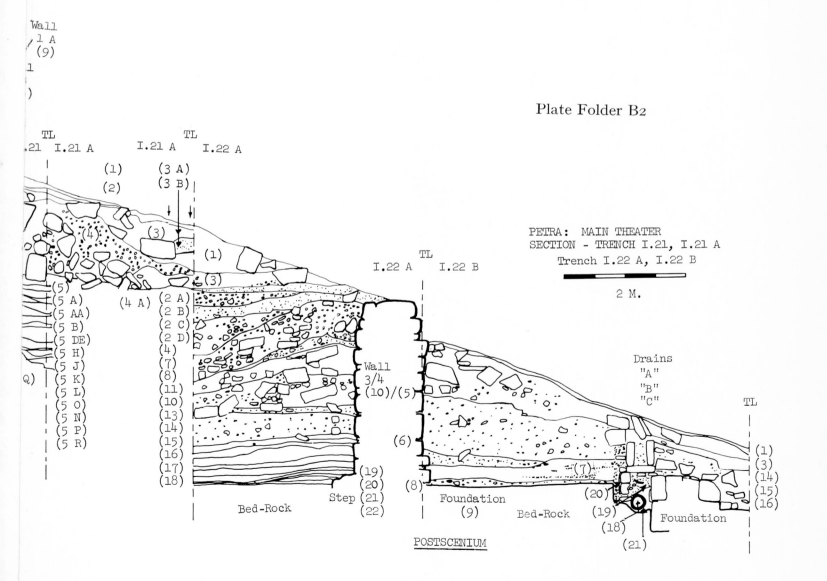

PETRA: MAIN THEATER
SECTION - TRENCH I.21, I.21 A
Trench I.22 A, I.22 B

2 M.

POSTSCENIUM

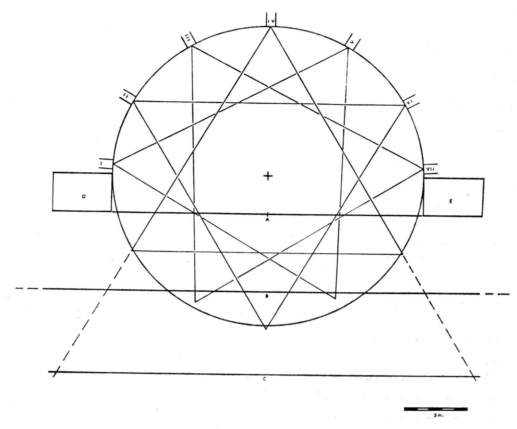

THE MATHEMATICS OF THE THEATER AT PETRA

Key to plan: A—line of *finitio proscenii*
B—line of *scaenae frons*
C—line of *postscenium* wall
D—*vomitorium dextrum*
E—*vomitorium sinistrum*
I–VII —*itinerae*

scaenae frons. This method permitted a much wider *scaenae frons* than the Vitruvian model, and was generally used.

Canon modifications were also made at Petra in regard to the stairways. The Vitruvian model would have called for additional, staggered, stairways above the *ima cavea*, but this was not followed.[8]

A banister, c. 35 cm. wide, of carved stone, built up of individual blocks, set end to end, was set into receiving recesses along the outer edge of the first stairways on each side (#1, #7). The angle of setting of these was such that none survived *in situ*, but a number were recovered in fall debris.

The point at which the *scaenae frons* line cut the *orchestra* circle was also roughly determinative of the inner edge of the first niche in the *scaenae frons* line at Petra.

The division of the *cavea* at Petra follows the usual pattern of the Roman 'class theater',[9] but no inscriptional evidence yet exists to clarify the distinctions implied by the plan. The classes represented in Roman society could be, and were, approximated socially in the provinces, but no basis is possible for their strict determination at Petra at this time. Since seats were usually without backs or arms, and since no numerical notations appear, the reservation of unrestricted seats possibly took place by reserving linear distances (i.e. 'feet' of seats) at particular points within a given section of each horizontal division, as was the case in other locations.[10] No evidence of 'tickets' was uncovered during excavation, although some means of seat purchaser identification may have existed.[11]

The seating capacity of the Theater at Petra, variously suggested in the past on the basis of estimates of seating rows visible above the surface, as noted above, must now be revised upward. When the row-count variations are averaged and the count rounded off, the *summa cavea* contained eleven rows, the *media cavea* nineteen rows, and the *ima cavea* ten rows that could be calculated. The gross linear seating capacity would therefore amount to 3,412.02 m. On the basis of c. 40–50 cm. for each seat, the Theater at Petra could probably have accommodated between about 6,824 to about 8,530 spectators, in addition to those smaller numbers accommodated by the *tribunaliae, orchestra* (?), and other special reserved areas.

It is not felt that these figures can be used for population estimates at Petra. In a monumental public building, accommodation is often made more spacious, not only for probable attendance, but also from factors of civic pride.

Acoustically, the Theater at Petra must have relied upon the massive back wall of the *summa cavea* gallery instead of the principles insisted on by Vitruvius. When the *cavea* section is compared with Vitruvius' acoustical canon of row-edge alignment from top to bottom,[12] it will be noted that this alignment ceases from about the eighth row of the *summa cavea* all the way down to the last row of the *ima cavea* (see Plate XVI). Hence, the back wall must have been an adequate substitute for the mathematical device.

At each side of the *cavea* area, beyond the seating rows, are series of wall complexes which appear to have served as blockades against casual entrance to the Theater (see plan, Plate Folder C, and Plate XVII, 1, 2). At the *media cavea* level these are related to the *tribunalia(e)*. Only one sure *tribunalia* was found, above the *vomitorium dextrum* (see Plate XVII, 3). On the NE end of the Theater no remains can be surely traced, and the installation may have been unfinished (note evidence of the *vomitorium sinistrum* below), or were robbed away (see Plate XVII, 4). The latter possibility exists because of the lack of rock available for rock-cut foundations at that point, which would have necessitated built masonry and hence later robbery quarrying of ready-cut blocks.

The *tribunalia* which does exist, at the S.W side was established squarely on the top of the *vomitorium dextrum*, using the bedrock at that point as the basis for both side walls, by extension of the *praecinctio* wall and the outer wall of the *vomitorium*. Entrance was presumably from the front, via the *praecinctio* dividing the *ima cavea* from the *media cavea*, but the rear wall also has a doorway. No boundary wall appears around the *tribunalia*, itself, but again robbery would account for lack of remains. The area measures roughly 4.20 m. on a side and at an elevation of about 3.03 m. from the stage floor, would have given a totally unobscured view of the stage area below. A similar area seems definite over the *vomitorium sinistrum*, but nothing except the platform remains.

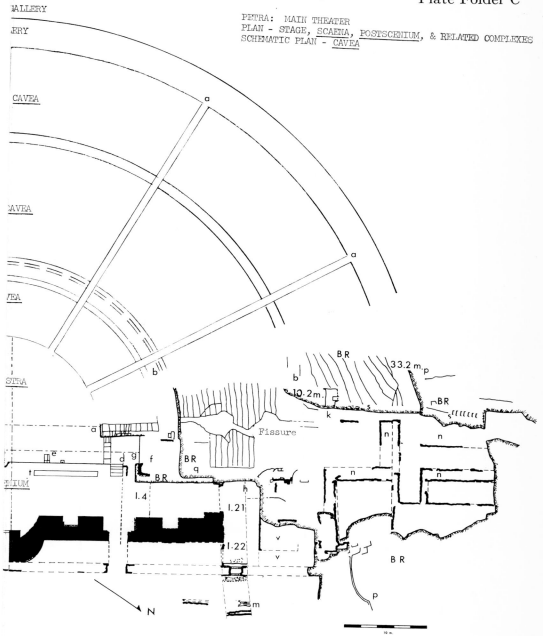

IE MAIN THEATER—PLAN

—SCHEMATIC PLAN ONLY)

Key

m	drain complex, *postscenium* ('A', 'B', 'C')
n	blockade wall
p	drain runnel
q	side wall, *media cavea*, lower level
r	side wall, *media cavea*, upper level
s	side wall, *summa cavea*, upper level
t	*auleum* slot, stage area
v	stair and roof (?) platform area
BR	bed-rock
Nos.	approximate heights above *orchestra* floor

eriod

Beyond the *tribunalia dextra* area, to the SE, a wall line continues along the bedrock line of the *vomitorium* below. This wall, of built masonry, extends roughly 26.10 m. to an outcrop of bedrock cut to receive it (see Plate XV, 1). The western side of this passage is bounded by a rock-cut wall of bedrock of which the outcrop noted above forms the corner and end. A break in this bedrock, c. 7.10 from the rear wall of the *tribunalia*, appears to have been filled with masonry build. About 14.30 m. from the *tribunalia* rear wall a natural cave, c. 2.40 m. deep and 2.10 m. wide at the back, was squared off. This may have been intended to penetrate the *aditus-vomitorium* passage, as an access point, but appears uncompleted (see below).

The floor of this long room-type complex remains roughly at the level of the *praecinctio*. Access to it, from the SW, was not determined by excavation, but may have existed in antiquity.

The *media cavea* area is also bounded by an eastern wall line, of rubble build along the bedrock top edge of the line which bounded the *ima cavea* complex. The bedrock cut rises with the *media cavea* from the *praecinctio* level (c. 8.65 from the *orchestra* floor) to roughly 14.10 m. above the *orchestra* floor, at which point a bedrock cut roughly marks the line of the *praecinctio* between the *media cavea* and the *summa cavea*. The seat cutting of the *media cavea* was poor at this side, with masonry seats presumably necessary in areas of bedrock faults, especially above the roof of the *aditus*, which opens to the *praecinctio* from the *vomitorium* below. The area of the *summa cavea* was vaguely bounded by built wall lines and rock-cut outcrops, which could not be completely traced.

The *aditus* mouth is set back, by staggered cuts, about 1.10 m. from the face line of the *praecinctio*, and is provided with three steps at that point (see Plate XVIII, 1, 2). From its mouth, the *aditus* passage descends through bedrock, on a gentle slope to the intersection of a stairway from the *vomitorium* passage and another stairway leading up to a transverse room, at right angles to the *aditus* line (see Plate XVIII, 2). The eastern end of that room was presumably the access point for entrance to the *media cavea* complex behind the *tribunalia*, but does not appear completed (cf. the cave extension noted in the bedrock wall at that point). These *aditus* passageways, excavated in bedrock, were some 3 m. to 5.10 m. in height, extend some 18 m. in length, and varied from 3 m. in width. Excavation of these passageways entailed the removal of something over 187.50 cu. m. of bedrock.

No *aditus* appeared on the NW side of the Theater, although the quarry marks of its beginning are obvious in the wall opposite the exit passage of the *vomitorium sinistrum*. A squared opening along the *praecinctio* between the *media cavea* and *summa cavea* on the NW side of the Theater may have been planned as the exit of this *aditus*, but at a higher level than on the other side, and was never completed (see Plate XIV, 4).

Above and behind the *vomitorium sinistrum* the blockade complex was much more definite and involved than on the side just described (see Plan, Plate Folder C). A series of parallel cross walls, on a rise with the *summa cavea*, extended back to the bedrock cliff face c. 42 m. from the arch line of the *vomitorium sinistrum*, to a point roughly against the *summa cavea* gallery wall. Longitudinal walls further complicated the plan, resulting in room-like chambers. Whenever possible, these walls were bonded into bedrock, with rock-cut recesses carved to receive them. Next to the *cavea* side of the bedrock boundary wall, an arched passageway seems indicated by the cuttings found. On the stage side of the area, bedrock was used as a boundary, supplemented with wall lines along its edge wherever necessary. It is fall from this area which complicated the stratigraphy in the Trench I.21–22 sector. The walls were from c. 1.50 to 2.40 m. in thickness, indicating probable wall height equal to the rise of the bedrock *summa cavea* area itself.

The *media cavea* area did not possess a passageway parallel to that on the other side of the Theater. Rather, the seating rows were extended to the edge of the bedrock cliff, along the line of the stage front. Whether this was deliberate asymmetry, or simply functionally taking advantage of the bedrock cannot at present be determined. This seating extension may, however, explain the planned (?) higher *aditus* noted above, but never completed. In any case, the rock fault through this area must have disturbed the cutting and was presumably filled with built masonry, since the seat rows continue in roughly straight lines on either side, indicating a continuation between.

Whether the *tribunalia(e)* at Petra were reserved for honored guests or officials cannot, of course, be determined. Their presence would seem to indicate the practice, however. The large stone-cut chair found by the clearance operations of the Department of Antiquities on the *orchestra* floor may perhaps indicate, by the find spot, that this may have been part of the *tribunalia dextra* furniture, and hence further strengthen the position of honor involved in the *tribunalia* complex (see Plate XVIII, 3).[13]

Various rock-cuttings were found throughout this upper area, including a drain-runnel leading over (?) the cliff edge on the eastern side.

2. *ORCHESTRA*

The *orchestra*[14] of the Theater was cut into bedrock and roughly levelled. The area was not paved, since related parts are simply tied in with plaster curbs reaching almost to the bedrock surface. A thick layer of extremely hard cement-plaster was used to cover the bedrock surface and building cuts made into it (I.1 (18), I.2 (16)).

The plan of the *orchestra* is a true semicircle, on a 24.50 m. diameter. Because of the position of the *vomitoria*, the 'model' Vitruvian plan was altered, in the usual way, by the setting back of the *finitio proscenii* 3.10 m., parallel to the diameter line. The total *orchestra* area was therefore about 2.36 hectares. This diameter places the Theater at Petra in the upper range of medium-sized Roman period theaters.[15]

Along the *orchestra* edge, at the juncture of Trench I.2 with *itinera* #4 (center) was found a boundary curb and wall line which are to be related to the latest phase of Period I (see below; see also Plate XIX, 2, 3).

The wall extended for only about 3.73 m., was a single course wide (c. 34 cm.), and stood 1.10 m. in height. Its face was 1.10 m. from the edge of the lowest seat in the *ima cavea*, with apparent rubble blocking between (see Plate XIX, 4). It was bonded, on either side, by a curved bond with the curb abutting the *ima cavea* line. The wall was well dressed, with cemented joints, and was carefully laid, with staggered coursing of joints. The exterior (i.e. eastern) face had been thickly plastered (c. 1 cm. thick), with a slight curb at its joint with the floor of the *orchestra* (see Plate XIX, 3). Four masonry steps rose from the *orchestra* floor, providing access to the *ima cavea* (Plate XX). Both treads and risers, as well as outside edges, were carefully plastered, with a curb again forming a curved joint with the *orchestra* floor. The curb, to which this wall bonded, was composed of blocks, curved to fit the *ima cavea* curve, 45 cm. wide, 70 cm. long, and 67 cm.

high. That this wall and curb represent a later phase of Period I will be shown below. The purpose of the wall cannot be explained functionally because of the Period II robbery wall activity directly behind this wall (see Plate XIX, 3).

The *orchestra* floor showed a series of rock-cut 'davits,' or tying anchors, cut into its surface (cf. also, S.W. stage floor), along with a series of cup-holes (see Plate XXI, 1 and Plate XVIII, 4). The davits varied in size, but approached 50 cm. in length and, originally, all must have had unexcavated 'handles' across their width. These proved to be one of the most puzzling features of the *orchestra* area and visitors provided all sorts of possible explanations. The reconstruction activities of the Department of Antiquities solved the problem by chance, but without doubt, however. In the course of that work, as the column drums were being restored into position, tripod hoists were erected and guyed to the davit holes by ropes—precisely the manner in which the original builders had done. Once this practice was observed, the mystery of the oddly placed davits disappeared! Such rock-cut tie-holes are still used today by the Bedouin, and other examples may be cited from stable areas of Crusader times. At the Theater, the presence of bedrock made stakes impossible for guying the hoists, and a reasonable substitute was found in the davits. Those were then hidden from view by the plastering of the *orchestra* floor.

A false door (?) slab was uncovered, *in situ*, during the course of excavation which is also of interest (see Plate XXI, 2). The slab, measuring c. 40 × 43 cm., was securely cemented into a slight recess in the *orchestra* floor made expressly for it. The purpose of this is unclear, although it may have been originally intended to represent 'Charon's door', sometimes actually built into an *orchestra floor* for theatrical-effect function.[16] That this was the pedestal remains of an altar does not seem probable. Rather, it may well have relation to still another feature of the *orchestra*, a rectangular trench excavated into bedrock, leading to and beneath the central niche of the *finitio proscenii*. This channel was c. 84–90 cm. deep, with slightly incurved sides (54 cm. at the top, 48 cm. at the bottom), and extended c. 2 m. from the niche face into the *orchestra* area (Plate XXI, 3–4). The attribution of this channel to the earliest phase of the Theater will be shown, stratigraphically, below, and the presence of a small piece of grey marble facing, still *in situ* on the side, further proves its relation to that phase. The entire canal was apparently covered over with concrete slabs, one of which was found still in place, when its function was no longer appreciated (see below). The fill of this trench was high in concentration of Nabataean-Roman Pottery fragments.

Drainage of the *orchestra* area was minimal, with only a single runnel found, at the SE side, leading to a drain led into the base of the *finitio proscenii* (Plate XLII, 2). The curbs (original) across the *vomitoria* entrances would have precluded drainage in that direction, but, as was noted above, the amount of probable rainfall, the probable amount of use of the Theater during that time of year, and the upper drainage system, were all factors which permitted so little need for direct drainage of the *orchestra* itself. Evaporation and absorption probably kept the area from being flooded for long, without the need for further devices.

On the *orchestra* floor level, at each side, were the *vomitoria* passageways already noted above (see Plate XXII, 1–2). The *vomitorium dextrum* had been cleared by the Department of Antiquities prior to the beginning of the present excavation, but the stratigraphy available in the area of the *vomitorium sinistrum* sufficed for relational purposes.

The *vomitorium dextrum* was planned in detail (Plate XXIII), because of its completeness in comparison with the other side. A description of it therefore provides the necessary detail. The passage, and its related *aditus* complex above, was rock-cut, with masonry vaulting provided over the *vomitorium* proper, and with supplementary masonry at the immediate entrance on the *orchestra* end. The entrance to the passage was set back 4.6 m. (*vomitorium dextrum* but 4.70 m. *vomitorium sinistrum*) from the *orchestra* line, in order to provide the necessary perpendicular springing height (i.e. one-sixth of the diameter, by the Vitruvian canon),[17] for the *vomitoria* arches. The builders at Petra should have cut back at least 5.82 m., to secure an impost height of 4.08 m. (one-sixth diameter), but only cut back the distance noted. The result of the impost achieved (1.6 m. in the rock-cut, but 2.02 m. for the first voussoir, which might be seen as a springer?) gave an arch height of 3.6 m. Whether this was dictated by the necessities of available bedrock, or other factors, cannot be determined. From the imposts, cut into the bedrock side walls, spring the segmented barrel vaults which roof the passages. Above the vaulting, masonry has been coursed, horizontally, in cement (concrete) to provide the horizontal floor of the *tribunalia(e)*. This consolidation also relieves the lateral thrust of the vaulting, especially against the masonry fill areas of the eastern wall of the *vomitorium dextrum*. On the right, the passage leads out of the *orchestra* area, joined by a groin with the barrel vault, perpendicular to it, leading to the common exit with the rock-cut *aditus* from the *praecinctio* above. The SE impost of this barrel vault is also rock-cut, with part of its northern side again resting on a supplementary masonry build.

The eastern faces of both *vomitoria* outer walls are studded with plugging holes for marble facing, all of which has been robbed away (see Plate XXII, 3). However, the pattern of the plugging holes is such that the pattern of the facing, and the dimensions of its slabs and moldings, may be completely restored.

The *vomitorium sinistrum* was completed, but its *aditus* passage never cut. The cutting marks for that passage are evident in the western wall of the passage, at its intersection with the transverse exit (see Plate XXII, 4). That this *aditus* would have exited on the *praecinctio* between the *media cavea* and the *summa cavea*, rather than at the lower level, as was the case on the other side, seems probable as was noted above.

Above the outer exit of the *vomitorium sinistrum* a circular rock cutting was apparent. That this served as the seat for some circular decorative medallion,[18] in stone or metal, may have been possible. Unfortunately no remains of such a decorative piece was found in the fall debris.

The arching of all *vomitoria* passages, because of the height of the springing and the height of the arch peak used, resulted in a 'circular' arch form, quite in keeping with Roman period architectural practice.[19]

The use of concrete to relieve the arch thrust is also a strictly Roman contribution. Such a consolidation no longer acts laterally (as an arch), but simply rests as a unit on the impost blocks or the wall, as Roman engineers soon discovered and widely applied.[20] That the Theater at Petra employed ashlar blocks instead of brick for their vaulting can be readily explained in terms of the relative availability of the material used. This procedure is noted in the case of other installations, however, even though as 'exceptional' and 'almost entirely limited to eastern countries'.[21] That the builders did not avail themselves fully of the concrete technique, using it only to consolidate the floor level above the arching, would seem to indicate a period when the use of this material was known, but the full structural value of the technique was not yet appreciated.

3. *PROSCENIUM*

The stage area[22] of the Theater is on a line parallel to the diameter of the *orchestra* circle, set back 3.10 m. The stage proper is a combination of built masonry and rock-cutting (the *hyposcenium*) (see Plate XXIV 1, and plan, Plate Folder E).

The *finitio proscenii* (i.e. the face of the stage elevation) rests on bedrock. The present height of the stage floor is roughly 1.20 m. above the *orchestra* floor level. Allowing for variations in subpaving and pavement, this height is roughly in accord with the Vitruvian maximum of 5 ft.[23] The relation of stage height to line of sight has not been fully determined for the Roman theater, in general, but some connection obviously existed.[24] Because of the length of the *orchestra* depth at Petra, a somewhat higher stage could be allowed (and still do no injustice to the *proedria* distance requirements), hence the 'maximum' height is approached. Whether this also implies the use of the *orchestra* area for seating at Petra would be questionable, especially in view of the *bisellium* near the foot of the *ima cavea*.[25]

The length of the stage, regardless of where terminal points are determined at the *versurae*, exceeds twice the diameter of the *orchestra*, in accordance with the Vitruvian canon.[26] To the far edges of the *versurae* outsets, in any case, the stage (i.e. paved) area extends c. 27.02 m. on the N and c. 27.18 m. on the S from the center. Obviously, however, a good part of that area, on both sides, would have been obscured from view by the *vomitoria* walls, except to those sitting on the *tribunaliae*.

The stage depth (from the *finitio proscenii* to the line of the *scaenae frons*) is about 6.32–6.36 m., or 26% of the *orchestra* diameter, closer than most theater buildings elsewhere approached the Vitruvian canon of 25%.[27]

The *finitio proscenii*, in terms of its original build, must be related to the evidence uncovered in the *hyposcenium* area behind the central niche of the stage front. This area was excavated stratigraphically (see Section Drawings, Plate XXV), and produced definitive information concerning the phasing of Period I as a whole. This evidence may be summarized as follows:

(i) Bedrock served as the floor level of the area behind the central niche (1.9 m. wide, 70 cm. deep) during all phases of Period I.

(ii) The excavated canal, noted in the *orchestra* description, was functionally related to theatrical effects, because of its penetration behind the niche area, during the earliest phase of Period I.

(iii) The canal was subsequently filled, and a sliding door arrangement opened through the central niche: two piers, 14 × 48 × 79 cm., with a base, showed slots in their inner sides able to accommodate a total door a bit over 28 cm. wide and 76 cm. high. Since the side slots were 4 cm. wide and that of the base 7 cm. wide, it is suggested that the closure device was double, and less than 3.5 cm. thick. The canal was filled (I.1 (19)), covered and its eastern end blocked (see Plate XXIV, 3–4).

(iv) At a later date, the sliding door device went out of use and the opening in the central niche was crudely sealed with re-used orthostat slabs (not squarely set—see Plate XXIV, 3).

On the basis of this evidence, the build of the *finitio proscenii* can be resolved. In its excavated state, the stage front showed a flush face, the evidence of plastering over, and filling of internally incurved blocks recessed into the edges of orthostats, with intervening blocking materials between the alternate orthostats. The blocking of the internally incurved blocks was especially poor, with crudely fitted fill blocks used, chinked with smaller stones (see Plate XXIV, 4; Plate XXVI, 1). The plastering was relatively thick, terminating in a curved join area and obviously designed to completely mask the (original) carved decorations on the orthostats (see Plate XXVI, 2).

Related to this phase were two post blocks set on the *orchestra* floor next to the stage front, made from rubble (one from a part of column drum), crudely plastered over and apparently designed to support posts, masts or standards. These may have been actually used for an awning support, but no further evidence was obtained as to function (see Plate XXVI, 3, 4).

Still further, the plastering technique, as well as the plan, in turn related the wall with stairway and the curb remains found in front of the middle stairway of the *ima cavea* to the orthostat plastering phase, along with two stairways of poor masonry build added to the stage front on each side about midway between the central niche and the original stairways at each side of the stage area. These stairways were heavily plastered, with the same curved join with the *orchestra* floor observed in the case of the one across the *orchestra*. Neither was bonded to the stage front, but were held in place by build and plastering (see Plate XXVI, 4).

That this represented the final phase of Period I use was obvious. In turn, it could be related to the blocking of the opening of the central niche by the use of discarded orthostats and plaster. Still further, excavation beneath the pavement near the juncture of the *finitio proscenii* and the *vomitorium dextrum* confirmed the phase. At that point (Trench I.24), it was found that an earlier rectangular niche (70 cm. × 1.40 m.) had been sealed by the use of an orthostat set across its mouth and pavement laid over an homogeneous fill, topped with concrete. The orthostat used to seal the opening broke the pattern of orthostat location and hence could not have been *in situ* of original build. Thick plaster over the base areas of the orthostats again related them to the final phase of use (see Plate XXVII, 1–2). This data clearly indicates a basic change in plan over the stage-front-*orchestra* area.

Since the internally curved blocks noted above were set into receiving notches cut into pairs of orthostats (see Plate XXVI, 1), alternating with unnotched orthostat pairs, the curved niche arrangement must again represent a rebuild phase. This phase introduced a *finitio proscenii* decorated with alternating rectangular and curved niches (see Plate XXVII, 3–4). Since the orthostats were still in use, it would therefore indicate that the larger rectangular niches at each end of the stage were open, and that the orthostat-blocked sliding door device behind the central niche was also open and in use. The build, especially in the notching of orthostat edges, was rather clumsy, and the face of the stage front was probably plastered, at least to some degree.

Finally, on the foregoing evidence, it is obvious that the original build of the *finitio proscenii* must have been composed of *only* rectangular niches, with orthostats c. 55 cm. × 110 cm. × 20 cm. set against the outset intervals between each pair. When the interior of the large niche at the stage side (I.24) was cleared, its sides still showed plaster. Since this plaster went behind the orthostats, it is obvious that the interior sides of the original niches were plastered to cover the ashlar coursing of the elevation build. In view of the finely cut decoration and polishing of the orthostats, themselves, it is doubtful that they were covered with plaster, however.

To this original phase must then belong the canal cut into the *orchestra* floor, as the functional device for theatrical effects for the phase, later closed off on its interior end by a slab, when the sliding door device replaced it.

Three phases of the *finitio proscenii*—and hence of Period I as a whole—are schematized on Plate Folder D. Briefly summarized, they are as follows:

(a) Original: a curved (?) central niche, c. 1.84 m. wide, flanked by nine rectangular inset niches (c. 70 cm. wide, c. 70 cm. deep), with plastered sides and with orthostats against the piers between pairs; wide side stairs (c. 1.5 m.) at each end, each flanked by a deep rectangular niche (70 cm. × 1.40 m.) with orthostats against all piers; and an open canal for theatrical effect purposes.

(b) A rebuild phase: with the central niche opened by a sliding door arrangement inside, the canal blocked and sealed, flanked by five rectangular niches alternating with four incurved niches (1 m. wide), the end stairways still in use as well as the wider end niches; face of stage front probably plastered.

(c) A rather complete rebuild and modification of both stage front and *orchestra* edge; additional stairways added to stage front, with related stair, wall and curb near center stair of *ima cavea*; standard supports added; all niches filled flush and thickly plastered; end niches filled and sealed; central niche opening sealed.

The sealed deposit of I.24 contributed pottery remains of chronological significance. The sherd content of the fill was high and produced most of the fragments of one cooking pot and a jar, as well as most of a Nabataean plain, thin, coarse ware bowl, along with a great concentration of thin fine ware (Roman), heavy, coarse, common wares, thin, coarse, ribbed wares, a fragment of yellow-tan (marl clay) ware with combed decoration, Nabataean fine, thin plain wares and, especially, late Nabataean *black* painted ware (see Plates LVIII, LIX, LII, 1–5, and section C of this chapter).

This deposit was quite different in make-up from that found in the canal (I.1 (19)), where thin common wares, mainly *red* ribbed wares, and worn Nabataean red painted, fine, thin wares predominated (see Plates LI, 1–2; LII, 4; LVII, and see section C of this chapter).

The presence of the combed decorated wares in both deposits, as well as in I.2 (15) would tend to place those two phases rather close together chronologically, but the black painted Nabataean sherds would indicate the niche fill to be the later of the two deposits.

Parallels to the *finitio proscenii* treatment in these phases are mixed in date. However, it may be noted that related to the phase (a) treatment are a number of largely Hellenistic (third–first century B.C.) examples: Epidauros,[28] Megalopolis,[29] Magnesia,[30] Ephesus,[31] and Eretria,[32] as well as examples from the early Imperial period: Pompeii (large theater),[33] Termessos,[34] Sagalassos,[35] as well as others. In every case, however, an exact parallel to all features is lacking, even though the general style is similar.

The phase (b) treatment also has a variety of related but not exactly similar parallels, beginning with the first century A.D., but coming mainly from the middle of the second century A.D. and continuing down to the third century: Herculaneum,[36] Khamisa,[37] Minturnae,[38] Merida,[39] Timgad,[40] Djemila,[41] Ostia, Dugga,[42] Leptis Magna, 'Amman,[43] Jerash (South Theater),[44] Aspendos,[45] Palmyra,[46] and Samaria.[47] To these must be added, however, the earliest of the Palestinian examples, Caesarea,[48] from the late first century B.C. The preponderance of examples would point to the late periods, however. That the rebuilding of phase (b) is as late as most of the examples with related styles is doubtful, however, for stratigraphic and historical reasons. Especially to be noted in the latter regard is the gap in Roman theater building from the Augustan period to that of the Antonines. Hence, a rebuilding earlier than or between those periods might simply have reflected an early phase of a new styling adopted for a new theater (as Caesarea and Herculaneum), but not found in other contemporary examples—and reappearing when new theater building again became common.[49]

The broad stairways (c. 1.5 m.) at each side of the stage (see plan, Plate Folder C), leading to it from the *orchestra* (and the *vomitoria*) were not only functional, but also served as part of the dramatic conventions of the day, informing the audience that actors ascending them came from 'distant places.'[50]

The stage floor was well paved in stone, in distinction to a number of other provincial theaters. The pavement of the far ends of the area is much better preserved than in the central part, since it was laid on bedrock at those ends and, hence, able to resist the impact of the fall (Period IV; see Plate XXVIII, 1–2). In addition, early re-use robbing (Period II) of the central area greatly weakened as well as depleted the paving stones there. Current restoration activities by the Department of Antiquities have (wisely) stripped the remaining pavement from the stage proper so that the sub-paving and supporting members of the *hyposcenium* may be strengthened once more.

The original pavement was of well polished limestone, not marl or sandstone, both of which were used by the builders only when facing could be supported or other protection offered. The paving slabs vary in size from c. 47 cm. × 65.5 cm., to 50.5 cm. × 72.5 cm., to c. 53.5 cm. × 87.5 cm. (see plan, Plate Folder E).

The slabs were laid in straight rows, lengthwise, from the *scaenae frons* inward, but the end joints are staggered according to slab size and the contours met. The facing slabs (*crustae*) of the *scaena frons* were first set in place and then the paving slabs butted against them. Cement appears to have also been used to level bedrock wherever the slabs were set directly on its surface, with runnels cut at various points to assist drainage beneath the slabs (see Plate XXVIII; and plan, Plate Folder E).

In the area of the stage proper, the paving rested on a sturdy sub-pavement of more roughly cut and less carefully joined slabs. These were, in turn, carried by supports above the *hyposcenium* (see Plate XXVIII, 3–4).

The *hyposcenium* was made by leaving two parallel sets of bedrock piers during the cutting of the *orchestra* (see Plate XXVIII, 4; XXIX, 1). These served as floors and arch imposts for the stage floor, augmented by built masonry generally composed of ashlar, column drums and similar debris. Where the bedrock piers were used, a series of small segmented arches was carried between them in the direction of the stage depth to serve as sub-pavement flooring joists. The springings were cut back into the piers (see Plate XXIX, 2–3). The rough sub-pavement was then laid over the arches, resting halfway across the width of the arch voussoirs on both ends, stretching along the direction of the stage width. At the sides, against the bedrock walls, the slabs were roughly chinked with small stones to prevent lateral movement. Their sheer weight kept the pressure arches in place beneath them, and this rough but massive construction was extremely rigid, preserving a firm foundation for the finished paving above and roofing the *hyposcenium* area below. Only when robbing occurred was the strength of the whole impaired by the loss of inter-related parts, thus causing a breakdown of the horizontal line.

The *hyposcenium* had a series of rooms between the longitudinal piers on each side of the stage center. Their purpose is unclear, but in other theaters they were used for storage, among other purposes.[51] No trace of any stage machinery was recovered either during excavations or clearance, however.

Related to the *hyposcenium* were the *auleum* slots of the stage, c. 50 cm. wide, set back from the *finitio proscenii* edge about 1 m. These slots had been excavated from bedrock at their lower levels and built up with masonry with the stage elevation. Near the bottom they narrowed to c. 25 cm. into three elongated pits c. 35–40 cm. deep (see Plates XXIX, 4; XXX, 1).

Such slots were standard features of the Roman theater plan,[52] and accommodated the stage curtain (*auleum*) which was lowered into the slots, on telescoping poles, at the beginning of perfor-mances and raised once again at their end to shield the stage from the spectator's gaze.[53]

It was in the slot at the northern end of the Theater that the Hercules torso was recovered in 1961. During the 1962 season that slot was excavated stratigraphically with the hope of recovering further parts of the statue and some remains of the *auleum* rods or their hardware. None of those expectations were realized, except for a few bits of the lower legs of the Hercules torso.

The slot excavated (I.23/B) was almost filled with wash-drift cover, indicating that it was open up to and during that period, as noted above in regard to the central niche area. The slot was connected to the central niche area by an arched passageway. This was filled with a wash and drift material, indicating that the paving immediately above it had not been robbed away as in the niche area itself.

The debris found in all related areas exactly parallels the Period IV material elsewhere (see Section Drawings, Plate XXV, 1, 3).

In the parallel walls of the arched passageway, leading from the *auleum* slot to the niche area, were found matching notches, c. 12 cm. × 10 cm. × 12 cm., near the top and bottom of the wall lines. These would suggest that a closure, perhaps a door, kept the two areas separate.

In the niche area, the fall debris was heavy down to a hard-packed level (I.25 (9)) below the sliding door base stone. It was in this level, which represents the depth of the fall and cover, that a second coin of Constantine the Great was found (#2069). Hence, this level must correspond with Period IV as in the north, and represent the cover wash and drift of Period V. However, the next levels (I.25 (11), 12), (13)) appear to represent conscious fill, and are therefore construed to be the fill placed beneath the sliding door base in the second phase (b) of Period I. However, the density of level (9) tends to indicate that its lowest part may have belonged to Period I, with wash and drift of Periods II–III packed down and the level penetrated by the fall, on which Period V cover was then deposited. Because of the essential likeness of the wash/drift of Periods II–III and V, differentiation is not possible, but some floor level is to be expected over the fill (11), (12), (13) of the sliding door phase.

Since levels I.25 (1), (2/3), (4), (6), (7), and (8) all showed considerable fall rubble, Periods II and III cannot be differentiated in this area.

On each side of the stage extensions are *versurae* outsets, extending from the *vomitoria* walls and from the *scaenae frons* (see Plates XXVIII, 2; XXX, 2). The southern end of the stage was intact, and permitted accurate planning of the features. The extensions from the *vomitoria* are outset c. 1.10 m., with an additional 15 cm. of plaster and facing. From the *scaenae frons* the extensions are c. 90 cm., plus the additional 0.15 cm. The northern *versura* build was less well preserved, with the marble facings and plaster gone; however, only about 5 cm. variation between the two sets of *versurae* openings is unaccounted for.

On the *vomitorium dextrum* end, the outset still had a column base (of the 53 cm. class) *in situ*. On the *vomitorium sinistrum* end, a base with one full drum and part of a second drum was also *in situ*. These provide data concerning the decoration of the inside of the *versurae* faces. The reconstructed southern theater at Jerash provides an exact parallel to the columnation. The presence of voussoirs near the *versura sinistra* indicates an arched doorway, again as the Jerash example. Socket holes in the floor next to the outside edges of the *versurae* outsets indicate a closure was used to bar entrance over the stage, keeping spectator traffic moving only through the *vomitoria*, with the possible exception of *orchestra* (?) and *ima cavea* seat holders.

The wall bar slots and pavement holes in the (southern) area just behind the line of the main stair from the *orchestra* to the stage would seem to indicate a barricade at that point, also (see Plate Folder E).

No evidence was found for any roofing, temporary or permanent, of the stage area.[54]

4. *SCAENA*

The *scaena* (see Plates XIII, 2, 3; XXX, 3, 4) of the Theater at Petra is composed of a single wall line, with outset foundation courses on its eastern side and a decorative *scaenae frons*. The distance between the *scaenae frons* and the outside line of the *postscenium* wall is c. 6.80 m. with long gallery rooms between the wall lines, c. 2.80 m. wide. These rooms appear to have had entry doors from the *vomitoria* passageways at each end, but may also have been blocked in between at the exit lines of the side doors of the *scaenae frons* as well. The exit passages leading from the *vomitoria* outside the *postscenium* wall were paved with a flagstone type pavement on a level with the stage floor (at least on the north end—see Plate XXXI, 1–2).

The *scaenae frons* wall is, of course, the more carefully built, and illustrates the building technique employed. This was the 'triple wall' type, wherein dressed faces on each side of the wall line are backed by rubble and cement between, as described by Vitruvius, but seen by him as a hasty method not to be recommended.[55]

Because of the direction of the fall (Period IV), i.e. toward the *orchestra*, the lower part of the *scaenae frons* was protected in detail. Standing courses, at various points along the line, rise four or five courses high (c. 1.20–1.50 m.), because of the fall direction and the thickness of the lower *scaenae frons* at that level. As a consequence, plan, building technique, facing and molding application, columnation podia, and other features of the lower *scaena frons* are all preserved.

Ashlar blocks of local sandstone[56] were used for the wall, squarely cut, with typical Nabataean dressing throughout. The effects of wear and, in the case of debris, destruction and erosion, caused some difficulty in securing exact measurements of original block sizes. However, when all measurements are compared, a series of rough dimensions appears as follows: 70/60/50/40/30/20/20 cm. These dimensions could therefore be interchanged to fit needed space, with cut blocks of the 60 cm., 50 cm., 30 cm., and 20 cm. dimension or multiples thereof, on one or more sides, predominating.

This *opus quadratum* appears to be coursed in a perplexing fashion, even though it is in the 'isodomon' coursing (i.e. blocks of equal height), until it is realized that corners are vertically coursed in an alternating header-stretcher pattern to give stability. Thus, where a corner has a header on its main face (i.e. toward the stage front), a stretcher butts it (see Plate XXXI, 3; XXVII, 3). Where a corner has a stretcher in that position, a header butts it on the main face.[57] This is the Vitruvian 'emplecton' ('weaving-through') coursing, which he saw as 'Greek' style.[58] Irregularities of the pattern are simply the result of the necessities of the dimensions involved. Because of the mathematics of the *scaenae frons*, a general irregularity of coursing appears across it, but this artistic defect was covered either by facing slabs or plaster applied over the ashlar. The building technique especially where possible in the lower courses of the *scaena*, gave the structure a great deal of strength and rigidity, as its present condition shows, and provided a stable base for the elevation. The neat header-stretcher coursing of the *opus quadratum* seen in structures in Rome is, however, absent.[59]

The face of the *scaenae frons* wall is pocked by plugging holes, some still retaining marble plugs and bits of the bronze fixtures (or their unmistakable green stains). Fall blocks also showed the same signs over the area (see Plate XXXII, 1). At the base of the *scaenae frons* and at various points along its second podium, facing marble is still to be found *in situ*, held by a thick layer of plaster (generally 9 cm. in thickness), with some bronze fixtures also still *in situ* (see Plate XXXII, 2–3). Moldings are also to be found *in situ* at some points, providing a complete picture of the technique employed. The amount of marble (white, gray, and veined), along with white mottled red (properly breccia) facing slabs, gives some indication of the elegance of the original decoration.

The plan (see plan, Plate Folder C) of the *scaenae frons* is symmetrical (although parallel parts may vary slightly in dimensions), as would be expected from the mathematics of the original layout (i.e. based on points determined by the equilateral triangle inscribed in the *orchestra* circle).[60]

A large Main Doorway (the *aula regia*, or 'royal door') is flanked by small rectangular niches. These are, in turn, flanked by stairways forming the conventional stage exits (*aulae hospitaliae*). Next to these are another set of small niches, followed by the *versurae* outsets and doors. These units measure as follows, including facings:

Main Door 9.72 m.

North side		*South side*	
Face	3.08 m.	Face	3.08
Niche	1.68 m.	Niche	1.66
Face	3.12 m.	Face	3.14
Stairwell	3.92 m.	Stairwell	3.95
Face	⎫	Face	3.24
Niche	⎬ 10.66 m.	Niche	1.66
Face	⎪	Face	3.08
Versura outset	⎭	*Versura* outset	2.86

These measurements make a total of 54.85 m. for the distance across the *scaenae frons*. The placement of both the first set of side niches closest to the Main Door and the inside edges of the side stairwells are about 20 cm. short of the mathematical locations (i.e. the niche edges at the point on the *scaenae frons* where the *orchestra* circle intersects and the points of extension of the sides of the central triangle inscribed in the *orchestra*).

The 'Royal Door,' conventionally representing a palace door, was set into a deeply incurved niche, with flanking piers (see Plate XXIV, 1). Since no curved pieces nor voussoirs were found in the fall debris near this door, it is concluded that it had a straight entablature (i.e. trabeated, not arctuated). The two side doors were considerably less imposing in size, although set off by insets, as befitted their roles. By the stage conventions of the day, these doors were for the use of secondary or tertiary actors, or were used to indicate conventionalized locations.[61] They were, however, wider than the purely decorative niches, for the sake of architectural emphasis. All three doors had steps leading to the exit floors. The entrances to the stage area from the sides, via the *versurae* doorways, were also conventional, leading from 'the Forum', or from 'the country' as the plot action demanded.[62]

The small rectangular insets in the face of the *scaenae frons* are seen by Fiechter as purely decorative, and as typically Roman ('western' style) features in eastern theaters.[63] This is borne out at Petra by the presence of a high concentration of breccia in the fall debris immediately in front of these niches. Apparently these were given this additional embellishment as part of the decorative emphasis. They were also arched, as is indicated by voussoirs in the fall debris below the two niches nearest the central doorway.[64]

Comparison of the *scaenae frons* of the Theater at Petra with other provincial theaters indicates parallels of varying degrees: Arles, Dugga, Orange, and Djemila all show the incurving niche for the main door, along with the rectangular stair wells, but without the decorative side niches; Aizano (Hadrianic) and Aosta also show the central niche and the side stairwells, but the latter are increased to four and the decorative side niches are again absent; Boṣra and Khamisa, on the other hand, while having the curved central niche, also have curved side niches as well. Herculaneum again (see above) furnishes one of the closest parallels to the Petraean plan, with a central door niche, rectangular side niches, and the flanking stairwells. The Neronian (?) or Augustan (?) rebuild of the large theater at Pompeii is also quite close to the Petra plan, as is a 'IV style' mural from there, shown by Fiechter, from Reg. VIII, insula 2, #23.[65]

Fiechter characterizes the niche type of *scaenae frons* as 'western', in distinction to the flat, unbroken type ('eastern'), and has established some chronological aspects.[66] Difficulty arises, however, in both terminology and typology in terms of this characterization when applied to the Near East, including Asia Minor. For 'western', another term, such as 'Italic', might be preferable in order to avoid geographical confusion in application. Still further, as was noted above, the chronological typology tends to break down in the Near Eastern areas, without clear chronological distinction.

In specifics of detail, however, the 'western' *scaenae frons* of the Theater at Petra most closely resembles the early imperial façades of Fiechter's typology (i.e. the Augustan).[67] This, coupled with the Herculaneum parallel, seems significant.

The development of the *scaenae frons* and its precise relation to the stage in the Roman theater plan is still a matter of some scholarly dispute. It has been seen as solely a decorative background in the classical Greek and Hellenistic periods; as a decorative background later united with the actual place of acting; and current opinion seems to consider it as having had an integral relation to the performance area from the very beginning.[68] In any case, by the Roman period the *scaenae frons* was the backdrop for the action on the stage, of which it had, indeed, become an integral architectural part. It was highly decorated and specifically formalized by the dramatic conventions.[69] Painted scenery supplemented it, in order to enhance action, supply a more exact locale, and provide variation in the setting. This scenery was shifted, like modern stage sets, by drawing one panel off, thus exposing the next one (i.e. the 'scaena ductilis'), or was simply revolved, in the form of painted prisms, at the sides of the stage area (the Greek *periactoi*, known to the Romans as 'scaena versilis').[70] No identifiable scenery remains were found at Petra, aside from the façade of the *scaena* itself.

The Department of Antiquities resumed their clearance activities at the far NE side of the Theater area, just beyond the trench lines of the 1962 season. In the course of that work a masonry extension of the cut cliff wall was uncovered, extending parallel to the exit line of the *vomitorium sinistrum* and then turning parallel to the *postscenium* wall line (see Plate XXXII, 4). At that point a stairway was let in, rising to a landing, continuing upward at right angles, parallel to the cliff face to a second landing, and then turning at right angles to a platform on top of the wall (see Plate XXXIII, 1). This complex was a massive end blockage to the whole *scaena* wall line, and must be related particularly to it. That it was not a public way, in spite of the use of plaster to finish the side walls of the lower stair, is obvious in terms of the terminal platform to which the stair system led. Further, because of the protruding rock-cut wall in the cliff side, at the NW side of the platform, no view of the stage was possible, and no access to the *cavea* offered. The mass of the build, however, suggests a functional reason for its erection. Since it butts the *scaena-postscenium* wall lines, and since those lines were probably connected by a spanning roof, the stair complex would give access to that roof, not for spectators, but for stage technicians. Even though no machinery was found, the possibility of its use for dramatic effect (i.e. cranes, etc. for hoisting men and gods 'heavenward' from the stage floor) cannot be discounted. Still further, access to the roof area would provide the means of access for repair of the upper story area at any time. The wall lines of this massive structure were, unfortunately, not completely intact, but on the basis of present height, it appears to have been c. 8.30–8.40 m. above the *orchestra* floor level, or c. 7.10–7.20 m. above the stage floor (see below). Such massive *parascenium* structures occur in other theaters where windows seem to have been let in, as well.

5. *EPISCENIUM*

The stratigraphic and clearance operations of the two seasons made it possible to investigate the details of the *episcenium* build for the first time since antiquity. The bulk of the data presented below therefore resulted from analysis of the fall debris (Period IV) and comparison with known related structures. Although individual components of the scenery wall were able to be isolated and their location noted, it was still found that certain gaps in specific data areas were impossible

4

to fill. The tumbled mass of fall debris made exact limits impossible to define in certain details, as might be expected when a mass of debris is deposited by fall.

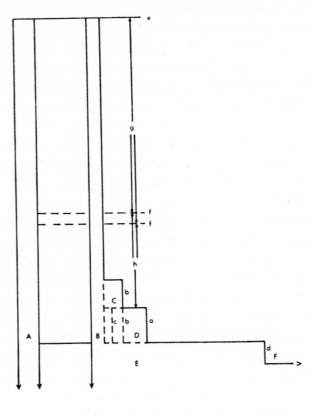

5 m.

SCHEMATIC ELEVATION: *SCAENA*

A — *Postscenium* wall
B — *Scaena* wall
C — Second podium, *scaenae frons*
D — First podium, *scaena frons*
E — *Proscenium* (stage) area
F — *Orchestra*

a — *scaenae frons* line, first podium
b — *scaenae frons* line, second podium and back wall of niches
c — *scaenae frons* line, at side doors level of first podium
d — *finitio proscenii*
e — roof line, second story (?)
f — *scaenae roof* level (?), first story
g — height of second story and attic of first story
h — height of first story order (?)

However, the fact of simultaneous fall of all parts, and its subsequent seal by non-occupational deposits, as well as the non-use (except for the robbery phase) of the area in general, permitted more specific data to be gained than has generally been the case with theater structures. Concentration peaks of debris were obvious, and careful analysis of their meaning provided access to further data.

For a variety of reasons, not every detail of the *episcenium* and other parts of the Theater could be secured in complete specificity. However, the amount possible quite adequately suggests what the structure did look like during its main period of use.

The ground plan of the *scaenae frons* has been discussed above, and attention must now be centred upon the elevation of the *scaena* wall. Following the ground plan, the first elevation of the *scaenae frons* consisted of a set-back of the *scaena* wall to form a podium, c. 1.90 m. high. This set-back followed the niche outlines of the plan, thus forming true niches in the wall face. The floor level of this podium was indicated by columns still *in situ*, found here and there along it (see Plate XXXI, 3).

From the level of this podium the *scaena* wall was again set back, this time on a line with the back wall of the niches of the level below. Thus the first podium was provided with a surface area for the columnar decoration c. 1.26 m. deep along its front edge.

Next to the side doors, the face plan of the first podium was also set back c. 60 cm. At the sides of the main door, the set-back was in a curved line. The *scaena* wall behind the first podium was therefore also set back, in a staggered line, following the lines of the podium face, c. 38 cm., providing an additional 98 cm., making the first podium depth c. 2.24 m. at those points. The floor level of the two piers flanking the main door were at the level of the first podium.

The set-back area of the *scaena* wall behind the first podium rose c. 1.50 m. to form a second podium, or, more properly, a parapet, 98 cm. deep, and c. 3.79 m. long between the side door and side stairway areas. No evidence was secured for the length at other points. This parapet had a marble base facing and molding, further indicating its line (see plan, Plate Folder E). In effect, this parapet actually formed a backing elevation for the niche areas, as well, with whose rear walls it formed a straight line at the upper level.

Above the upper parapet level the *scaena* wall was destroyed, for the most part, although the Department of Antiquitie's clearance uncovered a higher portion at the northern end of the stage (see Plate XXXI, 4; XXXIII, 2).

However, marble facing lines found near the northern side door area, on the parapet level, indicated that the *scaena* wall was again set back behind it, to the line of the doorway set-back, leaving the *scaena* wall only 68 cm. from that point upward. The clearance noted above shows that at the northern end of the complex, at least, this wall continued in a straight face. At that end, the *versura* outset area was well preserved, with facings and plaster fairly intact (see Plate XXX, 2).[71] The remains of the wall lines at that point, plus the massive blockade along the other side of the *vomitorium sinistrum* exit, suggest a height of c. 7.60–8.40 m. above the *orchestra* floor (i.e. c. 6.40–7.20 m. above the stage floor) for the possible roofing of the area between the *scaenae frons* wall line and the *postscenium* wall (see below). Destruction of the walls in both cases precludes an exact height determination, but the standing masonry platform of the blockade at the other side of the exit measures c. 5.80 m. above the stage floor, in present ruins, and thus the above estimate is not impossible, as other factors indicate, as well.[72]

The *postscenium* wall continues straight along the rear of the *scaena*, being interrupted only by door cuts. This wall was generally c. 1.10 m. in width, with outset lower foundation courses. In the model elevation, this wall should reach to the level of the upper gallery of the *summa cavea*, for acoustical purposes.[73] This was probably the case at Petra, since when the cliff sides were cut back for the *scaena* walls, outcrops were left along the elevation lines for bonding in the walls themselves (see Plate XXX, 4). Above the level of available bedrock, the remains of masonry built walls continue the lines so that the *scaena* was apparently carried to its full height, some 18.8 m. above the *orchestra* floor level. The *scaenae frons* wall, above the first podium, was relatively narrow for such a height, but with columnar buttressing along its lower face line, the probable support of roofing close to its mid-point, further colonnade and roofing support above that, and the firm buttressing by blockade cross walls at the end, a great deal of strength was actually achieved. Modern masonry construction calls for a 1:18 ratio of width to height—a ratio met by the *postscenium* wall and compensated for in the *scaena* wall.

The first podium, was probably provided with some molding treatment along its face line, as the quantity of such moldings in the fall (but none *in situ*) would suggest. The face of the *scaenae frons* shows plugging holes for marble facings to the full height of both the first podium and the parapet levels. The interior niche areas were plastered, and very probably painted as occasional painted plaster fragments indicate. The *postscenium* wall was not faced, but the diagonal dressing may suggest stucco plaster, although no distinct evidence was found to suggest this. Whether the *scaenae frons* was faced for its full height also cannot be determined.

The doors of the *scaenae frons* had moldings of white marble, but the details of architraves, if any, cannot be established. Gabled cornice fragments, found c. 4.10 and 4.30 m. from the *scaenae frons* line, near the doors, may suggest architraves like the side doors of the Khazneh (i.e. gabled—but cf. the main door which has a simple architrave).[74] But these elements may also be related to either the attic or the tympaneum (?) above the main door area, in the entablature. The *versurae* exits on the stage were probably arched, as elsewhere, as the presence of voussoirs in the fall indicates.

The dimensions of the floor surface of the first podium (1.26 m. deep to 2.24 m. at the door insets) preclude more than a single row of columns along the *scaenae frons* line, except in the doorway insets. This is established by the columns found with plinth, base, and drum parts *in situ* on the podium. These columns had plinths c. 92 cm. square, placed c. 14 cm. from the podium side edges and c. 6 cm. from the front edge (see below). The width of the podia could have permitted up to three such columns between each niche area, but the inter-columnation distances of such an arrangement would have been so scant that a crowded effect would have resulted.[75] Nor does it seem probable that columns flanked the niche areas, since no wall recess is indicated, but this may have been done. No column drums of suitable size were recovered to indicate this possibility either.

Single columns were set on the *versurae* outsets, both from the *scaenae frons* and the *vomitoria* walls. The piers extending from the main door could have each accommodated a single column, as well.

It will be noted that the first podium is slightly lower than called for by the Vitruvian canon,[76] lacking c. 14 cm. of the required height. Likewise, the parapet behind the first podium is higher than the canon allowed.[77]

Since the first podium could not have alone accommodated all the columns for which drums or partial drums were recovered, since the material of the recovered drums, as well as their sizes, show two distinct large groups of columns, and since the fall concentration peaks show fall ranges for four groups (see below) there must have been a second, upper story to the *scaenae frons*.

The fall debris (see Period IV, above) permitted the isolation of two main columnar types, on the basis of size and material: A 53–55 cm. group, uniformly of yellow marl, and a 59–63 cm. group, uniformly of a harder stone, with a grey patina suggesting local material. Since no obvious entasis could be detected, the variations within the size groupings may simply represent cutting variations—the regulation of which, in terms of an individual column was controlled by the drum letter and number carved into the yellow marl examples, at least.

Previous and succeeding clearance operations precluded an exact count of drums recovered, as did the robbery phase (Period VI).

All drums were unfluted and were generally well cut and finely polished. All had tie holes in their flat ends for lifting, aligning, and joining purposes (see Plate XXXIII, 3–4). The yellow marl group also supplied a good deal of epigraphic data in the form of masons' marks cut into drum ends. The larger size group was unmarked.

A third column group was represented by a few scattered drums of c. 36 cm. in diameter, coated with plaster, with sharply marked flutes. One 45 cm. plastered drum was also found. It is suggested that these, along with a single Corinthian capital, were later additions and may have served to decorate a few specific places without involvement in the general columnar pattern.

The column bases found in the course of excavation also varied in both size and material (see Plate XXXIV, 3 and Plate XXXVIII). All showed a double torus, with a sharply defined type of scotia molding between. The bases were set on plinths, as the ones *in situ* indicate. With the smaller column type, the bases were c. 50 cm. high, the upper torus c. 60 cm. in diameter, and the lower torus c. 70 cm. in diameter. Tie holes were again found in the upper centers. The bases of the larger group were c. 26 cm. high, c. 86 cm in diameter at the lower torus, set on plinths c. 94 cm. square and c. 30 cm. thick.

The capitals of the main column groups were, without any question, pure Nabataean. These capitals were represented by examples carved in one single block (c. 1.20 m. wide, from tip to tip and c. 30 cm. thick) or in two pieces apparently joined after cutting. The flat block-like nature of the Nabataean capital made such a procedure possible. The recovered examples were all starkly plain, lacking even the ornateness of the Khazneh façade types (see Plate XXXIV, 4). Since no other capitals were to be found for the main columnar types in the unrobbed fall debris, it is quite clear that the order of the Theater was originally Nabataean (Period Ia) and, logically, continued to be so during later phases. That additional columns may have been erected (see above) could only have been incidental, and could not have changed the original order without extensive dismantling of the entire *episcenium*. That the Nabataean order represents a local variation of the Corinthian is regarded as probable, in spite of the fact that the form of the capital is obviously quite different and varies from the usual canon. Unfluted columns are also a variant feature, but were often used in the Roman Corinthian order.[78]

Two other isolated capitals were also found. One was an example of what may perhaps be termed 'Ionic', although such designation is only approximate (see Plate XXXVII, 3–4). The capital was of soft stone, c. 50 cm. square, by c. 22–23 cm. thick. It was carved to resemble two round bundles of reeds, tightly bound in the centers, with the ends of the bundles squarely cut. That such was the clear intention of the carver is unmistakable, from the representation of the binding cords, the lines of the individual reeds compressed toward the center of each bundle, with round sections squarely cut. The find spot of this particular example suggested a location near the central door of the *scaenae frons*.

The only non-Nabataean capital recovered was found by the Department of Antiquities during clearance, and represents a pure Corinthian type. This may possibly come from the last phase of main use (Period Ic), or may even be intrusive, since its stratigraphic location is unknown.

The matter of column height, for both varieties of main column types, may be approximately determined from analysis of the fall debris, in terms of concentration peaks.

The gray column (60–63 cm.) group shows distribution in the fall from 0 to c. 5.10 m. from the *scaenae frons*. But overlapped peaks appear from 1.3–3.3 m., 0–3.10 m., 2–5.10 m., and 1.25–3.25 m. Bases were recovered from 0–2.5 m., and at 2.8 m. Therefore an overlap of individual column falls must be seen, separated by at least 1.08 m., the probable intercolumnation distance at points where two rows are possible (see above), which corresponds to the fall intervals between the two sets of related concentration peaks. Hence the theoretical height of the drums of one column would be c. 3.10 m. on the basis of the range of distribution.

Since at least one complete line of six drums can be postulated from related fall, and since the partial column *in situ* near the northern side door gives a drum height of 56 cm., six drums would be 3.36 m. in height, corresponding roughly to the theoretical height based on distribution peaks alone. Since some drums were recovered which ranged to 60 cm. in height, the actual drum height could be from 3.36 m. to 3.60 m. From the column fragment *in situ*, it can also be found that the plinth was c. 30 cm. high. Recovered capitals were c. 30 cm. high, hence the probable total height of this class of columns was between 4.22 and 4.64 m. The former height is some 58 cm. less than even a 1:8 proportion between column height and column diameter (the basis for classical reckoning). Hence the columns at the Theater, as at the Khazneh,[79] are shorter than those common in Roman architecture for the Corinthian order (1:10). No possibility seems indicated, however, to raise the column height by an additional drum, which would achieve (at 60 cm. diameter) the 1:8 ratio.

The marl columns (53–55 cm. diameter) were found at concentration peaks ranging from 6.30–10.80 m., 7–10.80 m., 9–10.80 m., and 6.50–9.80 m. from the *scaenae frons*. Marked drums were recovered at the following distances: #1/#2 (?) at 6.30 m., #5 at 7.50 m., #5 at 9.55 m., #6 at 10.80 m. Bases were found at 6.8 m., and capitals, or capital fragments, up to c. 9 m.

The two drums marked #5, found at points 2.05 m. apart, suggest that the columnar arrangement of these columns followed those of the gray variety—i.e. two rows, at least at certain points. Since bases were found at 6.8 m., the extent of the columnar row displacement must be reduced. In any case, the range from 6.30 m. to 10.8 m. (the edge of Trench I.3, beyond which no stratigraphic excavation produced data for Period IV), gives a distribution of 4.5 m., to which 1.55 m. to 2.05 m. (displacement range of first (?) drum to bases and displacement range of drums marked #5), or 6.05 m. to 6.55 m. for a theoretical height of overlapped drum fall.

However, since these drums were uniformly marked (from #1/#2 (?) to #6) and none beyond #6 in the lower fall range, six drums must represent the total in any given column.

Recovered drums were c. 50 cm. in height, therefore an actual column height should be 3.00 m., which correlates with the theoretical figure derived from the fall analysis. However, since in some cases bases were carved with partial (?) drums, as one unit, and the capitals were largely destroyed by the fall, no attempt will be made to postulate the total height of this second columnar type, but it is felt that a height close to about 3.70 m. (c. 83% of the lower order) is probable.

Since the first podium is 1.90 m. above the stage floor, the possible height of the lower order, without entablature, would be in the vicinity of 6.12 m. to 6.54 m. from the stage floor. The wall lines of the stage-*vomitorium* on the northern end of the Theater was seen to be c. 6.40–7.20 m. When the entablature is added to the column heights suggested above, the order rises to c. 7.17 m. to 7.59 m., with the first height out of line with the roof height postulated (i.e. 6.40–7.20 m. above the stage floor).

The entablature pieces recovered in excavation present some interesting variations from the classical forms also. These variations are probably the result of local interpretation, rather than local taste, or even conscious local innovation, since they are, basically, of classical *western*, not oriental, design. All members were uniformly of yellow marl.

The entablature fall debris was distributed over the entire range extending from the *scaenae frons* to c. 9.8 m. out. At first glance, this seems to violate the possibility of analysis, until it is remembered that the nature of this part of the structure varies greatly from that of the column lines, in that straight vertical fall is to be expected here, along with arc effects from the linear extension outward of column fall.

Since the cornice of the entablature is more distinctive (see below), and thus more easily recognized as to original position, analysis of the concentration peaks of that debris is more productive. Peaks were found in the stage area excavation, at c. 2–3.6 m., 4.5–5.6 m., 6–7.4 m., 7.7–8.9 m. Since the displacement, in depth, of the lines of the entablature would follow that of the columnation, a displacement between related parts would be set at least 1.02 m. (see above.) Thus, the peaks are probably to be related: 2–3.6 m. to 4.5–5.6 m., as belonging to the lower order, including sides; and 6–7.4 m. to 7.7–8.9 m., including sides, for the upper order. The second peak of each group would thus represent the outer face line of the fall. Within these ranges are also the remains from the attic between orders.

Inscription fragments were found at the edge of the *scaenae frons*, and at c. 1.1 m., 1.9 m., especially at 3–3.50 m., and some near 4 m., in very relative 'concentrations'. These in turn can be related to the cornice peaks as follows: c. 1.90 m. range to the inset face of the lower order, with the 3–4 m. range belonging to the front face of that order. The inscribed fragments at c. 1.10 m., and at 3.0 m. are both noted to have had traces of red paint in the carved letters. Since the inscribed frieze blocks were lower down on the entablature face, less outward fall than the cornice pieces would be expected. The blocks with red-painted letters appear to have been c. 50 cm. in height, whereas the main 'theater' inscription fragment was only c. 42 cm. high. That they should be attributed to the upper frieze of the entablature seems probable, on the basis of other parallels, but is conjectural.

Architrave debris, including plain frieze blocks, was also distributed over the entire stage area, but needs no particular analysis.

The complete entablature, including architrave, may be described from top to bottom as follows (see Plate XXXVIII):

Cornice:
  ovola corona with bead

plain fascia
modillion and disc with fillet
cyma recta
ovolo bed for dentils, with fillet
small ovolo with double bead
plain/inscribed fascia

Architrave:

tilted and splayed cavetto with fillet
cyma reversa with double fillet
fascia with bead
fascia

It is felt that the upper and lower entablature orders were the same, and nearly the same height, on the basis of the fall material and comparisons with the orders of the Khazneh (cf. Dalman, *Khazneh*, p. 106).

On the basis of members of the orders isolated, certain conclusions are possible, although gaps exist.

Cornice blocks were found measuring 40 cm. or 35 cm. from corona to the top of the fascia. Likewise, architrave blocks were found both 44 cm. and 30 cm. in height, cut as units with the fascia in the 36 cm. class, or individually (22 cm. each) in the larger size. This would therefore suggest a slight variation between the upper and lower entablatures (see also below).

No fascia blocks belonging conclusively to the upper frieze of either entablature were found, but the red-painted inscribed fragments (c. 50 cm. high) and the 'theater' inscription itself (c. 42 cm. in height) may again point to order size variations between the two levels. Since frieze fascia may equal the height of the total architrave, no problem would be presented in terms of the two sizes, as far as location is concerned.[80]

A critical problem does arise in terms of the lower fascia of the architrave, however, since blocks of neither 7.5 cm. nor 11 cm. were noted. Such sizes would be necessary if that fascia was half the size of the one above it, in the standard fashion. A higher corona would also be indicated, if that member were to be in proper ratio. A certain lightness would have resulted, if the above ratios did exist.

In any event, on the basis of the dimensions given above, the entablatures of the two orders would have been c. 1.45 m. and 1.17 m. respectively, with the gaps filled conjecturally. Since the lower order determines the height of the upper, the lower one would have had the former dimensions, with the upper one c. four-fifths of its height. This would make the ratio of entablature to column height over one-third—not at all in accord with the Vitruvian limit of one-fifth, but in accord with the Khazneh in both cases.[81]

Dalman[82] sees the architrave of the Khazneh as 'Ionic', because of the number of fasciae, and it is suggested that such is the case at the Theater as well. The addition of another fascia would raise the height of the entablature even more excessively and disproportionately.

The grooves of some of the architrave blocks showed traces of red paint, suggesting some decoration of that member.

The cornice remains uncovered in the excavations proved to be of definite interest, in terms of style and motifs, as well as size variations noted above.

The faces of these members, as all others of the order, were well cut and finely polished. The hidden parts displayed pick marks, however, giving an indication of the tools used in quarrying or rough cutting of the blocks to size (see Plate XXXV, 4). Such tools are noted in the literature concerning the period and their use at Petra, where stone cutting was so characteristic, is to be expected.[83] The marks are short and relatively narrow, indicating that a chisel-like blade was employed. These marks are quite unlike the pick marks to be seen under close examination in typical Nabataean diagonal dressing. This dressing, as has been noted before, was well represented on the Theater masonry as well (see Plate VI, 4; XXXII, 1). Guide lines for final cutting of details were scribed on the faces of the blocks, as one recovered sample shows (see Plate XXXVI, 2; and detail, 4). In the example in question an obvious error in scribing the corner treatment was made, with the corrections also scribed in. It would appear that generally these lines were polished out after the final cutting was done.

The dentiled members of the cornice (see Plate XXXVII, 1–2) were outset, cut into an ovolo bed, c. 8 cm. wide, and cut in a 2:1 ratio to the reserve of the bed between each dentil (Plate XXXVIII). For ease in handling, a number of such dentil members were found cut from separate blocks which could be lifted in place and aligned without too much difficulty. In these cases the higher members of the cornice were also cut as separate units with the corona.

The upper part of the cornice was occupied by a modillion-and-disc member which covered about half of the overhanging surface.

Very few of these members appear to have been cut as a single unit with the lower dentil members, as noted above, because of the sheer weight involved. One such monolith was well over a meter in length, however, and such blocks could have posed serious lifting problems, even with machines.

Cornice fragments in the fall debris permitted the isolation of four major types, differing only slightly in terms of their modillion-and-disc dimensions.

These size-types were as follows:

A. Modillion—c. 8 cm. wide × c. 10 cm. long.

   Disc—c. 12 cm. in diameter (see Plate XXXV, 1).

B. Modillion—c. 6 cm. wide × c. 15 cm. long.

   Disc—c. 14.5 cm. in diameter (see Plate XXXV, 2).

C. Modillion—c. 8.5 cm. wide × c. 16.5 cm. long.

   Disc—c. 15 cm. in diameter (see Plate XXXV, 3).

D. A crudely cut type:

   Modillion—c. 8 cm. wide.

   Disc—c. 10 cm. in diameter, poorly cut and sharply tilted downward (see Plate XXXV, 4).

It is suggested that 'D' was simply a poor specimen and was not to be included in the actual use typology, however.

Corner treatments were also isolated in the fall, and although they agree in modillions, variation is to be noted in the end discs. Again, three separate major groups were noted:

(1) Modillion—c. 6.5 cm. wide × c. 15 cm. long.

End Disc—in elliptical form, c. 4 cm. wide at the center and c. 11.5 cm. long (see Plate XXXVI, 1).

(2) Modillion—c. 8 cm. wide × c. 15 cm. long.

End Disc—elliptical, c. 6.5 cm. wide at the center, and c. 11 cm. long (see Plate XXXVI, 2).

(3) Modillion—c. 8 cm. wide.

End Disc—in crescent shape, with lance-like shaped appendage, c. 16 cm. wide × c. 18.5 cm. along the diagonal (see Plate XXXVI, 3).

These carved members show some degree of tilting from the horizontal, in accord with suggested practice to preclude foreshortening effect.[84]

Certain factors seem to indicate the correlation of the cornice block and corner treatment types. With the fall peaks of the entablature (see above), and the columnar arrangement in mind, it would appear that a similar relation of frontal face to inset face must be seen here. Inset face fragments from both lower and upper orders would show displacement in fall on the basis of position, once again.

Thus the larger modillion-and-disc type would be expected on the lower story, with a relatively smaller type on the upper story. At the same time, other elements would enter as factors in regard to side and corner treatments, as well as vertical position. The face lines of the cornice, upper and lower stories would present the cornice treatment frontally, as would the inset faces. Hence, in regard to the modillions, variation in depth would not be a factor, but size variations (edge width) would be. On the same basis, diameter variation would be critical for the discs. Along the inset sides, however, the situation reverses, where length variation in modillions would be visible, as would side-view diameters of the discs. Hence it may possibly be assumed that the original architects compensated for the side and corner views, as against a proportional variation for the stories in establishing their size criteria.

On this basis, therefore, it is suggested that cornice blocks of the 'C' type were on the frontal and inset face of the first story, with type (3) corner treatments; type 'A' cornice blocks, with type (1) corners were along the faces of the upper story; and type 'B' blocks with type (2) corner treatments were used for the inset side areas of either the lower or both upper and lower stories. Unfortunately the data secured does not provide positive evidence of either the architectural sophistication presumed or conclusive proof that another arrangement was not used (e.g. 'A' with (1) as frontal and near corners, 'B' with (2) as inset and far corners, and 'C' with (3) as inset and farthest corners, as a foreshortening device, or the possibility of an unidentified fourth group of both blocks ('D'(?)) and corners for the same purpose). The identification of type 'C' with the lower story and 'A' for the upper story does seem reasonable, however, on the basis of size variations to be expected for the two levels, since a third entablature cannot be reasonably assumed.

ut-set Foundat

Mai
("Roy
Door

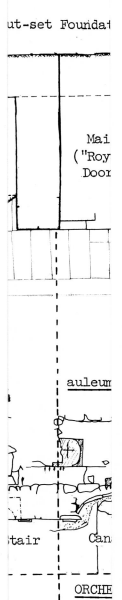

auleum

tair   Can

ORCHE

If this be correct, however, there is a disproportional variation in the reduction of modillion widths and disc diameters between the stories.

Obviously an attic must have separated the two stories of the *episcenium*, but the details of this feature can only be conjectured. Following classical patterns, and seen on the Khazneh as well, this feature should have been composed of a reserved band of masonry with a corona. Since fascia blocks and architrave corona blocks would have been indistinguishable, except possibly by position, no judgement can be made concerning the attic details. Two blocks with narrow double rows of dentils, found at c. 4.3 m. and 5.4 m. from the *scaenae frons* may be related, possibly, to the attic corona, but cannot be definitely assigned there (cf. the attic of the Khazneh). If the relation of parts in this case again correlates with the Khazneh, an attic of c. 1.40 m. would be anticipated.[85]

Likewise a tympaneum above the entablature of the main door area would be expected, since such gabled features occur over both classical and Nabataean structures in general. Again, no definite evidence exists, although the two blocks noted above, as well as the gable fragment also previously noted from the main door area, may perhaps be related here, rather than to either the main door architrave or the attic corona.

6. CONJECTURAL RESTORATION OF
SCAENAE FRONS

On the basis of the foregoing data, with the assumption and selection of conjectural factors, the parts of the *scaenae frons* of the Theater at Petra would have had the following elevation:

Lower order:		Upper order:	
podia	1.9 m.	columns	3.70 m.
columns	4.22 m.	entablature	1.17 m.
entablature	1.45 m.		
roof	7.17 m.		
attic	1.40 m.		

In terms of the elevation above the stage floor, the Lower Order would have risen 6.12 m., its entablature to 7.57 m., with the roof beams inserted at c. 7.17 m., and its attic to 8.57 m. The Upper Order would have its columns (without podia) at 12.67 m., and its entablature to 13.84 m. If the *scaenae frons* and *postscenium* walls continued to the *summa cavea* gallery level, a total of 17.6 m. was reached in height. Whether any additional attic rose above the Upper Order to complete the *scaenae frons* architectural decoration cannot be determined. Nor can it be determined whether the Upper Order was roofed. This possibility seems indicated, however, as a completion of the *parascenium* complex, at least at the northern end, indicates.

At least the face of the Lower Order seems to have been faced with decorative marble *crustae*, along with the external walls of the *vomitoria*. The second podium of the Lower Order would seem to have been left without columnar decoration, but may have served as a plinth for statuary (e.g. evidence of the two Hercules statues recovered).

The order of the architecture is related to the classical Corinthian, but ought to be properly called Nabataean-Corinthian. It seems to have some affinities with Greek Corinthian, as against the Roman, but these affinities may be merely the chance results of local interpretation.

IV

THE HYDRAULIC SYSTEM

John Haralson Hayes

A significant feature of the Theater at Petra was the associated hydraulic system. The hydraulic features not only served as an ordinary drainage faculty but also constituted a complex flood control system to prevent the water erosion of the Theater area. The hydraulic features were noted and explored, primarily during the 1962 season, in conjunction with the over-all survey and planning of the Theater and as a result of the excavation of an area outside the *postscenium* wall at the northern end of the stage area on a line with the *vomitorium sinistrum*.

Two factors made the flood control system a necessity during the period of the Theater's original usage. These were: (1) the nature and location of the Theater itself, and (2) the turbulent rainstorms which plague the area during their sporadic occurrences in the rainy season of the year. Since the Theater was carved into the side of a mountain, the control of run-off rainfall was an acute problem necessitating feats of hydraulic engineering at which the Nabataeans excelled. A number of flood control devices were found throughout the Theater.

In the upper gallery, some 15 m. above the *summa cavea* gallery, a drainage canal was cut to prevent water from flowing into the *summa cavea* area and to divert it around the *dextra* side of the Theater. This canal was hewn out of the bedrock of the upper gallery floor (Plate XIV, 1, and Plate XLII, 1). This chiselled canal in the upper drainage gallery, however, did not encompass the entire Theater. At the present time, 60 m. of the canal are visible, although the upper gallery is badly eroded at the *dextra* side of the Theater area, making measurement in this vicinity impossible. No doubt, the canal originally diverted water completely around the *dextra* portion of the Theater, either emptying into the *wadi* bed, or else connecting with a constructed drainage system which ran parallel to and outside the *postscenium* wall. The destroyed nature of the gallery at the *dextra* side makes it impossible to decide which was the case although the latter is the most probable. Apparently, no canal was utilized on the *sinistrum* side of the Theater as no evidence of such is traceable in the upper drainage gallery, although the beginning of the diversion canal for the *dextra* side is clearly obvious. Because of erosion damage, it is difficult to determine the exact dimensions of the drainage canal. In one reasonably well preserved area, the floor of the canal measured 61 cm. in width, with walls 38 and 15 cm. in height.

In the *summa cavea* gallery, a runnel was utilized to divert the water away from and around the seating area in a manner similar to that described above (Plate XIV, 3).

In addition to the runnels and the drain canal in the upper and *summa cavea* galleries, a number of runnels were found in the stage and *orchestra* floors (Plate Folder E, 1, 3). Still well preserved was a drain at the *dextra* side of the stage, built to conduct water underneath the *finitio proscenii* (Plate XLII, 2). This rectangular drain, measuring 16 cm. in height and 24 cm. in width, carried run-off water away from the *orchestra* floor and into the *hyposcenium* area, emptying into the *auleum* slot. In association with this drain, which ran under the wall of the stage front, were two rough-hewn runnels. One ran parallel to the *finitio proscenii* in order to conduct accumulated water out of the *orchestra* area. The other runnel emptied into the main drain from the general area of the *vomitorium dextrum*. This drainage canal built into the *finitio proscenii* may be compared with a similar type noted in the excavation of the Theater at Caesarea.[1]

The most significant and important hydraulic remains in the Theater area were a series of well preserved drain rebuilds excavated at the *sinistrum* side of the stage area between the *postscenium* exit and the *wadi* bed. This series of three superimposed drains was uncovered in Trench I.22B during the 1962 season. The trench, in the vicinity of the drains, was part of a trench complex which extended from the bedrock face into which the *vomitorium sinistrum* had been cut, through the *scaena* wall remains, and across the *postscenium* wall. Surface remains of the top drain were partially visible along the *wadi* east of the *postscenium* wall prior to the actual commencement of excavation. However, the visible portions of the drain were located north of the confines of trench I.22B.

The uppermost drain emerged in level (4) of Trench I.22B and at the eastern end of the trench. This top drain, referred to as Drain 'A', was roughly constructed, built with irregular stones, which had been smoothly worked on only two sides, and rested on a rubble fill (Plate XLII, 3). The stone bottom and side panels were mortared together and covered with plaster. The side panels were chinked with small stones and braced with a rubble fill to give support to the structure. The construction and position of Drain 'A' are shown in the section drawing (Plate XLIII, 4). This drain was part of the Theater installation during the time of main use and is to be associated with Period I(c).

Underneath Drain 'A' another drain of a totally different type was discovered (Plate XLII, 4). Drain 'B' was made of circular ceramic tile of which three sections were *in situ*. The major portion of Drain 'B' had been destroyed in the construction of Drain 'A' and partially incorporated into the rubble foundation for the upper drain. Drain 'B' was inserted into, but extended above, the top of Wall V which formed part of the build belonging to a still earlier drain. The one unbroken drain pipe recovered measured 37 cm. in length from center of joint to center of joint with an inside diameter of 22 cm. The thickness of the tile was approximately 1 cm. although the pipe was slightly thicker at the ends. The reddish ware of the tile showed a sprinkling of white grit and a thick (0.5 cm.) black core. The drain sections had an outer jacket and an inner case at the joints and were bound together by mortar placed between the overlapping jacket and the inner case. Drain 'B' belonging to Period 1(b) of the Theater's main use.

The ceramic tile drain employed in Drain 'B' was of a type used for water conveyance known and discussed by Vitruvius.[2] Similar type drains have been excavated elsewhere in Palestine from the Roman period.[3] Dalman noted the existence of such tile water pipes in the Siq at Petra, and shows a photograph of one example in his 1912 publication on the Nabataean site.[4]

Underneath Drain 'B', a third ceramic drainage system was discovered completely intact (Plate XLIII, 2). Drain 'C' was set into a foundation cut in the soft red sandstone bedrock (Plate XLIII, 1). The bedrock served also as the floor to the *postscenium* exit located in Wall III. Associated with the drain was a foundation and retainer wall built in step fashion from large, finely finished stones. This foundation wall served not only as protection against water from the *wadi* but also provided steps leading toward the *postscenium* exit. Portions of the foundation build lay to the east of the area excavated in Trench I.22B and were therefore not exposed by the excavation. The tile sections in Drain 'C' were 44 cm. long and the inside diameter measured 18.5 cm. The tile was 0.75 m. in thickness with a reddish ware showing a moderate sprinkling of white grit. A very thin, grayish core was also noticeable. The tile sections were joined socket-fashion and mortared with a very black cement containing charcoal grit similar to the mortar used elsewhere in the main Theater construction. Drain 'C' was the original drain constructed during the first build of the Theater and belonged to Period I(a).

The relation of the hydraulic system of the Main Theater at Petra to the over-all system of the site, itself, was beyond the scope of the excavation reported in this study. That some direct relation must exist, however, seems obvious and awaits further general study of the site's water-control system.

NOTE: Subsequent clearing conducted by the Department of Antiquities in the vicinity of the excavated drainage system have revealed the relation of this system to the over-all piping system at Petra to be seen carried along the wall lines near the Theater and, presumably, also related to the piping systems seen in the walls of the Siq.

P.C.H.

V

CHRONOLOGICAL CONCLUSIONS

The 'Roman' character of the visible remains of the Theater at Petra, along with the documented fact of Roman occupation of the site in A.D. 106, have been the primary factors in the generally held datings of the site. The actual evidence for such dating, while the structure was unexcavated, had thus been without a firm basis.

That the plan and general arrangement of the Theater is, indeed, 'Roman', has been shown to be correct. Hence, the Roman period must be the one in which a more definitive chronology of the Theater must be sought. Within this period two further points must be established, however. First of all, Blake[1] has noted that, by the time of Augustus, the colonial enterprise of Rome had 'doubtless' supplied most provincial areas with places of amusement, and, hence, that few such installations were probably built following that period. Secondly, Bieber[2] indicates that the establishment of purely Roman theaters took place in those areas which had developed a progressive civilization only after Roman conquest and settlement.

In the case of Petra, both of these viewpoints offer chronological implications, within the Roman period, when viewed in terms of the history of Syro-Palestine and of Nabatene proper. The apparent gap in theater building, implied in Blake's assertion, has already been noted. Following the Augustan period, a definite hiatus in such construction is seen in the Near East until c. A.D. 150, in general, with a few exceptions. Hence the chronological position of the Theater at Petra must be found either early in the Imperial Period, or later, toward the middle of the second century A.D.

Bieber's statement would seem to indicate the latter chronological setting—i.e. sometime after the Roman occupation of Petra in A.D. 106. On the other hand, that statement also presents a contradiction, in that it depends on the matter of the *purely* 'Roman' character of such installations. When that aspect is introduced, certain factors already presented in the discussion of the Theater at Petra must be evaluated, and set against Blake's statement concerning building activities, as well as Frézoul's study noted earlier, the stratigraphic and other evidences from Petra, and the known history of the area and era.

As was shown in Chapter III of this report, the 'Roman' character of the Theater at Petra emerges as definite, but at the same time is overlaid with specific and definite localisms which are equally obvious. Thus the architectural data of Chapter III is vital in establishing the chronological setting of the Theater, especially in Period I (a) and (b).

Among the specific localisms to be noted are the following:

(1) *Site location:* aside from geographical necessity (i.e. the geological situation), the Theater at Petra meets the criterion established by Frézouls,[3] namely that location in regard to main streets is of importance in relation to local evaluation of a monument.

At Petra, no other similar location could have been found which would have placed the monument so completely in the public view, from the *local* point of view. That the Theater is extra-mural is to be considered a geologic, rather than a sociological, factor, in view of local preferences in building technique (see below). Even in its present location, it was necessary for the builders to hew into the sides of a number of rock-cut tombs to achieve the full extent of the desired *auditorium* circumference. Thus this extra-mural aspect has no negative relationship to the popular evaluation of the monument's significance, but rather must be seen as a positive indication.[4]

That Roman builders would also have chosen the specific site cannot be denied. Yet, if Frézouls is correct, the extra-mural location of the Theater, which could have been vaulted on level ground inside the city proper, is called into question. This is further supported by the locations of other 'civic betterment' projects of undeniable Roman authorship inside the city area (e.g. the Street, the Gate, the Qaṣr).

That the Siq entry represented the main entry to the city, and that a location along its inner course inside the eastern ridge would present a main street attitude, can only be seen as the result of long-term acquaintance with that attitude. That this area would be seen as extra-mural, and hence would represent a non-indigenous viewpoint, cannot be proven, but seems psychologically defensible. In favor of the argument is the location of the Khazneh and other monuments along the same trail—even though their purpose is funerary, as well as public ostentation.

Likewise, the size of the Theater, in relation to other sociological factors known at Petra, must also indicate the desire to embellish the city, positively. Here, again, Frézoul's[5] view that the appearance of such a monument is related to a sense of 'urbanisme' must be considered as validated. When the total building plan of Petra is viewed, even in ruin, it must be admitted that the Theater represents a particular architectural triumph, which could only have been achieved when an urban consciousness had been reached. The necessity for a specific place of assembly and entertainment, in an area with as much open ground for popular assembly, and with a tradition of open air, non-structurally confined assembly, indicates that the psychological level of urbanism had been reached along with the *de facto* condition forced by the change from nomadism, or semi-nomadism, to sedentary and finally urbanized living.

If the Theater is indeed a monument '*par excellence*' of the true city,[6] the example at Petra confirms the final urbanization of the inhabitants.

Likewise, if the appearance of a theater has relation to geographical distribution of population density, as Frézouls has suggested and seems also to have proven,[7] the Theater at Petra not only confirms his thesis, but likewise provides chronological indications by the very fact of its appearance.

When the historical material concerning the rise and decline of Petra is viewed, certain specific periods emerge as probable periods when a sense of urbanism and the population density factors merge—and could have provided the incentive for the building of the monument.

Still further, the fact that theaters were found only in places of some importance,[8] gives further hypothetical data for the placing, chronologically, of the example at Petra. That Petra was a Nabataean capital of first rank, that the Nabataeans passed from nomadism or semi-nomadism into urbanism well before the first century B.C., and that eclectic art and foreign influences of all types were incorporated into their culture, must be balanced against the fact that during the Roman occupational period the height of local culture—and the centrality of the site as a dense population center attracted by commercial vigor—had already suffered severe decline, in spite of the fact that the (rather hollow) title of *colonia* had been conferred. This may also be set against the fact of the theater building at Boṣra—which had become Nabatene's second capital, and royal residence, as early as Malichus and Rabbel II. Still further, the building activities of local monarchs,[9] in the immediate neighborhood of Nabatene, and with competitive connections with the Nabataeans, especially in the case of Herod the Great, provides precedent for early native theater building in the area, in the Roman period, but without specific occupation by Roman administrators.

(2) *The cavae:* although the Romans also did build into hillsides the (equivalent of cutting into cliff sides), the 'model' preference stated by Vitruvius was building upon level ground, via arched vaults for the *cavea* elevation. That this would have been possible at Petra is not to be denied. The supply of stone, the availability of terrain, and other factors would have made this an option for the architect. That the specifically Nabataean preference for rock-cutting—as against their own less proficient skill in masonry work—was employed, and thus the *cavea* was rock-cut, not built on vaults, would seem to indicate local indigenous control of both site choice and building technique.

Against this is the fact that Nabataean tombs had to be destroyed in order to accomplish the rock-cutting operation. This objection has been pressed as an indication of specific Roman control of the operation, since the native population would have been loath to desecrate its own necropolis. That tombs were generally respected in Semitic contexts is an assumption, however, stemming from non-Semitic, religious perspectives. This is borne out by the rifling of tombs in the Near East from pharaonic times onward, from the necessary precaution of supplying tombs with curses against defilement (cf. the Turkmaniyeh Tomb inscription), and from a host of devices used to conceal or barricade tomb chambers in eastern (and western) areas. That, however, an 'official' desecration of a necropolis would take place, would seem to be a different matter. Hence, the conclusion that a foreign (i.e. Roman) element must have been responsible, since the project was a public work, has been reached in the past.

In actuality, the matters of 'desecration' and chronological relationship are not sequential, but depend upon other factors. Foremost among these is the matter of Nabataean tomb-cutting chronology, itself. This is, in fact, unresolved. That later generations would not 'desecrate' earlier tombs depends, to a great extent upon the antiquity of the tombs in question. Still further the matter of 'desecration' depends upon whether the tombs in question were actually 'desecrated', or not. Two elements must be considered here. First, were the tombs of the *cavea* areas desecrated—or could they not have been cleared, with proper ritual and formality, with reinterrment of any remains? This question cannot be answered, except by analogy to modern public works procedures where entire necropolis areas are moved with little public outcry. In addition, the matter also rests upon the degree of respect for the dead held by a culture. The assumption has always been that, since the Nabataeans carved enormous tomb façades and chambers, respect for the dead must have been great. This assumption is also tenuous not only in view of Strabo's[10] eyewitness source (early first century A.D.), who reported that the Nabataeans considered dead bodies 'no better than manure' and that they buried kings 'beside their privies', but also in terms of the class structure of the Nabataean kingdom, about which little is known except for the egalitarianism reported by Strabo. Hence both the charge of 'desecration' and the assumed reluctance of Nabataeans to move or remove Nabataean tombs cannot be defended as an evidence of the

5

foreign origin of the Theater. Thus the local preference for rock-cutting can at least stand as a possibility, in terms of architectural control of the operation.

Still further, the use of hillsides is seen by Vitruvius as a 'Greek' phenomenon in theater building. With the marked Hellenistic features obvious in Nabataean coinage, royal titles, ceramic prototypes, and other areas, even a 'Roman' plan might well be executed according to Hellenistic tendencies. This argument, however, is not as important as the other factors discussed above.

(3) *Local architectural features:* Among these must be noted the order, the hydraulic system, the acoustical system, the masonry techniques, the epigraphic data, and local climatic adaptation of plan.

Against this body of apparently local architectural features must be set the possibility of the foreign planning and supervision of the operation using local craftsmen. Primary here is the plan, quite obviously a Vitruvian adaptation common throughout the Roman provinces. This relationship has been noted in Chapter III at a number of points: The general layout of the plan, the general mathematics of parts (stage height, stage length, stage depth, seat and *praecinctio* wall measurements, *cunei* division, both horizontally and vertically; *scaenae frons* layout and elevation) and in actual building techniques (wall building, coursing). On the other hand, both the slavishness to the Vitruvian canon—and departures from it—are significant. The Theater was a foreign element in Near Eastern culture, hence some foreign architectural assistance was necessary as a building guide, either a foreign standard work or a foreign architectural consultant, or both. That the Vitruvian canon was followed, at certain points, to the degree of slavish adherence, would seem to indicate a stage of theater building in which conscious innovation had not yet taken place. Hence, a period close to the earlier stage of Vitruvian model building description might be in turn indicated. At a later time, advanced knowledge of techniques might be expected, especially in the provinces, where Roman domination could compel both the labor and financial expenditures necessary. Still further, advanced (i.e. later) technical ability would preclude undue expenditure of labor and finances, since advanced techniques (i.e. architectural short-cuts) would be known.

Yet, the Theater at Petra betrays ignorance of certain of those possibilities: the cement/concrete technique used over the vaulting of the *vomitoria* passages appears to have been employed only to provide a flat base for the *tribunaliae*—not for actual consolidation of the vault thrust downward against the imposts to preclude horizontal displacement; the cut-back for the *vomitoria* is exaggerated, whereas closer mathematical calculation, with higher arching, would have accomplished the same result; the acoustical system conforms to local custom, not mathematical computation; the hydraulic systems are not only the usual Nabataean ones, but conform to local weather conditions; the stone dressing is purely indigenous, wherever exposed faces are not finished; the epigraphic evidence found on the column drums establishes a probable date within the known Nabataean epigraphic range; the order of the *episcenium* is non-Vitruvian, conforms to Nabataean usage in many details, reflects a Corinthian style which is not altogether Roman in parallel, and shows a pure Nabataean form, especially in its capitals.

Still further, certain features of the Theater are variants from even generally made Vitruvian adaptations in the Roman plan: The canal, under the *finitio proscenii* and running into the *orchestra*, is paralleled only at Epidaurus; the sliding-door in the niche of the *finitio proscenii*

(Period I (b)) is unusual; the marked asymmetry of the *cavea*, the blockade walls and the position of *aditus* passageways are all irregular features of plan.

Against the latter points, it may be argued that local architects were consulted by the foreign builders, in order to make best use of locally known techniques. It would be anticipated, in such a case, however, that such advice would only be taken where *efficiency* would result. The localisms noted above do not contribute to such an end, but, rather in certain respects, produce opposite results.

Likewise, it might be argued that foreign conquerors might wish to appease local populations by catering to local tastes in architecture. This cannot be documented from Roman practice, and, indeed, would not seem to have been general Roman practice, at all. In the case of the non-Roman elements noted above, little popular approval is at stake, as over against considerable loss of aesthetic and technological advantage. That Roman engineering skill would have been sacrificed to pander to less efficient, but more 'local' techniques and tastes does not seem indicated, historically.

At the same time, the known Nabataean architectural eclecticism must be considered. As any survey of tomb façades will indicate, the architectural tastes of the Nabataeans were derived from, and were overlaid by, local modifications which suggest interpretation, not innovation. Hence, in interpreting the Vitruvian canon, modifying to fit local conditions, and adapting to the stone-cutting technique especially, the 'local' elements present in the Theater at Petra are not aberrant features. That basic Roman model mathematics were employed in layout would be expected; that masonry coursing would be Vitruvian is to be anticipated from the technology of the culture; that local weather conditions dictated adaptations (and deletions) of Roman standards would be logical; that local taste would be observed must be admitted, if local authority was in ultimate control. Still further, but less provable, that Hellenistic elements seem latent again follows from the historical picture.

(4) *Stratigraphic evidences:* the stratigraphic indications of the three phases of Period I of the Theater site should be considered in a discussion of apparent localisms and their chronological implications. The cement/concrete fall evidence (Period IV, Period VII), bearing upon the original build of the Theater, plus the ceramic remains of the secondary phases of its main use, would seem indicative of chronological setting and progression. The cement/concrete remains found *in situ* and in fall periods shows that Nabataean sherds were used as filler. When these sherds are surveyed, it is found that they were generally of the fine, thin wares, and, where painted, of the red-painted variety. Lamp fragments are generally of the voluted (first century A.D.) types known since Horsfield as local products. The ceramic materials in the fill of the canal (Period I (b)), likewise show finer red and red-painted examples, as well as other sherd materials within generally accepted Nabataean types. Finally, the sealed deposit filling the niche of the *finitio proscenii* also shows Nabataean wares, even if markedly degenerate, with (late) black-painted varieties of the painted ware series predominant. If these separate groups of sherd materials all represented chance fill, removed from surface deposits without any chronological relationship, it would be expected that all three would include at least some examples of the same sherd types. That a *progression* of types is involved would indicate, however, that contemporary wares, available from contemporary dumps, were being used. Hence, chronologically discrete building phases are indicated, as did the architectural evidences of the *finitio proscenii* build, in a time when the various types of chronologically distinguishable Nabataean wares were in production or use.

It may be immediately pointed out that the whole question of Nabataean ceramic chronology, as a whole and within series, is still unresolved. As a consequence, it would be possible that Roman builders, at successive stages following A.D. 106, were using contemporary deposits of still continuing Nabataean wares of distinctive varieties. At this point, this argument cannot be denied. However, on the basis of work done on Nabataean ceramics as a whole, the fact of a progression and the degeneration of the wares, *within* the Nabataean period is maintained in this report.[11] Hence, the presence of such remains would indicate a chronological position closer to the Nabataean period of Petra's history, *per se*, and especially close to the height of that period, rather than its declining years already evident prior to A.D. 106 historically.

Furthermore, the fact of the three phases of Period I must also be considered as chronologically relevant. The modification of the Theater, from Period I(a) to its form in Period I(b) was relatively slight. In actuality, Period I(b) did little else but remove an earlier theatrical device (?) in favor of a simpler, but more advanced one (the sliding door in place of the open (?) canal), and bring some degree of embellishment to the austerity of the *finitio proscenii*. The plan of the *finitio proscenii* was now in accord with other 'Roman' stage fronts (e.g. Caesarea, Samaria-Sebaste, Jerash, and the later ones of 'Amman and Palmyra). The change from I(b) to I(c) was radical, however. This is seen not only in the complete redoing of the *finitio proscenii*, in the addition of parts (the stairs, boundary wall, and the standard supports) but also in the *manner* in which these modifications were done (i.e. re-use of debris, heavy plaster, lack of bonding, etc.). Such a modification would seem to represent, when compared with the original build and its subsequent modification, the introduction of a markedly different point of view, architecturally, which, by virtue of the impossibility of modifying the *scaena*, made itself felt in those areas where modifications could be carried out most fully. That Roman architects, after A.D. 106, changed thier perspective so drastically is not borne out by known data. By that time, the 'modifications' seen in the Theater at Petra would have been better accomplished at the time of original building —and a long enough time for further developmental modifications, after Trajan, is difficult to fit into the known Roman occupation chronology of the site. This argument is the least effective, in terms of evidence for indigenous building of the original Theater structure, but, taken with the factors noted above, is still seen to be persuasive. Especially is this the case in regard to the *finitio proscenii* plan related to the stratigraphy of Period I as a whole. The stage front and canal of Period I(a) has its most interesting parallel at Epidaurus (Hellenistic–Early Imperial periods) while the *scaena*, and stage front, of Period I(b) can be compared favorably with Pompeii (large theater) and Herculaneum, as well as with (more closely related geographically) parallels at Caesarea and Jerash. When the historical aspects of Petra's position are in turn related, the stratigraphic and typological possibilities become more meaningful (see below).

(5) *Local Architectural needs:* it must be assumed that the Nabataeans, sometime after their settlement of Petra and their subsequent rise as a commercial power, encountered specific architectural needs, necessitated by urbanization and by its concomitant sophistication. This is most apparent in the cultic devices, cultic installations, and funerary architecture of the site as a whole. Added to the needs of cult and funerary structures must also have been the civic. As was noted previously,[12] the Theater structure becomes *the* civic structure, *par excellence*. As capital of a major commercial empire, with relations with the Greeks as early as 312 B.C. and with the Romans from the time of Pompey onward, it is difficult to consider that this need for civic architecture was not met. This is a phenomenon surviving from Hellenistic times in the Near East, and is most strikingly illustrated by the extensive building activities of Herod the Great.[13] In meeting the local architectural needs, therefore, the Nabataeans, in their funerary and cultic installations borrowed eclectically, interpreted locally, and modified existing parallel plans to fit their needs. Hence, it is (therefore suggested that the Theater at Petra in its original form, followed the same development.)

Against the assumption of this need must be raised the lack of documentation in proof of it, the question of engineering architectural ability necessary to accomplish it, and the cultural level demanded for its inception.

In answer to the first of these objections, the excavation of the Theater furnished no positive evidence. The presence of masons' marks in Nabataean script could be the result of the expected use of local labor; the Greek inscriptions are paralleled in language, if not in script elsewhere on the site and in other locales; and the numismatic evidence relating to Period I(a) and I(b) is indeed scanty. No external documentation is available, and no locally written history has yet been found to argue for or against the assumption. At the same time, this lack of documentation cannot be a valid argument *against* Nabataean building of the installation. Still further, no evidence exists in documented form *for* Roman origin of the installation. The fact of Nabataean script, suitable to the Nabataean period, proper, and of Greek lapidary script also suitable to the first century A.D., as well as the lack of later coins, coupled with the presence of those of Aretas and Rabbel, are all indirect, but cumulative, factors in regard to documentation. When they are taken with the architectural and other evidences, their tenuousness is reduced and their indirect contribution made more positive.

In answer to the matter of engineering/architectural skills requisite for the task of originating the Theater without foreign supervision, more definite data may be furnished. At its most basic level, the skill of the Nabataean architects, engineers and stone-cutters is illustrated by their combined works over all the site and over the whole range of Nabataean territory. The tomb façades of Petra and Medain Selaḥ, the cultic carvings and installations of Petra, itself, and the hydraulic systems of the entire kingdom, offer conclusive proof of ample skills already developed by the first century A.D. and at their height by that time. Comparable Roman engineering feats can indeed be adduced, but the stone-cutting techniques of Petra offer indisputable proof of local knowledge and skill already present on the site prior to Roman occupation.

The question of cultural level necessary to require the establishment of a civic center—or even demanding it—can only be answered in terms of known Nabataean history and intercultural relations. The dispersion of Nabataean commercial interests brought the kingdom into contact with most of the great civilizations of the ancient Near East, either directly or indirectly (e.g. the observation of ruins), as well as contact with the western world. The latter contact was made at least by 312 B.C. and its influence grew with the rise of the Nabataeans, themselves, in the commercial sphere primarily. The impact of Hellenism has been noted previously. The impact of Roman culture, itself Hellenized, also came at an early date—as early as Pompey's intervention in the Near East and the coming of the Roman period. Regardless of the isolation or the semi-independence of Nabatene from Rome, once the contact was made, the Nabataeans maintained close relations with the new power. Especially is this true in the Augustan age, when Rome claimed Nabatene as a dependent, regardless of how that claim was received. This is illustrated by Herod's difficulties over collecting taxes from Aretas, in the name of Rome, the prior question of Syllaeus, and even the accession of Aretas himself. Extra-territorial Nabataean inscriptions are known on the Roman routes, and Roman authorities of the first century onward note the presence of the kingdom.

That this exchange brought cultural sophistication to the Nabataeans may be seen not only in the contrast between the reports of Diodorus and Strabo, but in Nabataean numismatics, inscriptions, politics, and trade. Hence, cultural ineptitude, as a factor precluding local desire for a 'foreign' civic center cannot stand as a valid argument against its possibility.

Still further, and perhaps more relevant, is the relationship which existed between Nabatene and the Jewish state, particularly under Herod the Great. No question can be raised concerning Herod's proclivity for erecting civic installations (e.g. the Temple in Jerusalem as his major local contribution), many of which were decidedly 'foreign' in their purpose, and designed solely for civic (i.e. cultural) ostentation. Among these must be noted the theater at Caesarea Maritima, the works at Samaria-Sebaste, and other architectural efforts even more distant from his own borders. That one monarch in close connection with the Nabataeans (e.g. by kinship (?) and political necessity) showed the requisite 'cultural' level for such building, therefore provides the evidence that other, related, local rulers could have done likewise, and were even provided with the impetus of competition to do so. The continual rivalry, commercially and otherwise between the Jewish state and bordering Nabatene is fully documented and offers still further evidence of the possibility of Nabataean civic consciousness being stirred by such a close example of its results. Such international rivalry, even to architectural matters, is not without parallel throughout all history and cannot be precluded in the present instance, as well. That Roman (or Hellenistic) cultural impetus was necessary must be admitted, but the actuality of local response to example is also documented.[14]

On the basis of the foregoing, therefore, it is suggested that the Theater at Petra, in its original form (Period I(a)–(b)) was a local architectural product, with the assistance of either some form of the Vitruvian canon, or of consultant (Roman) architects, designed to meet the civic needs of the capital city of a major semi-independent commercial kingdom, at the height of its prosperity, population density, and civic (urban) sophistication. The 'Roman' features of the installation are admitted, but the localisms noted above are seen to be firmly rooted in the techniques, architectural form, and stratigraphic evidence resulting from the excavations, and to be borne out by the psychological, sociological, and historical data of the Nabataean period, itself.

If then, an original Nabataean origin for the Theater at Petra is indicated, the point within the chronological range of Nabataean history in which the work was done must be sought. Because of the lack of absolute evidence in the excavations, no precise date can be assigned.

However, on the basis of the excavations, as indicated above, certain definite historical factors must be met, if the Nabataean period is the period of origin, and if the drastic plan modifications of Period I(c) are to be explained. These would seem to be as follows:

(1) A sufficient period of Hellenistic and specifically Roman cultural contact to account for acceptance of the concept, degree of urban sophistication, and familiarity with techniques foreign to the originating culture. Related to this would be the necessity for a political climate not adverse to foreign innovations in public architecture. Related to this would also be the need for a government sufficiently stable to accomplish the task.

(2) A period of local prosperity sufficiently high to afford the expenditures of labor and materials of such an enterprise, at public or private (i.e. royal) expense.

(3) Preferably, a period in which competition with neighboring groups would provide sufficient impetus for such an extensive project as a sign of civic pride. To this aspect might be related also the necessity for sufficient population density and area importance to justify the competition, regardless of whether or not the size of the finished installation gave a true picture of civic need.

(4) A period in which sufficient parallel structures, or standard architectural works, would provide data for the engineering and architectural problems involved.

(5) Specifically, in regard to the Theater at Petra, a sequence of historical events must be found which might account for the mild modification of the plan from Period I(a) to I(b) and the drastic introduction of the features of I(c).

Obviously other factors are involved in the question, but the above elements are seen to be basic demands to be set against the known historical period involved.

Consideration of these factors will now be taken up, in order of their listing with no precedence of weight or rank involved.

Since the period of Roman influence on the specifically Nabataean context begins only with Pompey's arrival in the Near East in 64 B.C., the factor of Hellenistic-Roman cultural contact must begin from that point. The impact of Hellenism, as a softening influence to intercultural exchange had already made its impression on the Nabataeans, however, and 'Roman' influence could therefore accelerate rapidly.

Relations between Nabatene and Rome continued to grow, and became especially favorable with the accession of Aretas IV (9 B.C.–A.D. 40) becoming strained only during the reign of Tiberius Caesar, when an expedition was dispatched against Aretas, but never reached Petra,[15] because of the death of Tiberius. With the reign of Aretas, therefore, the Nabataeans entered a period of close relations with Rome which was to be without incident from c. 9 B.C. to A.D. 37. Aretas was followed by Malichus II (A.D. 40–70), who in turn was followed by Rabbel II (A.D. 70–106). In this latter period, however, Nabataean fortunes declined commercially, and Petra began to be deserted, as a royal residence, in favor of Boṣra to the north.

Thus the main period of Petra's specific connection with Roman influence, prior to occupation in A.D. 106, was the reign of Aretas IV, and, to a lesser degree, the reign of Malichus and Rabbel.

Thus the period 64 B.C. to 9 B.C. provides a period of developing Roman cultural contact, the period 9 B.C. to A.D. 40 provides a period of close intercultural exchange, continued from A.D. 40 to A.D. 106, but with a lessening of Petra's Nabataean stature in the latter period. The length of the reign of Aretas IV, at the height of close relations would therefore, provide a stable reign in which to seek both a climate favorable to architectural innovation and sufficient power to accomplish building plans of great scope. This could be said of the reign of Malichus II, but the attractions of Boṣra would seem to have diverted attention from Petra. More so was this the case in the reign of Rabbel II.

The reign of Aretas IV also represents the peak of Nabataean prosperity, just prior to an economic decline, based on trade route shifts by the Romans.[16] That this was not serious during the reign of Malichus is possible, but the peak period demanded for great public works, plus the (negative) growing interest in Boṣra, would seem to indicate any major works must be assigned to the reign of Aretas, rather than his successors.

Likewise, the reign of Aretas IV meets the next point raised as well, namely a period in which competition between local rulers might spur competition in the architectural, or civic beautification areas as well. The building activities of Herod began well after his establishment as king, because of internal disputes at home and civil disorders in Rome.[17] From about 24 B.C. Herod began a series of building activities which extended well outside of his borders.

These projects were seen as a sign of Herod's 'ambition' to have monuments of the greatness of his government to posterity, according to Josephus, and probably had definite relation to his status with Rome. With such an example of both the gratification of personal ambition to fame and as a means of currying favor with Rome, other powers in the area might also have been spurred to erect suitable civic buildings. Although the prosperity of the reign of Obodas II (30 B.C.–9 B.C.) could well have allowed emulation of Herod, relations with both Rome and Herod were not good and the commercial future of Nabatene appeared threatened in the midst of prosperity. In the more settled and more Romanized period of Aretas IV, matching the building projects of Herod's reign, now in decline and in a state of unrest, while Nabataean fortunes rose, would again seem more probable for a time of civic pride as well, especially since Nabataean relations with the Jews steadily worsened. In the latter part of the Augustan age, theater building in the provinces seems to have halted, hence basic technical knowledge had been attained and was more widely known throughout the provinces, and could be made available to a favored local monarch. Roman architects might also be more inclined to act as consultants elsewhere, once the number of specifically Roman enterprises began to lessen.

Finally, the necessary succession of economic, political, and other considerations necessary to explain the building phases of Period I(a)–(b) may be found in this time, as well. The establishment of a large civic center, at a time of prosperity, when technical knowledge was available, in a city of importance with high population density, under a stable monarch favorable to foreign architectural innovations could only have been done under Obodas II, or Aretas IV, when the history of Petra is considered. Again, certain elements relating to the reign of Obodas (especially his relation with Rome, as well as the height of Augustan building projects, and the threat of economic decline) would tend to focus probability on the reign of Aretas IV. By that time, most of the objections raised concerning the situation during Obodas' reign were settled and Petra was at her zenith.

A second period, in which civic interest was still high, and public works were still being undertaken at Petra, must then be found. The ceramic evidence points to a period not far from that of the original building, and before the degeneration of Nabataean fine wares took place. The single coin found in relation to this phase of Period I indicates only that it was deposited, after the reign of Rabbel II had begun. During the reign of that king interest was centered more upon Boṣra than upon Petra, however. Hence it might be suggested that Period I(b) should be assigned to the reign of Malichus II. The probable sequence of red-painted–black-painted Nabataean wares noted above would be in accord with that possibility, also.

Finally, the drastic change of plan, seen in Period I(c) must be accounted for. Since Rabbel II practically deserted Petra, and the sealed deposit of Period I(c) indicates a later time than Period I(b), it is suggested that Period I(c) represents Roman refurbishing of the Theater. Since a great deal of new building was done on the site after the Roman occupation in A.D. 106, such a refurbishing of a standing public building could be expected. Precisely when this took place is not able to be determined. However, the rather poor job done might tend to indicate an early date in the period, when compared with the other known Roman work on the site.

In conclusion, therefore, the following chronological sequence is suggested for the Theater at Petra:

Period I(a)—Aretas IV: possibly between 4 B.C. (the death of Herod) and A.D. 27 (the beginning of military actions once more).

Period I(b)—Malichus II: after A.D. 40 and perhaps before A.D. 53–63 when Nabataean affairs began to decline once more.

Period I(c)—Roman: after A.D. 106 and probably by c. A.D. 150, when the city again rose to some prominence under the Antonines.

If the Theater was indeed destroyed by the earthquake of A.D. 365, and further demolished by the severe quake of A.D. 746–748, the periods of re-use (Period II(b)), and disuse (Period III) would fall late in the Roman period, the robbery periods (Period VI(a/b)) would be Byzantine, followed by disuse of the area during the later Byzantine—early Islamic periods (VII), culminating in the final destruction (at the end of VII) and disuse until modern times (Period VIII).[18]

VI

MISCELLANEOUS SMALL FINDS

METAL ARCHITECTURAL FIXTURES

P. C. Hammond

The copper (*sic!*) and iron architectural fixtures recovered in the excavation of the Theater were all badly oxidized. In the case of the copper fixtures, however, the oxidation readily responded to treatment (electrolysis) and the fixtures could be returned to original condition. The iron fixtures, both the nails and the brackets, had all lost too much core metal to be reclaimed.

The copper fixtures measured from about 9.6 cm. to 13.2 cm. in length, and were about 1.30 cm. wide, with some variation in the latter dimension. Thickness averaged about 0·2 cm., with thickening at the pronged end to about 0.35 cm. The form (i.e. single or double prongs) depended upon use. At molding levels, single prong fixtures simply held the top of the facing slab in place, with the carved moldings set above; in the case of successive levels of facing rows, double pronged fixtures held the top of each lower level slab and the bottom slab of the next row above. The ends of the fixtures were inserted into receiving holes of the ashlar masonry and secured by plugging with plaster or marble chips, with or without doubling of the fixture ends before plugging. Various specimens are shown on Plate XLIV.

The iron nails appear to have been rather thin in section, but with large heads. These nails were undoubtedly used to key plaster to the masonry and could easily have been inserted between courses of masonry for that purpose. Recovered nails ranged from about 7.3 cm. to about 10.5 cm. in length and would thus have been long enough to extend most of the way through the (generally) 9 cm. plaster undercoating of the facings. The action of the original wet plaster, as well as later water action on these fixtures oxidized them almost completely, so that little core metal remained. This factor also precludes any accurate determination of the original cross-section dimensions. Specimens are shown on Plate XLV.

The iron angle brackets recovered were in a similar state, and likewise did not respond to treatment. One example, however, measured some 22 cm. in length, 4.5 cm. in width, and 1.5 cm. in thickness in its recovered (oxidized) state. The rarity of these brackets, and their find spots (about 5.5 m. to 9 m. from the *scaenae frons*), suggests that they were used for special tying needs only, as the occasion demanded. The lack of any clear bolt holes, or oxidation traces, in any of the architectural blocks found in excavation leaves the question of the precise use of these angle brackets unanswerable. Typical iron specimens are shown on Plate XLV.

The use of facing stone, especially marble, plaster bedding, and metal tying and keying fixtures at the Theater at Petra is clearly Roman in origin and in keeping with the other architectural aspects of the construction. Marble was in use in Rome about the beginning of the first century B.C.,[1] and the use of sawn facing slabs is noted at least from the time of Julius Caesar (the house of Mamurra).[2] In specifically theater architecture, marble was employed as early as the Theater of M. Scaurus, in 58 B.C.[3]

The use of bedding plaster, bronze fixtures and iron keying nails goes hand in hand with the use of facing marble in Roman architecture. The cost of marble soon suggested the *crustae* technique, and marble facings, or veneers, with their associated fixtures became common.[4] A preference for bronze as the metal for the attaching fixtures seems to have arisen, especially in the better types of work, although iron was generally used for keying plaster bedding and stucco.[5] Examples of the use of these metal devices may be cited from a number of buildings: the Forum Julium (House #29—49 B.C.), the Rostra (c. 44 B.C.), the Regia, Septa Julia (27 B.C.), the Baths of Agrippa (21 B.C.), the Forum of Augustus (c. 2 B.C.?), the Augustan Arco de' Pantami, the Temple of Ceres (partly rebuilt by Augustus and rededicated by Tiberius in A.D. 17), the Temple of Concord, Nero's 'Golden House', the Temple of Minerva, the Temple Sacrae Urbis, the podium and niches of the Colosseum, the Poseidonium, the Baths of Caracalla, the Pantheon, the villa of Sallust, the Hadrianic Temple of Venus, the Vespasian Forum, the Baths of Titus, Caligula's palace and other public buildings, the Flavian palace on the Palatine, among others. Likewise, the House of the Vestals also shows 'T' and angle bracket clamps in use in the stonework.[6] Middleton illustrates the use of the facing-bedding-fixture system in use during the Augustan age,[7] as it was also found in use in the Theater at Petra.

A total of seventeen copper fixtures, single or double pronged, intact or fragmentary, with or without associated plugs, were recovered in the course of the excavations near the *scaenae frons* (Register Nos. 20, 30, 31, 79, 83, 84, 85, 140, 141, 142, 134, 135, 136, 137, 138, 162) from levels I.1 (1–1A), I.1 (x), I.1 (3), I.4 (2), I.5 (2), I.6 (2), I.6 (7), and I.7 (8). Nails and nail fragments (Register Nos. 74, 75, 77, 78, 81, 146, 148, 154, 155) were recovered from levels I.1 (x), I.3 (7), I.4 (2), I.5 (3), I.6 (2), I.7 (8). Iron brackets, with two or three bolts (Register Nos. 32, 147, 150, 156, 163, 170) were found in levels I.1 (4), I.1 (6), I.5 (2), and I.6 (2).

The copper and iron fixtures from the Theater have been analyzed, semi-quantitatively,[8] with the following results:

Copper		Iron*			
Fe	0.1% or less	Al	0.4–4%	In	<0.05
Pb	0.3	As	0.01–0.05	Mg	0.2
Al	0.01	Ag	<0.02	Mn	<0.02
Si	<0.01	Au	<0.02	Mo	<0.02
Mn	<0.01	B	<0.005–0.01	Na	<0.03–0.04
Zn	0.06	Ba	<0.01–0.04	Ni	>0.1 (0.2–0.3)
Sb	<0.5 (?)	Be	<0.01	Nb	<0.1
Ca	0.005 > 0.3	Bi	<0.005	Pb	<0.01–0.03
Su	0.08	Ca	0.3–0.4	Pt	<0.04
		Cd	<0.01	Sb	<0.01
		Cr	<0.05	Sn	0.08
		Co	0.04–0.1	Sr	<0.1
		Ge	<0.01	V	0.1–0.5
		Hg	<0.1		

* Quantity levels of calcium, magnesium, and arsenic indicate lack of refinement. Aluminum quantities vary in samples from 0.4 to 4.0%, further indicating the same factor. The high silicon content is seen as an unusual feature reducing conductivity and making the metal brittle and black.

MARBLE FACINGS

A great deal of thin marble facing slabs (*crustae*) was found in the course of the excavations, as would be expected from the amount of area so covered (i.e. the *vomitoria* sides, and parts of the *scaenae frons*—see Chapter III).

The marble varied from pure white, finely sawn slabs about 1 cm. thick, to dark gray slabs, with a variety of veined types in between. In addition, a quantity of excellent white mottled, dark red (*breccia* type) was also found.

The facings were applied to the ashlar blocks of the *scaenae frons* base areas by first applying a thick coat of plaster (generally 9 cm. thick) and then attaching the facing with tanged bronze fixtures firmly tied into the walls with plugs. The plugs holding the fixtures in place were often bits of cutters' marble refuse which were admirably suited, after being roughly squared, for driving into holes bored in the softer sandstone masonry. The forward tips of the fixtures, whether with a single prong or double ones, were left protruding from the plaster and then bent into rough cuts in the facing edge to secure the latter. The combination of close fitting plaster adhesive, and bronze clamps was more than sufficient to hold the facings in place. The lowest courses were put in place prior to the laying of the upper pavement and thus were further supported. A white marble molding topped the base facings, but whether further moldings were used appears doubtful, at least on the *scaenae frons* face.

The tie-holes cut into the *vomitoria* walls facing the stage were so patterned as to permit reconstruction of the facing design employed. A molding in an horizontal line, c. 8 cm. wide, applied in 20 cm. strips, went along the wall about 1.25 m. from the pavement. Below it, panels of facing slabs 60 cm. long by 40 cm. wide were mounted horizontally in three rows, with occasional vertical rows of panels used to break up the face. Above the molding strip the panels were only about 40 cm. × 28 cm., and were mounted in horizontal rows along the length of the panels. At the base, the usual outset base molding appears to have been used.

It has already been noted that the *breccia* type red marble occurred in heavy fall near the inset niche north of the main door. This suggests that the niche areas were decorated in this manner, making an impressive (but economical) display of lavish color in contrast to the other facings of the *scaenae frons*.

Along with the bronze fixtures, a quantity of iron nails, with large heads, was also recovered. These undoubtedly were used to key the plaster to the face of the ashlar blocks (see page 66). Somewhat similar in nature, if not in function, were iron angle brackets, with bolts or rivets protruding from their sides. Since these were few in number, and found scattered in the fall debris, their *loci* and exact function remain in doubt. Most probably, however, they served also as tying devices of some sort, perhaps of architectural elements where deemed necessary.

In addition to the facing marble, marble moldings were also found, *in situ* over the base facing course, and along door edges, thus clarifying their use. These were all of fine white marble, with a minimum diversity of profiles (see Plate XXXVIII and Plate XXXIX, 4).

TILES

Also uncovered in the fall debris, in some quantity, were a variety of tile fragments (see Plate XXXIX, 5, 6). These were all generally heavy, rather coarse, and crudely formed, although with some uniformity. Finger marks (from molding?) were found on the backs of some, indicating rather careless manufacture. These may have been used as drainage, tiles[9], or may even have served as roofing tiles (see Chapter III).

PAINTING

Only two examples of painting were recovered in the fall debris, on two plastered building blocks. One block was discovered in the dump which resulted from the clearance prior to the 1961 season, and no record of its find spot exists. The surface was so badly worn that no recognition of its design was possible.

The second block (see Plate XXXIX, 3), emerged in the fall level of the *scaenae frons*. A thin layer of fine plaster had been applied to the block and an architectural drawing of a column and its entablature made in black paint. Again, the surface was so worn and mutilated by the fall that complete detail was not able to be made out. Whether or not this block served, as such, as part of the decoration of the *scaenae*, or whether, as is also possible it represents the re-use (in the *scaena* build) of a decorative block from elsewhere, cannot be stated.

Other traces of paint, but no outline nor consistency, appeared on bits of plaster from the deep end niche debris.

The relation of such plaster painting at Petra to the 'Painted Temple (tomb)' at El-Barid is an interesting one, particularly in view of the relation of both to Pompeiian styles.[10] This relationship is especially interesting in view of the chronological conclusions above (see Chapter III).

STATUARY

Only one piece of statuary was recovered in the excavations (Plate XL, 1), with an additional (identical?) example uncovered during the clearance operation prior to the 1961 season.

The stratified piece was found in the curtain slot of the stage across from the first inset niche in the *scaenae frons*, north of the Main Door. It was of fine white marble, well modeled and finely polished. The statue was headless, with legs and feet broken off just below the knees, along with the right arm and left hand (Plate XL, 2–3, XLI; 2). The head had originally been carved separately and affixed to the torso by a bronze pin, traces of which remained (Plate XLI, 3). Over the left arm was hung a lion's skin, which identifies the statue as Hercules, however (Plate XL, 3–4; XLI, 2). Trace of the right arm support may be seen on the right thigh, indicating the position of forearm and hand (Plate XLI, 3). The weight of the statue is upon the right foot, with the left leg slightly advanced. A heavy support extends along the right leg, on the outside from the hip down. Comparison with one of the fragments from the other statue (Plate XLI, 4) and the further fragments found in 1962 (Plate XLI, 1) show that the statue stood on a plinth c. 8 cm. high, and confirms stance and the club held in the missing right hand.

In spite of the damage, the total height of the original statues can be determined from the torso recovered. Since a circle scribed with the navel as its center and a point just below the kneecap for a radius, will then touch the crown of the head, the height of the missing head can be calculated (27 cm.), and then that figure used to calculate proportions. As a result, the full size of the statues was c. 1.89 m., or about 7 ft. 5 in.

The closest parallel to both the style and the type of the Petra Hercules seems to be the Doryphorus of Polycleitus, a much copied figure in the Attic Revival in Roman art. The emphasis on musculature, the rendering of the fat rolls on the hips, the conventions, and the stance (although reversed in the Petra examples), all are most faithfully copied, but with a certain vitality and skill. When this work is compared with other sculpture at Petra, its decidedly non-oriental and non-Petrean origin is indicated, and both pieces were probably imports. The loss of both heads seems to indicate vandalism prior to the fall of the *scaenae frons*, since both torsos were well in the fall debris. The separate heads would therefore be expected, had they still been affixed to the torso at the time of fall. The intervening Periods II and III provide the necessary time for such vandalism and for the mutilation of the torso obvious in the photographs.

The Petra Hercules is similar to the Roman statuette in the Boston Fine Arts Museum, which is a copy of a fifth-century bronze original attributed to Myron and executed in the Hadrianic or Antoinine period.[11] Either period would also be suitable as the time of execution of the Petra statues, in view of the chronological suggestions made for Period I(c) above. The Boston example also suggests the disposition of the missing hands, and the instruments held in them: the usual club of the hero-god in the right hand (see Plate XLI, 1) and the bow in the left. Another more specific stylistic parallel is an unidentified Boston torso 'in the style of Polykleitos'[12] which would also seem to be a Doryphorus or Hercules. A still more striking parallel, also in marble, and similarly defective in parts, has just recently been published,[13] but without details.

Hercules was 'evoked' from Tivoli in 338 B.C., and brought to Rome, thus becoming 'Roman' from that point on.[14] Once within the Roman fold, Hercules began to acquire characteristics of certain vague spirits, became the patron of various crafts and professions (e.g. of traders), and even became the referent of imperial divinity (e.g. the godly counterpart of Augustus).[15] If the Petra Hercules was original to the first Theater (Period I(a)), rather than later, it is conceivable that another chronological indicator to that period is given. The statue of the divine counterpart of a reigning emperor, placed in a public building of a semi-dependent kingdom might represent the same type of flattery to be found in Herod's dedications at Samaria-Sebaste.

Because of his 'adventures' and legendary feats of wile and strength, Hercules became popular with the masses at large, and finally became a much approved comic figure. By that route he entered stage comedy, became a common figure in stage decoration, emerged as a stock comedy figure in plays and was also featured in formal, non-comic, theatrical and non-theatrical decoration.[16]

As patron of both drama and traders, and as the divine counterpart of Augustus, Hercules was an appropriate motif for the decoration of the Theater at Petra, one of the major cultural and commercial centers of the Near East of the Roman period. Still further, as a comrade of Bacchus-Dionysus, the connection is made more specific, since Dushares, the ancient god of the Nabataeans, appears to have been identified with Dionysus in the Roman period as well.[17]

FIGURINE FRAGMENTS

Only five figurine fragments were recovered in the course of the excavations (see Plate XXXIX, 1, 2): Register #22, #27, #207, #208, and #246. Two of these, (#22, #246) were fragments of the familiar nude female figure (a goddess?) seated upon a block. These figurines were in the round, but molded in two parts and joined before firing. That they may be identified with Atargatis is suggested by the results of the Eṭ-Ṭannur excavations, but some earlier, indigenous identification is also possible. One of the pieces (#246) was in very poor condition (cf. #27 for same type).

A third fragment (#208) was also of a human figure, male, with arm and wrist bracelets, but too crudely made for any detailed study (cf. #69, #165).

The remaining two fragments (#22, #207) were of horse figurines, with parts of the trappings preserved (on #207, cf. #240).

VII

GREEK EPIGRAPHIC MATERIALS FROM THE EXCAVATIONS

James Steel, Allison Cunningham,
Philip C. Hammond

The Greek epigraphic materials recovered during the course of the excavations included some twenty fragments of carved stone, mostly composed of fragments of individual letters, Plate XLVI. Because of their fragmentary nature, no readings could be obtained, with minor exceptions, and the value of these epigraphic materials is relatively slight and consists only of limited chronological and architectural evidence.

The largest single fragment, discovered during the 1961 season, was a block found in the fall level (5) of Trench I.1 in the niche of the main doorway of the *scaenae frons*. When the block was cleared and lifted, Greek capital letters, 23 cm. high and 9 cm. wide, were found inscribed on its finished face. The letters ThEAT were legible and promised the possibility of some dedicatory inscription of chronological importance, still to be recovered from adjoining blocks. The further discovery of a partial block, bearing the remaining corner of the *taw* of the first block and a probable *rho*, further strengthened that possibility. Unhappily, no further adjoining blocks, in either direction, were recovered. Since the second block was uncovered to the north of the first one, however, it appears indicated that this inscription may have come from the *postscenium* face, not the *scaena* face, and would thus have fallen, in the main, into the wadi bed which runs before the Theater. The two blocks give some indication of the type of epigraphic work done on the Theater, however, as well as some indication of the method employed. In the latter regard, the first block gives evidence that the inscription was carved after the blocks had been set in place (the joint cuts into the *taw*, but the join of the two blocks is exact, hardly to be expected in coursing alone).

The remaining fragments recovered present a few legible letters, but no connected reading, or suggested sense, would seem possible from them. The presence of red paint in some of the incised lines of some of the smaller fragments recovered, along with their related find spots, suggests that a frieze inscription was incorporated into the *episcenium*, or that a series of (dedicatory?) inscriptions, as at Jerash, *inter alia*, had been placed along the length of the *scaenae frons*.

Comparison of the script of the larger fragments with that of the Jerash materials, especially, as well as with others does not provide any conclusive chronological evidence as to the period of the Petra fragments. However, such a comparison would seem to indicate the first century A.D. as not impossible for the Petra script, which negative evidence does agree with other chronological data secured and presented elsewhere in the final report of the excavations. The Greek epigraphic fragments are presented on the accompanying plate without further comment, Plate XLVI.

VIII

NABATAEAN EPIGRAPHIC MATERIALS
FROM THE EXCAVATIONS

John M. Salmon

The constructors of the Petra Theater used a system of location marking which contributes far more epigraphic data than any other of the Roman-period theaters excavated to date. The system employed combinations of Nabataean letters (for the most part) and slashes, inscribed on the end of column drums, on column bases, and (in four cases) on pieces of the entablature.[1]

Most of the numbered pieces found in the Theater debris were column drums of yellow marl, one of two main types of column used in the Theater, of diameters ranging from 52.5 cm. to 62 cm. Thirty-one drums (whole or fragmentary), six bases, and four pieces of entablature (also of the yellow marl) were found to bear the markings.

In most cases, the number was inscribed on the flat surface of a piece, on one end of a drum, on the drum-supporting surface of a base, or on one flat surface of a piece of entablature. Two column drums, however, bore markings on the side, near one end. One of these drums (Plate XLVII, 6) was of an entirely different order of columns, plastered and much slimmer (36 cm. in diameter). The letter is a squared *beth*, with three slashes meeting the bottom horizontal (compare Plate XLVII, 2 and 3). The other drum (Plate XLVIII, 15) is of the marl type, numbered also on one end. The numbers are not identical, however; the end of the drum is inscribed *samekh*-five, but the number on the side is a combination of a Nabataean *teth* and some other symbol partially broken off and unidentifiable. Why the same drum should bear two different numbers is inexplicable.

When the first pieces bearing the letter-slash combinations were found, it was tentatively suggested that the masons had employed the dual system to indicate the linear location of a column and the position of the specific drum in its elevation. This hypothesis was proved to be substantially correct when, at a later stage of the excavation, three lines of numbered column drums were found in the fall debris, with each drum in a line bearing the same Nabataean letter (or other symbol) and successive numbers of slashes (see Plate XLIX, 23, showing drums *kaph*-two, -three, and -four; and Plate L, 39, showing 'double-quadrant' -five and -six).

In the numbering system, bases were marked only with the letter designating the column; drums were marked with the letter and numbered from one to six, from the bottom. In most cases, the position of the drum in its elevation was indicated by the appropriate number of slashes. In four instances, numerals were used: three times the x-mark representing the numeral four, and once the numeral five (see Plate XLVII, 9; Plate XLVIII, 14; and Plate L, 32 and 34). At the same time, other drums bear four and five slashes, rather than numerical symbols, indicating that the usage was not uniform.

While the numbers of slashes thus proved to indicate the position of a drum in its elevation, the evidence seemed to show that the letters (or symbols) did not designate the linear location of

6+

the column. The evidence was somewhat limited in this respect: of the forty-one numbered pieces in the fall debris, sixteen were removed from their fall position in clearing operations carried out before the beginning of the excavations and between the 1961 and 1962 seasons. There is thus no indication of their original position in the original plan of the Theater. On three others (not shown; Plate L, 40 should probably be added as a fourth), only slashes, or slashes and unintelligible fragments of letters or symbols, remained. Of the remaining twenty-one (or twenty-two) pieces, the smaller column and the entablature pieces can be used as evidence for column location only in a very general way, since their relation to the regular column which bore the same letter designation cannot be definitely ascertained.

Excluding those pieces whose location in the fall debris cannot be known, we are left with pieces bearing only five letters (six, if the small column and entablature pieces bearing the *beth* are added) but all of the non-alphabetic symbols (see below). The distribution of these pieces in the fall debris is shown on the accompanying Schematic Diagram. Despite the limitation of the

SCHEMATIC DIAGRAM: LOCATION OF MARKED PIECES

Approximate location of marked pieces shown in relation to line of *scaenae frons*. Only excavated pieces indicated.
(face line, first podium, *scaenae frons*)

{ Center of Main Door }

					#14		
1 m.	#28		#40	#23			#25
2 m.			#18	#31			
3 m.	#26	#24		#35			#30
				#36			
4 m.			#38				
5 m.							
6 m.				#27			
					#21	#22	
7 m.		#39		#32			
8 m.	#29			#33			
9 m.				#34			
10 m.	#16						
	#15						

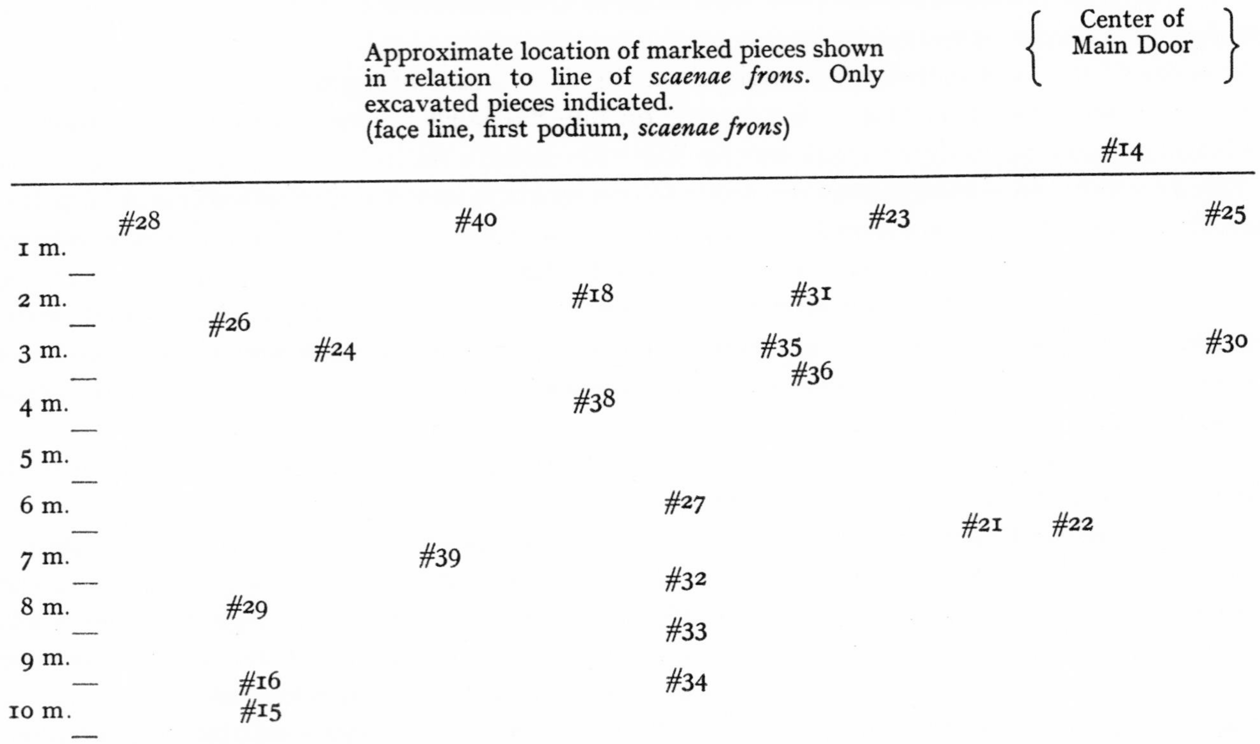

evidence, it appears virtually certain that the columns were not arranged in alphabetical order, or in any other discernible pattern. Apparently the letters (and symbols) served only to keep together the drums cut for each particular column, without necessarily designating the location of the column.[2]

Twelve (possibly thirteen) of the twenty-two letters of the Nabataean alphabet are represented in our material: *aleph, beth, gimel, daleth/resh, he, waw, ḥeth, ṭeth, kaph, samekh, ṣadhe,* and *taw.* One fragment (Plate L, 40) may preserve part of an '*ayin,* but the letter (or symbol) is not complete enough to permit identification.

That all twenty-two letters (with the probable exception of *zayin*, which is only a slash in Nabataean) were originally used, however, is made certain by the presence among our repertoire of letters from the last half of the alphabet (including *taw*), plus the use of some symbols other than letters. These include a circle (Plate L, 30, and possibly 31, although both are bases), a diamond-shaped figure (Plate L, 32, 33, and 35; also 34?), and a bisected semicircle, or 'double quadrant' figure. The origin of the latter is unknown. No comparable symbol is known to exist in any Nabataean inscription, nor anywhere else in the Middle East. The closest approximation (other than a Greek *theta*, which this definitely is not) is a symbol found in a Sinaitic Nabataean inscription, published in Euting's *Sinaïtische Inschriften*, no. 469.[3] The Sinaitic figure does not have the straight line across the diameter of the semi-circle, however, and the short inscription which it accompanies is unintelligible. It is likely that the 'double-quadrant' figure, as well as the other non-alphabetic symbols, were arbitrarily selected as designations of columns when letters had been exhausted. Since, as we have seen, the letters most probably did not serve to indicate linear location of columns, the use of arbitrary symbols would pose no problem.

Some attention must now be given to the form of the letters. In general, our material fits a date during the reign of Aretas IV quite well, although it must also be said that most of the forms, if not indeed all, could fit practically any date within the first century of our era. Nevertheless, there are some indications that a date in the first part of the century (although not too early) would be the most likely time to look for the origin of our material.

Datable Nabataean inscriptions available for comparison now number almost eighty, spanning a period of more than three centuries, from 90 B.C. to A.D. 328. All but a dozen of these, however, fall within the period from 9 B.C. (the beginning of the reign of Aretas IV) to A.D. 150. Nor is the latter part even of that period well represented: there is a gap from A.D. 76 until A.D. 90 in which no definitely datable inscriptions occur (although three inscriptions datable only to the reign of Rabbel II, A.D. 70–106, may come from this part of his reign), and only one inscription represents the period from A.D. 110 to A.D. 147. A dipinto (painted inscription) from Jebel Ramm of A.D. 147, an inscription from Boṣra of A.D. 148, and a graffito from Sinai dated A.D. 150, represent the middle of the second century.[4]

The geographical distribution of datable Nabataean inscriptions is fairly broad, and not particularly favorable for our investigation. The greatest concentrations are found at El-Ḥejr (= Medain Ṣaliḥ) in the Ḥejaz region of Saudi Arabia, and in the Ḥauran region on the Jordan-Syria border. Five out of the hundreds of graffiti in the Sinai peninsula are datable, but none predate A.D. 150. Other datable inscriptions occur in 'Abdeh, at various sites along the trans-Jordanian plateau, in Sidon and Dumeir (near Damascus) in the north, at the oasis of Jauf in the Arabian desert, and even as far afield as Italy, where two inscriptions from the first quarter of the first century have been found at Puteoli. From Petra, the capital of the Nabataeans, we have a scant half dozen datable inscriptions, two of which—the Aṣlaḥ inscription of 90 B.C.[5] and the Rabbel statue of 70 B.C.[6]—are the oldest we possess. Other than these two, we can refer to one[7] dated A.D. 5 and another dated A.D. 20.[8] Two inscriptions which we can date only some-time within the reign of Rabbel II[9] round out the half dozen. The largest known Nabataean inscription, the so-called 'Great Petra Inscription', found on the façade of a tomb in Wadi Turkhman,[10] is unfortunately not internally dated.

The geographical distribution would present no problem if the development of the Nabataean script were uniform throughout the area covered by the inscriptions. However, as has been often noted,[11] such is not the case. The development of the script in the Ḥauran, for example, in many respects lagged as much as a generation behind its development elsewhere.[12] This factor of local variation must, then, be borne in mind throughout our comparison.

Studies of the Nabataean script are relatively few. In the first place, the inscriptional material is widely scattered in publication. Part Two of the *Corpus Inscriptionum Semiticarum* includes only forty-eight of the datable inscriptions now available; the others are scattered through a large number of publications. A new fascicle of the *Corpus* which we have been promised[13] should make the inscriptional material more readily accessible. Among analyses of the script, the observations made by Lidzbarski[14] and Cantineau[15] are very helpful, but refer mainly to overall trends in the script, without attempting to fix a date when any given development took place in a given area. Albright,[16] Cross,[17] and Starcky[18] have more recently supplied us with studies which attempt some dating of developments of the script, and their work is of the extraordinarily high quality we would expect from them. All three, however, concentrate primarily on the earliest inscriptions, so that our understanding of the script before the turn of the era is now well advanced, but developments during the period of greatest inscriptional activity, from the beginning of the reign of Aretas IV until roughly the end of the first century, remain obscure.

Such are the resources for comparison. We now turn to the letters found in our material.

Concerning some of them, there is little to note. The forms of the *gimel* (Plate XLVII, 7–9), *daleth/resh* (the two are generally indistinguishable in Nabataean; Plate XLVII, 10), *he* (Plate XLVIII, 11 and 12; also 17? see below), *kaph* (Plate XLVIII, 19, 20; XLIX, 21–23), *ṣadhe* (Plate XLIX, 26), and *taw* (Plate XLIX, 27–29) occur as in our material throughout virtually the entire period covered by the inscriptions.

Variations of the forms of these letters do occur, but with no discernible pattern. The *gimel* of the Aṣlaḥ inscription (90 B.C.) is different, but in the other early inscriptions the letter does not occur. From 5 B.C.,[19] and probably earlier, the form of the *gimel* represented in our material is standard wherever it occurs, with only occasional variations.[20] Several forms of the *he* other than that found in our material also occur, but appear to be only variations in style occurring contemporaneously. A different form of the *taw* also develops, in which the left leg becomes a loop. This form apparently developed first as a final form, but subsequently is found in other positions as well. The looped-leg form, however, never seems to have replaced the form found in our material, which continued to be the most common. Our *waw* (Plate XLVIII, 13) is of the hook variety, which is earlier than the looped form. However, the latter form, apparently developing first as a final form, or at least one connected by ligature with the letter preceding, occurs as early as 5 B.C.[21] Thereafter both forms occur at least until the middle of the second century, although the looped form becomes more and more common.

Of the remaining letters, the *'aleph* (Plate XLVII, 1 and 2) provides probably the best indications for establishing a *terminus post quem* for our material. Our form does not occur in the earliest inscriptions,[22] and at Si', in the Ḥauran (where we have noted that the development of the script lagged behind other areas), a clearly transitional form occurs in two inscriptions dated, respectively, 5 B.C. and 2 B.C.[23] A form of the 'aleph in which the upper right arm intersects the oval is probably to be considered sequentially prior to our 'aleph, but apparently did not precede it much in time. In any case, a form comparable to ours occurs as early as the el-'Ula (Dedan) inscription published by Euting,[24] which dates from the first year of Aretas IV, in the inscription left by Syllaeus in Miletus just prior to that time,[25] and then in an inscription in Sidon to be dated 4 B.C.[26] Nevertheless, we would probably be well advised not to press this evidence too far. Most of the early examples of this form are still fairly awkward; the arm extending upward to the right is still relatively independent, made in much the same way as in the forms in which the arm intersects the oval. In most of the examples, the arm is not yet, as it is in both of our 'alephs, a smooth continuation of the movement used in forming the oval. While a date at the beginning of the reign of Aretas IV is therefore not excluded, it is perhaps not quite as probable as one somewhat later in his reign.

Our *beth* (Plate XLVII, 3–6) agrees well with a date in the reign of Aretas IV. This form is the one found uniformly in all positions in the earliest inscriptions (Aṣlaḥ, 90 B.C.; Rabbel, 70 B.C.; Tell esh-Shugafiye, 48 B.C.). In initial and medial positions, it was replaced in most inscriptions by a 'cursive' form—a slightly curving diagonal slash—early in the first century of our era. The older form continued in use in many inscriptions in the final position, however, although in this position, too, it was partially displaced by a form retaining the long bottom horizontal, but without the top horizontal part. The older form seems to have survived into the latter part of the first century A.D. in final position at el-Ḥejr[27] and occasionally in the Ḥauran[28] and at Petra, itself.[29] In other positions, the older form is the exception[30] rather than the rule.

The *ḥeth* (Plate XLVIII, 14–15) of the Theater material exhibits the common Nabataean ductus, although a well-formed one. The bend of the left leg is well developed in our form, but the top projection of the left leg has not yet been lost. This development apparently began as early as the beginning of the reign of Aretas IV,[31] and became more and more common during the first century A.D.,[32] but the older form (as in our material) persisted in some inscriptions to the end of the first century[33] and even beyond.[34]

Two variant forms in our material may be briefly noted here. Plate XLVIII, 16, is a variant form of the *ḥeth* which is infrequent, but not rare. Comparable forms occur in Petra,[35] Shobek,[36] and Sinai.[37] Plate XLVIII, 17, is more difficult. It may be either *he* or a *ḥeth*, but the former seems more likely. In either case, it is quite singular.[38] Its presence alongside the regular *he* (or *ḥeth*) is puzzling.

The *samekh* found in the Theater material (Plate XLIX, 24 and 25) is the most common Nabataean type. A smaller, flatter form, which came to be open on the left,[39] appears as early as 4 B.C. in Sidon,[40] and shortly after the middle of the first century A.D. seems almost completely to have displaced the older form in some regions. In the inscriptions from el-Ḥejr, for instance, the older form is uniformly used in inscriptions before the middle of the century,[41] but in five inscriptions dating from A.D. 49 to A.D. 75/76 the form has begun noticeably to change. After A.D. 50, forms comparable to our *samekh* occur only in the Ḥauran.[43] At Petra, however, this evidence cannot be pressed. In neither of the inscriptions datable after A.D. 50[44] does a *samekh* occur. Moreover the later form of the *samekh* does not occur in any of the more than 150 undated inscriptions from Petra, while there are more than two dozen examples of the earlier form.

The evidence suggests strongly that the older form may not have been displaced at all in the Nabataean capital.[45]

The remaining letter of our material, the *teth* (Plate XLVIII, 18), is the most striking of all. Our form bears little resemblance to the classic Nabataean ductus for this letter, with the straight vertical arm on the left and the elongated (often exaggeratedly so) loop to the right. The closest comparable forms occur in the Sinai graffiti,[46] but unfortunately not in any dated inscriptions from that region. Nevertheless, the Sinai forms are probably late. Otherwise, we can refer to isolated examples in the Ḥauran,[47] to Syllaeus' inscription at Miletus,[48] and to one inscription from Petra itself.[49] The character of most of these inscriptions suggests that a form such as ours may have continued to exist, latently and in disuse, through most or all of the period of Nabataean inscriptional activity, coming to use now and then in 'informal' writing, such as graffiti or our material, but overshadowed in all, or almost all, formal inscriptions, and in most other instances as well.

There remain to be considered only the numerals used in the columnar numbering system. Since the numeral 4 in Nabataean is a simple x, it affords no basis for comparison. The numeral five (Plate L, 32), however, may be compared with three examples from the el-Ḥejr inscriptions.[50] Although the material is quite limited, the numeral 5 in our material is clearly much closer to the earliest of these (1 B.C.) than to the others.

We may sum up our observations as follows: most of the forms exhibited in the Theater material fit well into a date during the reign of Aretas IV, 9 B.C.—A.D. 40. The development of the 'aleph provides some basis for preferring the latter part of that period, while considerations of the forms of the *beth* and *ḥeth* argue against a dating in the latter part of the first century, if this were permitted by the archaeological evidence. The *samekh* we have seen to be of use in some areas in dating Nabataean inscriptional material, but apparently not at Petra. Finally, the *teth* of our material may hint at the survival of some forms other than those prescribed for the letters by the norms of Nabataean lapidary writing.

IX

THE POTTERY OF THE SEALED DEPOSITS: PERIOD I b—c

Frank Garcia

The operations of the rebuilding stages of periods I(b) and I(c) produced two 'sealed' deposits of pottery sherds: I.1(19) and I.24 respectively. These deposits are of obvious importance for the dating of their periods of provenance and the building periods they reflect, and we turn now to their characteristics.

I.1(19) (cf. Plates LVII; LI, 1, 2) consists of the pottery found in the filling of the canal which, in the earliest period of the Theater, stood open in the *orchestra* floor, going beneath the central niche. In Phase I(b) this canal was filled and covered over with stone slabs and cement (cf. Plate Folder D).

Most of the fragments are from cooking-pots of the general type found from the Hellenistic to the Byzantine periods in Palestine (rims drawn in Plate LVII, 1–25). The wear is generally red, with a beige or tan slip, though there are examples of red ware with black slip (#16, 18, 25), of tan ware with beige or tan slip (#4, 10, 11, 19, 22) and even of black-slipped black ware (#14). Some of the sherds are ribbed (cf. Plate LI, 2), the ribbing being closer to the 'delicate but fully rounded and closely spaced' variety of the Roman, than to the 'heavy broad corrugations of the Byzantine period'.[1]

The handle fragments in this group belong to the 'ridged elliptic' and 'grooved' varieties, and some to the 'square topped', described by Kelso[2] as characteristic of the Roman period; the 'ridged elliptic' and 'square topped' being predominantly early, the 'grooved' predominantly late. The rims are mostly of the type grooved at the top (e.g. Plate LVII, 2, 6, 14, 20) or with a rather squarish or blunt band on the exterior immediately below the edge (e.g. Plate LVII, 1, 4, 5). For related forms, cf.[3]. The rim forms correspond to type series which have been identified as 'Nabataean II' or 'Late Nabataean'[4] and have obvious parallels in the pottery of trenches H51 and H56 of the excavations carried out at Dhiban in 1954–55 (unpublished). A few bowl fragments also occur (rims drawn in Plate LVII, 26–29), of typical late Nabataean ware.

In general, all fragments show the typically good levigation of the period, with small grits, and well-controlled firing. Throwing, turning, and drying errors do not show in any of the recovered sherds and cores are uniform. I.(24) (cf. Plates LVIII; LIX, LII, 1–4). This group of pottery sherds was found sealed in the filling of the stage front which occurred in Period (Ic) (cf. Plate Folder D). With the exception of several occurrences of fine Nabataean painted ware bowl sherds, the fabric is generally quite poor, warped, blistered, and with black cores due to defective firing. The coarse grits used as filler are readily noticeable, in particular in an extremely poor, coarse yellowish ware. A sherd of this 'marl' ware is shown Plate LII, 2, in second row far right, presenting the combed decoration usual to it.[5] Most of the cooking pot fragments, however, are of coarse red gritty ware with a light beige or tan slip, and show ribbing of the finer, rounded variety (cf. Plate LII, 1, 2, 4, 5). The examples on Plate LII, 4, 5 (drawn in Plate LVIII, 1, 10, cf. also 16, 21) show a type of ridged loop handle similar to those found in Qaryet el 'Enab, soundings VI A and VI C[6], of Early Byzantine origin. Ribbed, flat strap handles such as that depicted on Plate LII, 1, also continue into the Early Byzantine period.[7] Some double handles also appear (cf. Plate LII, 1, bottom row, second and third from left) which are characteristic of the late Roman Period.[8] Small, flat strap handles also occur (cf. Plate LIV, 2, second row, second row left) of the type depicted in Pritchard, *op. cit.*, Plate 39, no. #1, from N. T. Jericho.[9] Cooking-pot rims (drawn in Plate LVIII) show for the most part a rather sharp overhanging rim, continuing Hellenistic and Early Roman forms,[10] though in a poorer variety of ware. The type series parallels in Nabataean pottery extend, where datable, to the Late Nabataean or Early Byzantine periods.[11]

A number of bowl fragments were found also in this deposit (rims drawn in Plate LIX, 1–23). Among these there were several examples of fine Nabataean 'black-painted' ware (#13–17), but for the most part the bowls were of plain, coarse, red ware, sometimes with a slip or wash. The rim profiles fit into type series which occur in the Late Nabataean II Period.[12]

Three jug rim fragments also appear in Plate LIX (24, 25, 26) for which there are certain late parallels. For #24, with an everted overhang rim, ribbed, cf. a Byzantine jar from Khirbet En-Nitla[13] and a jug, perhaps Early Byzantine, from the Tyropoeon.[14] For #25, with an everted flaring rim, there are close parallels in form—even though without a spout or ornamental ribbing as in our example, from Kh. Qumran.[15]

PERIOD I: Additional Pottery Notes

Period I (c)—Sealed Deposit, Trench I.24 (all levels): Lamp fragments from this deposit may be compared with Horsfield, #161[16] (after first half first century A.D.), with Murray & Ellis,[17] Plate XXXVI, #16 (end of first century A.D., early second century A.D. ?), with Antioch Type 44[18] (late first century A.D., early second century A.D.), with Beit Nattif examples (first–third century A.D.), with Jerusalem specimens[19] mainly third/fourth century A.D. types, p. 45, but a bit late for I (c)), and with Tyropoeon Valley shapes.[20]

The Nabataean bowl pieces from this deposit are almost identical in ware composition, technique, firing, and all other features with the cooking pot and other wares represented, indicating a complete degeneration of technique in regard to the thin (common) bowl types so characteristic of Nabataean factories.

Period I (a)—Fall cover of Period V: Lamp fragments from this context may be compared with Horsfield, #45[21] (seen there as Broneer XXII—c. first quarter first century A.D.), with Horsfield, #42[22] (seen as a variation of Broneer XXII, but probably before the middle of the first century A.D.), with Murray & Ellis,[23] (there without volutes and hence dated second century A.D.), with Horsfield, #419[24] (with ovules inside the discus border; this parallels Broneer XXI, early—c. early first century A.D.), and with Murray & Ellis,[25] (seen there as c. A.D. 130–150, but probably dated too late?).

P.C.H.

NOTES: CHAPTER I

1. Diodorus, XIX.94–97.

2. Diodorus, II.48, XIX.99; Phillip C. Hammond, 'The Nabataean Bitumen Industry At the Dead Sea', *BA*, XXII (1959), pp. 40 ff. and notes.

3. Strabo, *Geography*, 783–784.

4. See especially, Gus W. Van Beek, 'Frankincense and Myrrh', *BA*, XXIII (1960), pp. 70 ff. and especially pp. 75–82, 76.

5. Starcky, Jean, 'The Nabataeans: A Historical Sketch', *BA*, XVIII (1955), pp. 85–86.

6. *Contra* Sir Alexander Kennedy, *Petra, Its History and Monuments*, p. 29.

7. Josephus, *Antiquities*, XII.5 (Hyrcanus); II Macc. 5:8 (Jason); I Macc. 5:24 (Judas & Jonathan); II Macc. 12:10; *Antiq.*, XIII.1 (John); I Macc. 9:36–42; *Antiq.*, XIII.9 (Jonathan); *Antiq.*, XIII.17 and *Wars*, I.2 (Hyrcanus); *Antiq.*, XIII.21–23 (Jannaeus); *Wars*, I.2, 3, 4; *Antiq.*, XIII.24 (Alexandra); *Antiq.*, XIV.2–4, *Wars*, I.5 (Hyrcanus); *Antiq.*, XIV.25, XV.4–6, 8, 9, XVI.13–16, XVII.1, 4, 12–13, 16 (Herod); *Wars*, I.12–14, 17–20; *Antiq.*, XVIII.7 (Agrippa I); *Wars*, II.3 (First Jewish Revolt).

8. *Antiq.*, XIV.2–4, 18; *Wars*, I.5–6, 7.

9. *Antiq.*, XIV (Scaurus' abortive campaign); *Wars*, I.6; *Antiq.*, XIV.12 (Gabinius); *Wars*, I.6; *Antiq.*, XV, 4–6 (Anthony & Cleopatra); *Wars*, I.13–14; *Antiq.*, XV (Augustus); and see also *Antiq.*, XVI.13–16, XVII.4, 12, XVIII.7: *Wars*, II.3, 7–8, VI.8, 15.

10. Starcky, *op. cit.*, pp. 88 ff. and see note.

11. *Idem*, pp. 88 ff.; and see also Howard C. Butler, *PAES*, II, pp. 310–311, 324–325, 317–318, *inter alia*.

12. Starcky, *op. cit.*, p. 94.

13. *Idem*, p. 97.

14. *Idem*, cf. pp. 97–98.

15. *Idem*, pp, 101–103.

16. *Idem*, pp. 103–104, 106.

17. *Idem*, p. 105.

18. On general discussion of Arabia Petraea and Petra, see the following:

Ben-Dor, Stella, 'Petra Colonia', *Berytus*, IX, (1948–49) pp. 41–43.

Bliss, Frederick Jones, 'Narrative of an Expedition to Moab and Gilead in March 1895', *PEFQS* (1895), pp. 203–35

Brünnow, Rudolf Ernst and Alfred V. Domaszewski, *Die Provincia Arabia*, I, II, III.

Gesenius, William (transl.)—*Johann Ludwig Burckhardt's Reisen in Syrien, Palästina, und der Gegend des Berges Sinai*, I, II.

Butler, Howard Crosby, 'Section B: The Expedition of 1909', *Publications of the Princeton University Archaeological Expeditions to Syria in 1904–1905 and 1909. Divisions I-II.*

Cantineau, J., *La Nabatéen*, I. II.

Conway, Agnes Ethel, 'Exploring "A city of Mystery"', *Illustrated London News* (Feb. 1, 1930), pp. 160 ff.

Dalman, Gustaf, *Petra und seine Felsheiligtümer*.

——, *Neue Petra-Forschungen*.

Erskine, Mrs. Stuart, *The Vanished Cities of Arabia*.

Evenari, Michael and Dov Koller, 'Ancient Masters of the Desert', *Scientific American*, (April 1956).

Glueck, Nelson, 'Explorations in Eastern Palestine, I, II, III, IV.' *AASOR*, XIV (1934), XV (1935), XVIII–XIX (1939), XXV–XXVIII (1945–49)—among others.

—— 'Nabataean Syria', *BASOR*, 85 (1942), pp. 3–8.

—— 'Explorations in Western Palestine', *BASOR*, 131 (1953), pp. 6–15.

—— 'Further Explorations in The Negeb', *BASOR*, 137 (1955), pp. 10–22.

—— 'The Third Season of Exploration in the Negeb', *BASOR*, 138 (1955), pp. 7–29 and succeeding accounts.

—— 'Nabataean Syria and Nabataean Transjordan', *JPOS*, XVIII (1938), pp. 1–6.

Harding, G. Lankester, *The Antiquities of Jordan*.

Horsfield, G. & A., 'Sela-Petra, The Rock, of Edom and Nabatene', *QDAP*, VII, (1937), VIII (1938), IX (1941).

——, and Agnes Conway, 'Historical and Topographical Notes on Edom: With An Account of The First Excavations at Petra', *The Geographical Journal*, LXXVI (Nov. 1930), pp. 369–88.

Hammond, Philip C., 'The Excavation of Petra, 1959', *BASOR*, 159 (1960), pp. 26–30.

——, 'Petra', *BA*, XXIII, (1960), pp. 29–32.

——, 'The Excavation of the Main Theater, Petra', *American Scholar*, 32 (1962), pp. 93–106.

——, 'The Roman Theater of Petra Excavated', *Illustrated London News* (May 25, 1963), pp. 804–5.

——, 'Rose-Red City of Petra', *Natural History*, LXXIII, (Feb. 2, 1964), pp. 14–25.

Jaussen, A. and Savignac, *Mission Archéologique en Arabia*, I, II.

Kennedy, Sir Alexander, 'The Rocks and Monuments of Petra', *The Geographical Journal*, LXIII (1924), pp. 273–301.

——, *Petra, Its History and Monuments*.

Kergorlay, Cte. Jean de, 'Pétra', *Revue des Deux Mondes*, 38 (1907), pp. 894–923.

Libbey, William and Franklin E. Hoskins, *The Jordan Valley and Petra*, I, II.

Millard, Alan, 'A Seal From Petra', *PEQ*, (1961), p. 136.

Moritz, 'Ausflüge in der Arabia Petraea', *Mélanges de la Faculté Orientale, Univ. St.-Joseph*, III (1908), pp. 387–436.

Morton, William, 'Umm il-Biyara', *BA*, XIX (1956), pp. 26–36.

Murray, M. A., *Petra, The Rock City of Edom*.

———— and J. C. Ellis, *A Street in Petra*.

Musil, Alois, *Arabia Petraea*, I, II, III.

Parr, Peter J., 'Excavations at Petra, 1958–59', *PEQ*, (1960), pp. 124–135.

————, 'The Capital of the Nabataeans', *Scientific American*, 209, 4 (1963), pp. 95–102.

Savignac, R., 'Notes de Voyage de Suez au Sinai et á Pétra', *RB*, X (1913), pp. 429–42.

Sourdel, Dominique, *Les Cultes du Hauran À L'Époque Romaine*.

Szczepanski, Landislaus, *Nach Petra und zum Sinai*.

Clermont-Ganneau, Charles, 'Les Nabatéens en Égypt', *Revue de L'Histoire des Religions*, 80 (1919), pp. 1–29.

Wiegand, Th., *et. al.*, *Petra* (Deutschtürkische Denkmals Schutz-Kommando. 3).

Wright, G. R. H., 'Petra, The Arched Gate, 1959–60', *PEQ* (1961), pp. 124–135.

————, 'Structure of The Qasr Bint Far'un, A Preliminary Review', *PEQ* (1961), pp. 8–37.

NOTES: CHAPTER II

1. Musil, Alois, *Arabia Petraea, II, Edom*, plan of the area, 1:20,000.

2. Burckhardt, John, *Travels in Syria and The Holy Land*, p. 427.

3. Irby, P. L. and J. Mangles, *Travels In Egypt and Nubia . . .* , p. 131.

4. Robinson Edward, *Biblical Researches In Palestine*, p. 134.

5. Kinnear, J., *Cairo, Petra and Damascus in 1838*, pp. 147 ff.

6. Ehni, J., 'Souvenirs du Mont Hôr et des ruines de Pétra', *Le Globe, Journal Géographique*, XXXIII 5th series, V (1894), pp. 120 ff.

7. Wilson, Edward L., *In Scripture Lands, New Views of Sacred Places*, pp. 95 ff.

8. Lenoir, Paul, *Le Fayoum, le Sinai et Pétra*, p. 300; Viscount Castlereagh, *A Journey . . .* , II, p. 176.

9. Bertou, Comte Jules de, 'Itinéraire de la Mer Morte à Akaba . . . et retour à Hebron par Pétrá', *Bulletin de la Société de Géographie*, XI (1839), p. 315.

10. Kinnear, *op. cit.*, pp. 147 ff.

11. Morris, Edward J., *Notes of a Tour . . .* , I, p. 133.

12. Wilson, *op. cit.*, p. 317.

13. Visconti, G. A., *Diario di un viaggio in Arabia Petrea* (1865), p. 335.

14. Roberts, David, *The Holy Land . . . .*

15. Musil, *op. cit.*, II, p. 107, Fig. 74.

16. Wiegand Th., *et al.*, *Petra* (*Deutschtürkische Denkmals Schutz-Kommandos*, III), Fig. 23, p. 30.

17. For previous preliminary reports, now superseded in all details, see: Hammond, Philip C., 'Excavations of The Roman Theater At Petra', *Yearbook, The American Philosophical Society* (1962), pp. 545–549; 'The Roman Theater of Petra Excavated', *Illustrated London News*, (25 May, 1963), pp. 804, 805; *Sciences et Avenir*, 198, pp. 574–575; 'The Excavation of The Main Theater, Petra', *American Scholar*, 32 (1962), pp. 93–106; 'Rose-Red City of Petra', *Natural History*, LXXIII (2/1964), pp. 23–24.

18. Dr. Awni Dajani, Director.

19. The major earthquakes of the first century A.D. onward (before which the Theater could not conceivably have been built, rebuilt, and fallen into disuse) were as follows: A.D. 19, 30, 33 (the latter two of slight intensity), 48 (moderate), 130 (strong), 306, 344, 362, 365 (which caused damage to the walls of Kerak), 419 (moderate to severe), 447 (strong), 498, 502, 551 (very severe), 554, 580, 583, 631–632 (a month of tremors), 637, 641, 658 (moderate to strong), 659/660, 672 (strong in the south), 710 746/748 (intensity range of 18.1; causing the destruction of Jerash)—so D. H. Kallner-Amiran, *Israel Exploration Journal*, I, (1950–51), pp. 225–226.

20. *Idem*, pp. 225–226; cf. the earthquakes of A.D. 419 (moderate to severe), 447 (strong), 551 (very severe), 631–632 (a month in duration), 658 (moderate to strong), 672 (strong near Gaza), 756 (strong), 750–780 (very severe), as against that of 746/748.

21. See also, Parr, Peter J., 'Rock Engravings From Petra', *PEFQS* (1959), p. 108; and 'Excavations at Petra 1958–59', *PEQ*, 1960, pp. 127–28.

NOTES: CHAPTER III

1. Brünnow, Rudolf Ernst, and Alfred v. Domaszewski, *Die Provincia Arabia*, I, Plate VII, p. 256; Alois Musil, *Arabia Petraea*, II, Fig. 74, p. 107; Theodor Wiegand, *et. al.*, *Petra*, Fig. 23, p. 30.

2. Nicoll, Allardyce, *The Development of The Theatre*, p. 55; August Mau, *Pompeii*, p. 144.

3. Vitruvius, V.iii—on site arrangement.

4. Note accordance with Vitruvius' canon—V.iii.

83

5. Vitruvius, V.vi; note also that at Pompeii, for example, seat width was not of Vitruvian standard—so Mau, *op. cit.*, p. 143.

6. Vitruvius, V.vi.

7. See Lepik, Wilhelmina, *Mathematical Planning of Ancient Theatres*, VIIb, p. 29; and cf. Vitruvius, V.vi on the necessity for modifications.

8. Vitruvius, V.vi.

9. The term coined by Margarete Bieber, *The History of The Greek and Roman Theater*, p. 203; on the date of the institution of class distinctions in places of public amusement, see Suetonius, *Augustus*, 43–45 and cf. Livy, XXXIV.54.

10. Cf. the Porta Portuensis inscription (*Corp. Insc. Lat.*, VI, i, p. 506) cited by J. Henry Middleton, *Ancient Rome in 1885*, p. 307; cf. Ovid, *Am.*, III.ii.19.

11. Cf. ivory tickets at Frosinone, noted in Mommsen, *Berlin Sachs Gesell.*, p. 286, with inscription: CVN:VI·IN·XVIII (Cuneus #VI, lowest row, seat #18), so Middleton, *op. cit.*, p. 306; also used at the Colosseum.

12. Vitruvius, V.iii.

13. At Pompeii, and elsewhere, the *tribunalia* areas were reserved for important personages: at Rome for the magistrate giving the play and for the Vestal Virgins—so Mau, *op. cit.*, p. 145.

14. On the general history of the *orchestra* development in the Roman theater type, see Ernst R. Fiechter, *Die Baugeschichtliche Entwicklung des Antiken Theaters*, pp. 99 ff. and citations made earlier.

15. E.g. Marcellus—c. 34 m.; Orange—30 m.; Caesarea—30 m.; Aspendus—c. 27 m.; Tralles—22 m.; Athens (Dionysus)—21.86 m.; Pergamon—21 m.; Timgad—20 m.

16. Cf. Eretria, where the passage leading to the 'door' is actually cut; see Nicoll, *op. cit.*, p. 34.

17. Vitruvius, V.vi.

18. Cf. the medallion over the southern side door of the Khazneh entry—Gustaf Dalman, 'The Kahzneh at Petra', *PEF Annual* (1911), Plate XVII.

19. Robertson, D. S., *A Handbook of Greek & Roman Architecture*, p. 236; on the role of the barrel vault in the period of the Empire, see Frank G. Moore, *The Roman's World*, p. 362.

20. Middleton, *op. cit.*, p. 33.

21. Bailey, Cyril, (ed.), *The Legacy of Rome*, p. 447.

22. On the problem of terminology, see Fiechter, *op. cit.*, pp. 97–99.

23. Vitruvius, V.vi—as against the Greek theater stage height of 10–12 ft.

24. Cf. Mau, *op. cit.*, p. 150; Lepik, *op. cit.*, pp. 31, 32, 33.

25. Nicoll, *op. cit.*, p. 51; Vitruvius, V.vi.

26. Vitruvius, V.vi.

27. Lepik, *op. cit.*, Table V, p. 19 and Table VI, p. 21.

28. Fiechter, *op. cit.*, Fig. 20; Nicoll, *op. cit.*, p. 24.

29. Fiechter, *op. cit.*, Fig. 22; Lepik, *op. cit.*, p. 14; c. third century B.C.

30. Fiechter, *op. cit.*, Fig. 25; Lepik, *op. cit.*, p. 14; c. second century B.C.

31. Fiechter, *op. cit.*, Fig. 27; Lepik, *op. cit.*, p. 14; c. first century B.C.

32. Nicoll, *op. cit.*, Fig. 6, p. 24; Lepik, *op. cit.*, p. 14; third century B.C.

33. Fiechter, *op. cit.*, Fig. 69; Mau, *op. cit.*, Fig. 64; *Dict. des Antiq. Grecq. et Rom.*, V, Fig. 6864; Lepik, *op. cit.*, p. 19; Augustan remodeling?

34. Fiechter, *op. cit.*, Fig. 89; Lepik, *op. cit.*, p. 21; *DAGR*, V, Fig. 6861 and p. 189; Augustan.

35. Fiechter, *op. cit.*, Fig. 90; Lepik, *op. cit.*, p. 19; *DAGR*, V. p. 189; early Imperial?

36. Fiechter, *op. cit.*, Fig. 73; Charles Waldstein, *Herculaneum*, Plate 12.

37. Fiechter, *op. cit.*, Fig. 81.

38. Second century A.D. rebuild.

39. Bieber, *op. cit.*, p. 202—Hadrianic rebuild, c. A.D. 135.

40. Fiechter, *op. cit.*, Fig. 82; Lepik, *op. cit.*, p. 19; Robertson, *op. cit.*, p. 343–c. A.D. 150?

41. Fiechter, *op. cit.*, Fig. 79; Robertson, *op. cit.*, p. 343–c. A.D. 150?

42. Fiechter, *op. cit.*, Fig. 80a; Robertson, *op. cit.*, p. 343–c. A.D. 150?

43. Robertson, *op. cit.*, p. 343–c. A.D. 150?

44. Late first century A.D.

45. Fiechter, *op. cit.*, Fig. 91; *DAGR*, V, p. 189; Lepik, *op. cit.*, p. 19; Robertson, *op. cit.*, p. 343–c. A.D. 150.

46. Bieber, *op. cit.*, Fig. 707; c. A.D. 200.

47. Crowfoot, J. W., *et. al.*, *Samaria-Sebaste I: The Buildings*, Fig. 24, p. 58—third century A.D.

48. Frova, A., 'Gli Scavi "Della Missione Archeologica Italiana A Caesarea (Israele)"', *Annuario della Scuola Archeologica di Atene*, XXXIX–XL, N.S. XXIII–XXIV (1961–62) Fig. 3, p. 654; Anna Albricci, 'L' Orchestra Dipinta del Theatro Erodiano di "Caesarea Maritima",' *Bollettino d'Arte*, IV (Oct.–Dec. 1962), Fig. 2, p. 290.

49. See also Bieber, *op. cit.*, pp. 200, 202, and Fig. 694.

50. Mau, *op. cit.*, p. 146.

51. *Idem*, p. 146, and Fig. 65, p. 145, p. 147; Nicoll, *op. cit.*, pp. 51–52—and especially his detailed description, p. 34.

52. Bieber, *op. cit.*, p. 179, and see p. 170; see also Fiechter, *op. cit.*, Figs. 119, 120, 121, and 122.

53. Mau, *op. cit.*, p. 146; Nicoll, *op. cit.*, p. 55.

54. Nicoll, *op. cit.*, p. 50; and cf. Aspendos, Orange, etc.

55. Vitruvius, II.viii.

56. It will be noted that, in place of the variety of local stone available near Rome, for instance, the Petraean builders had a limited choice; namely, the soft local sandstone and marl, along with a short supply of harder limestones and some available, though not local, marble.

57. Vitruvius, II.iii, viii.

58. *Idem*, II.iii.

59. Cf. the Tabularium, for example—Middleton, *op. cit.*, pp. 25–26.

60. I.e. the three of the five remaining angles of the inscribed triangles determine the lines for door arrangement.

61. Vitruvius, V.vi—for 'strangers'; also Nicoll, *op. cit.*, p. 32 and note (1), citing the *Onomasticon* of Pollux, IV.

62. Vitruvius, V.vi.

63. Fiechter, *op. cit.*, p. 90; however, the term 'Italian', following Bieber, would seem preferable to 'western', and leads to less confusion.

64. Fiechter, *op. cit.*, Fig. 110.

65. *Idem*, particularly Figs, 77, 80a, 78a–b, 88a–b, 81, 93 (= Brünnow, III, Fig. 982), 66 and 117; Bieber, *op. cit.*, Fig. 707, pp. 210 and 173; Waldstein, *op. cit.*, Pl. 12; with these cf. Bieber, Fig. 707 Palmyra, early third century A.D.

66. *Idem*, pp. 112–113.

67. *Idem*, Figs. 107–110—especially Fig. 109, without the modifications to be seen in 110, but moving in their direction. However, the gap in theater building, noted earlier, must also be kept in mind in the comparison of plan refinements.

68. Bieber, *op. cit.*, p. 114—summarizing the arguments of Dorpfeld, von Gerkan, and the current schools of Riechter, Dinsmoor, and herself; see also the views and summary of position by Fiechter, *op. cit.*, p. 99, and his arguments *contra* Dorpfeld, pp. 100–101.

69. Vitruvius, in his description, calls it a 'royal palace' façade; cf. that at Orange as a good classical example, along with others, including, in the Near East, the restored theater at Jerash done by Diana Kirkebride and the Department of Antiquities of Jordan.

70. Mau, *op. cit.*, p. 147; cf. also Greek usage—Nicoll, *op. cit.*, p. 32; Vitruvius, V.vi.

71. Note also such a room behind the stage at Pompeii—Mau, *op. cit.*, p. 146.

72 For this arrangement, cf. especially the *scaenae frons* of the large theater at Pompeii and a modified arrangement at Jerash.

73. Vitruvius, V.vi—where the *scaena* wall height is so set.

74. Cf. also Fiechter, *op. cit.*, Figs. 78b (Orange), 88b (Aizanoi), 89 (Termessos), 90 (Sagalassos), and, less closely, 80b (Dugga).

75. *Idem*. Figs, cited above, and Fig. 110 (second century A.D.) arrangement.

76. Vitruvius, V.vi—one-twelfth of diameter of *orchestra*.

77. *Idem*, V.vi—first podium, one-twelfth of *orchestra* diameter—here only c. 0.078 of *orchestra* diameter; parapet, one-half of podium height—here c. 79%.

78. Moore, *op. cit.*, p. 352; and see Dalman, *op. cit.*, pp. 102, 104, on height, entasis, and order of Khazneh columns.

79. Dalman, *op. cit.*, p. 102.

80. *Idem*, p. 102 in regard to the 1:2 ratio kept at the Khazneh.

81. *Idem*, pp. 102–103.

82. *Idem*, p. 102.

83. Blake, E. G., *Roman Construction In Italy From Tiberius Through The Flavians*, p. 84.

84. Vitruvius, III.v.

85. Dalman, *op. cit.*, pp. 102–103.

NOTES: CHAPTER IV

1. Frova, A., 'Gli scavi della Missione Archeologica Italiana a "Caesarea (Israele)"', *Annuario della Scuola Archeologica di Atene*, XXXIX–XL (1961–62), p. 654 and A. Albricci, 'L'orchestra dipinta del teatro erodiano di "Caesarea Maritima,"' *Bollettino d'Arte del Ministero della Pubblica Istruzione*, IV (Ottobre–Dicembre, 1962), p. 290.

2. *De Architectura*, viii.6.5–6.10.

3. Aharoni, Yohanan, 'Excavations at Ramat Raḥel,' *BA*, XXIV (Dec., 1691), p. 97, Fig. 1.

4. *Neue Petra-Forschungen*, Leipzig, 1912, p. 18, Fig. 6.

NOTES: CHAPTER V

1. Blake, Marion Elizabeth, *Roman Construction in Italy from Tiberius Through the Flavians*, p. 75.

2. Bieber, Margarete, *The History of the Greek and Roman Theater*, p. 190.

3. Frézouls, Edmond, 'Recherches sur les Théâtres de l'Orient Syrien', II, pp. 75 ff.

4. *Idem*, pp. 71 ff., and compare.

5. *Idem*, p. 54.

6. *Idem*, p. 63.

7. *Idem*, pp. 66 ff.

8. *Idem*, p. 61.

9. *Idem*, pp. 56–57 and note (1)—cited as a phenomenon surviving from Hellenistic times and widespread.

10. Strabo, *Geog.*, 783–784.

11. Hammond, Philip C., *A Study of Nabataean Pottery* (unpublished dissertation, Yale University, 1957) and see 'Pattern Families in Nabataean Painted Ware', *AJA*, 63, p. 373; also see 'A Classification of Nabataean Fine Ware', *AJA*, 66, pp. 172–173.

12. Frézouls, *op. cit.*, pp. 54, 63, 66 ff., 71 ff.

13. *Idem.* pp, 56–57, and note (1); cf. Josephus, *Antiquities*, XV, xi, XVI, v; and note other private patrons responsible for civic buildings throughout the Near East at this time and following.

14. Frézouls, *op. cit.*, especially pp. 56–57, and Josephus, *Antiq.* as cited above.

15. *Antiquities*, XVIII, v.

16. Starcky, Jean, 'The Nabataeans: A Historical Sketch', *BA*, XVIII (1955), pp. 101–102.

17. *Antiquities*, XV, ix—from his thirteenth year.

18. This would therefore tend to reduce the apparent disparity in the datings of other materials related to the later history of Petra, as well as to assist in the clarification of the sequences of that history, itself.

NOTES: CHAPTER VI

1. Middleton, J. Henry, *Ancient Rome in 1885*, p. 10.

2. *Idem*, pp. 11, 38.

3. *Idem*, p. 11.

4. *Idem*, cf. pp. 36, 38; J. H. Middleton, *The Remains of Ancient Rome*, II, p. 10 and I, Fig. 2, p. 43.

5. Middleton, *Ancient Rome*, pp. 36, 38, 311; Middleton, *Remains*, II, pp. 91, 92; William J. Anderson and R. Phené Spiers, *The Architecture of Greece & Rome*, pp. 170–171; Marion E. Blake, *Ancient Roman Construction From The Prehistoric Period To Augustus*, p. 65.

6. Middleton, *Remains*, pp. 2, 3, 6, 7, 10–12, 18, 36, 37, 97, 113–114, 123–125, 135, 143, 150, 162, 167–168, 171–172, 174–175, 194, 210, 221, 245; Middleton, *Ancient Rome*, pp. 19, 21–22, 141, 160, 162, 187, 210, 353, 368.

7. Middleton, *Ancient Rome*, pp. 38–39, and Fig. 3, p. 39.

8. Arranged through the courtesy and facilities of Dr. Howard Cox, Moravian Theological Seminary.

9. Cf. Vitruvius, VII.iv and V.x; R. Savignac and G. Horsfield, 'Le Temple de Ramm', *RB*, XLIV (1935), pp. 252–253, 257–258; James L. Kelso *et al.*, 'Excavations at New Testament Jericho . . . ', *AASOR*, XXIX–XXX (1955), p. 9; N. C. Debevoise, 'The Origin of Decorative Stucco', *AJA*, 45 (1941), p. 54; Nelson Glueck, *The Other Side of The Jordan*, p. 168; G. and A. Horsfield, 'Sela-Petra . . . ', *QDAP*, VII (1938), pp. 20–21, 24, 25; M. Abel, 'Le Monument Funéraire Peint d'El'Bared', *RB* III (1906), pp. 591, 598 ff.

10. Moore, Frank G., *The Roman's World*, pp. 323 ff., and Nelson Glueck, 'A Nabataean Mural Painting', *BASOR*, 141 (1956), pp. 12–23 and elsewhere.

11. Caskey, L. D., *Catalogue of Greek & Roman Sculpture . . .* , pp. 133–135.

12. *Idem*, p. 142, INV. 01.8190.

13. A torso of Alexander the Great as Herakles-Dionysos, found at Delos, now in the Mykonos Museum, attributed to the school of Scopas—so A. N. Oikonomides, 'Notes On Portraits of Alexander The Great', *Athene*, XXIII, 1, pp. 29–30 and Fig. 9, p. 27.

14. Moore, *op. cit.*, p. 119.

15. *Idem*, p. 127; Peter Hommel, *Studien zu den römischen Figurengiebeln der Kaiserzeit*, p. 18.

16. Bieber, Margarete, *The History of The Greek and Roman Theater*, pp. 129–134, 216, 226, and Figs. 479a ff., 539; and cf. the formal appearances, as near the Theater of Pompey and the Baths of Caracalla—see J. Henry Middleton, *Ancient Rome in 1885*, pp. 295–296, and 368.

17. Cf. Kammerer, A., *Pétra et la Nabatène*, I, pp. 397–399, 415; Sourdel, Dominique, *Les Cults du Hauran à L'Époque Romaine*, pp. 33, 35, 39, 40–41, 59, 62–64, 68–69, 73; Dalman, Gustaf, *Petra und seine Felsheiligtümer*, pp. 50–51; McCowan, C. C., 'A New Deity in a Jerash Inscription', *JAOS*, 54 (1934), p. 185; Murray, Margaret A., *Petra, The Rock City of Edom*, p. 28; Glueck, Nelson, *The Other Side of The Jordan*, pp. 178, 184, 189; Littmann, E., *Publications of The Princeton University Archaeological Expeditions . . .* , II, IV, A, pp. xxx–xxxi; Clermont-Ganneau, Charles, *Recueil d'Archéologie Orientale*, IV, pp. 397 ff.; Seyrig, Henri, Antiquités Syriennes: Héraclès-Nergal', *Syria*, XXIV (1944–45), pp. 79–80; among others.

NOTES: CHAPTER VIII

1. The use of alphabetical markings on building stones and on ivories to indicate order or position is known from Jerusalem, Samaria, and Megiddo, from earlier periods. See G. R. Driver, *Semitic Writing* (2nd edition; London, 1954), pp. 115–118, and references cited there. See also now A. R. Millard, 'Alphabetic Inscriptions on Ivories from Nimrud', *Iraq* XXIV (1962), pp. 41–51, especially figure 2; and P. J. Parr, 'Recent Discoveries at Petra', *Palestine Exploration Quarterly* 1957, p. 11 f, No. 18 and Plate XIIb. The latter is a Nabataean capital bearing a Greek *rho* as a 'mason's

mark'. There is no evidence one way or another, however, to show whether this is just a mason's mark, or part of a numbering system. In any case, the capital is apparently from a period considerably later than the probable date of the construction of the Theater.

2. Compare Driver, *op. cit.*, p. 117 f.

3. (Footnote #1 on original copy) Berlin, 1891.

4. Aside from the two from Petra mentioned below, *CIS* II, 185, from Boṣra, dates from sometime in the reign of Rabbel II. After A.D. 110: No. 27 in Enno Littmann, *Nabataean Inscriptions* (*Publications of the Princeton University Archaeological Expedition to Syria in 1904–1905 and 1909*, IV–A; Leiden, 1914; hereafter Littmann *Nab. Ins.*), from Deir el-Meshquq, A.D. 124; the dipinto published by M. R. Savignac and G. Horsfield, 'Le Temple de Ramm', *Revue Biblique* (hereafter *RB*) XLIV (1935), pp. 265–268, from Jebel Ramm, A.D. 147; the inscription published by Savignac and M. Abel, 'Inscriptions Nabatéenes', *RB* XIV (1905), pp. 592–596, from Boṣra, A.D. 148; and the Sinai graffito *CIS*, II, 1325, A.D. 150.

5. Dalman, Gustaf, *Neue Petra-Forschungen* (Leipzig, 1912; hereafter Dalman), No. 90.

6. *Corpus Inscriptionum Semiticarum* (*CIS*), II, 349, following the early dating of Starcky *et al.* Compare the views of Albright and Cross in the articles cited in footnotes 11 and 17, below.

7. *CIS*, II, 442.

8. *CIS*, II, 354.

9. Dalman, No. 92; No. 7 in Milik, J. T., 'Nouvelles inscriptions Nabatéenes', *Syria* XXXV (1958), pp. 227–251.

10. *CIS*, II, 350; see also below, footnote 29.

11. Lidzbarski, Mark, *Handbuch der Nordsemitischen Epigraphik*, p. 195; Albright, W. F., 'A Biblical Fragment from the Maccabaean Age: The Nash Papyrus', *Journal of Biblical Literature* (hereafter *JBL*), LVI (1937), p. 167 f.

12. Albright, *ibid.*

13. A communication of Starcky, J., and J. T. Milik in *RB*, LXIV (1957), p. 223 f.

14. *Op. cit.*, p. 195 f.

15. Cantineau, Jean, *Le Nabatéen* (Paris, 1930), I, pp. 27–36.

16. *Op. cit.*

17. Cross, F. M., Jr., 'The Oldest Manuscripts from Qumran', *JBL* LXXIV (1955), pp. 147–172, especially 160–162.

18. Starcky, Jean, 'Inscriptions archaïques de Palmyre', in *Studi Orientalistici in onore di Giorgio Levi della Vida*, (Rome, 1956), II, 509–529. See especially the chart on p. 522. See also by the same author, 'Un contrat Nabatéen sur papyrus', *RB*, LXI (1954), pp. 161–181 and plates.

19. No. 2 in Littmann, Enno, *Semitic Inscriptions* (*Publications of an American Archaeological Expedition to Syria in 1899–1900*, IV; New York, 1904; not to be confused with the volume by the same author, *Nabataean Inscriptions*, for which see footnote 4, above) (hereafter Littmann *Sem. Ins.*); from Siʿ.

20. Which might be explained by the form of the letter, *per se.*

21. Littmann, *Sem. Ins.*, No. 2.

22. Aṣlaḥ and Rabbel (see footnotes 5 and 6, above); also the Tell esh-Shugafiye (Wadi Temilât) inscription published by Clermont-Ganneau in *Recherches d'archéologie orientale*, VIII (1919), pp. 229–257; dated probably 47 B.C.

23. Littmann, *Sem. Ins.*, Nos. 2 and 1.

24. Euting, Julius, *Nabatäische Inschriften aus Arabien* (Berlin, 1885; hereafter Euting *Nab. Ins.*), No. 1 (= *CIS*, II, 332).

25. Published in *Recherches d'archéologie orientale*, VIII (1919), p. 144.

26. *CIS*, II, 160.

27. Euting, *Nab. Ins.*, Nos, 26 and 27 (= *CIS* II, 223 and 224); A. Jaussen and M. R. Savignac, *Mission archéologique en Arabie*, I, Nos. 22 and 38.

28. *CIS*, II, 174; Dussaud, R., and Macler, F., *Voyage archéologique au Safa et dans le Djebel ed-Drûz* (Paris, 1901), No. 36.

29. Milik, J. T., *op. cit.*, No. 7. It is noteworthy that all the instances of *beth* in the 'Great Petra Inscription' of the Wadi Turkhman tomb façade are 'cursive' forms; even the one instance of the letter in the final position (line 5) is only a diagonal slash. This inscription was conjecturally dated by de Vogüé in *CIS*, II 'a few decades' before the turn of the era. This dating is almost certainly much too early, and most scholars would now date it sometime within the first century A.D.

30. *CIS*, II, 174 (Boṣra, A.D. 50); Dussaud and Macler, *op. cit.*, no. 36 (Imṭan, A.D. 93); Euting, *Nab. Ins.*, Nos. 4, 5, 9, and 16 (all from el-Ḥejr from the reign of Aretas IV). The inscriptions from 'Abdeh published by Jaussen, Savignac, and Vincent in *RB* (N.S.) II (1905), pp. 238ff. are problematical. No. 2 is dated to A.D. 203/4 (= 99 of the era of Boṣra); the others are undated, but the script appears comparable. The classic form of the *beth* appears in both final and initial position in the undated material, which is quite exceptional if the inscriptions are all generally contemporaneous. These inscriptions also display other peculiarities: an instance of the letter *he* in what appears to be a Jewish hand, alongside regular Nabataean forms of the letter; and an apparent confusion of the regular *taw* form and the later form of the *ḥeth*, if the name (or word) which begins Nos. 2 and 3 is the same, and accurately copied.

31. The Syllaeus inscription (see footnote 25, above); see also Littmann, *Sem. Ins.*, No. 2 (and No. 1?).

32. Littmann, *Nab. Ins.*, No. 101 (Ḥauran, 29/30 A.D.); *CIS*, II, 170 (?) (Hebran, 47 A.D.); Milik, *op. cit.*, No. 5 (Mu 'arribah, in the Ḥauran, 48 A.D.); *CIS*, II, 182 (Salḥad, A.D. 56); all these from the Ḥauran region. Also: M. R. Savignac, 'Le sanctuaire d'Allat à Iram', *RB* XLII (1933), 405–422 (Jebel Ramm, 70 A.D.); Dalman No. 92 (Petra, 76–105

A.D.); Milik, *op. cit.*, No. 1 (= *CIS* II, 184–183; Salḥad, 95 A.D.); Dussaud and Macler, *op. cit.*, No. 62 (Tell el-Ghâriye, in the Ḥauran, A.D. 96). The Syllaeus inscription may suggest that the form had a cursive origin, if the traditional account of the carving of the inscription (by one ignorant of Nabataean, from a copy in Syllaeus' own hand) is correct.

33. Savignac, M. R., 'Le sanctuaire . . . ' (see above, footnote 32; one example of the older form occurs alongside the examples of the later form; Jebel Ramm, A.D. 70); Milik, *op. cit.*, Nos. 7 (Petra, A.D. 70–106) and 2 (provenance unknown, A.D. 75); Littmann *Nab. Ins.*, No. 2 (Umm es-Surah, A.D. 71/72); Euting, *Nab. Ins.*, Nos. 27 and 28 (el-Ḥejr, 73 and A.D. 75); Kraeling, C. H., *Gerasa, City of the Decapolis* (New Haven, 1938), p. 371 f. (A.D. 90); Dussaud and Macler, *op. cit.*, No. 36 (Imṭan, A.D. 93); *CIS*, II, 161 (Dumeir, A.D. 95).

34. Savignac and Horsfield, *op. cit.* (Jebel Ramm, A.D. 147); Savignac and Abel, *op. cit.* (Boṣra, A.D. 148); compare *CIS*, II, 1325 (Sinai, A.D. 150).

35. Dalman, nos, 31, 58, 70; *CIS*, II, 394 (?) and 461 (?); none are dated.

36. *CIS*, II, 488. Not dated.

37. Euting, *Sinaïtische Inschriften*, Nos. 202, 363, 426. None dated.

38. Compare *CIS*, II, 444 and 454. Neither inscription is dated, and in neither is the letter identified by the editors. Both seem quite late. It is possible that this particular drum in the Theater remains is of a later date than the rest of the material, perhaps used in repair of the colonnade. But this does not seem probable.

39. Savignac, M. R., and Starcky, J., 'Une inscription Nabatéene provenant du Djôf', *RB*, LXIV (1957), 196–217 (A.D. 44) (?); Milik, *op. cit.*, Nos. 2 (provenance unknown, A.D. 75) and 1 (= *CIS*, II, 184–183); Salḥad, A.D. 95; Savignac and Abel, *op. cit.* (Boṣra, A.D. 148); *CIS*, II, 963 (Sinai, 204 or A.D. 211); Jaussen and Savignac, *op. cit.*, II, No. 368. Compare also the undated Sinai graffiti in Euting, *Sinaïtische Inschriften*, Nos. 542 and 580. The papyrus contract published by Starcky (see above, footnote 18) suggests that the later form of the *samekh* may be due to cursive influence.

40. *CIS*, II, 160.

41. Euting, *Nab. Ins.*, Nos. 4, 5, 8, 9, 10, 15, 16.

42. *Ibid.*, Nos. 23 (A.D. 49), 24 (A.D. 51), 27 (A.D. 73); Jaussen and Savignac, *op. cit.*, I, Nos. 38 (A.D. 64) and 22 (A.D. 75/76).

43. Littmann, *Nab. Ins.*, Nos. 23 (Salḥad, A.D. 66); and 27 (Deir el-Meshquq, A.D. 124); Savignac and Abel, *op. cit.* (Boṣra, A.D. 148).

44. Dalman No. 92; Milik, *op. cit.*, No. 7. Both datable only in the reign of Rabbel II (A.D. 70–106).

45. Dalman, *passim; CIS*, II, Nos. 349 ff. *passim*.

46. Euting. *Sinaïtische Inschriften*, Nos. 116, 205, 206, 210, 397, 438, 492, 531, 560.

47. *CIS*, II, 174 (Boṣra, A.D. 50); Dussaud and Macler, *op. cit.*, No. 62 (Tell el-Ghâriye, A.D. 96); Littmann, *Sem. Ins.*, No. 58 (undated).

48. *Recherches d'archéologie orientale*, VIII (1919), p. 144 f. (9 B.C.).

49. Milik, *op. cit.*, No. 7 (A.D. 70–106).

50. Euting, *Nab. Ins.*, Nos. 3 (B.C. 1), 7 (A.D. 16), 15 (A.D. 36); the numeral in No. 25 (A.D. 57) is unclear. Compare also *CIS* II, 161 (Dumeir, A.D. 95) and Euting, *Sinaïtische Inschriften*, No. 463 (A.D. 189).

NOTES: CHAPTER IX

1. Kelso, James L. and D. C. Baramki, 'Excavations at New Testament Jericho and Khirbet En–Nitla', *Annual of the American Schools of Oriental Research.* XXIX–XXX (1955), p. 25.

2. *Idem.* p, 30.

3. Hamilton, R. W. 'Excavations against the North Wall Jerusalem', *Quarterly of the Department of Antiquities in Palestine.* X (1941), Fig. 14, Nos. 3, 7.
Crowfoot, J. W. and G. M. Fitzgerald, 'Excavations in the Tyropoeon Valley, Jerusalem. *Palestine Exploration Fund Annual*, V (1929), Plate XIII, No. 9.
Kelso, James L. and D. C. Baramki, *op. cit.*, Plate XIII, No. X122.
Murray, Margaret A. and J. C. Ellis, *A Street in Petra*, London, 1940. Plate XXX, Nos. 102, 103, 104.
Crowfoot, J. W. *et al.*, *The Objects from Samaria*, London, 1957. Figs. 71, Nos. 6 and 72, No. 14.
Pritchard, James B., 'The Excavation at Herodian Jericho, 1951', *Annual of the American Schools of Oriental Research*, XXXII–XXXIII (1958). Plates 58, Nos. 3 and 59, No. 1.

4. Hammond, P. C., *A Study of Nabataean Pottery*, unpublished dissertation, Yale University, 1957.

5. Pritchard, James B., *op. cit.*, Plate 51, Nos. 1–5. Cf. these for examples of this type of decoration of sherds from N. T. Jericho.

6. de Vaux, R., O.P. and A. M. Steve, O.P., Fouilles à Qaryet El-'Enab, Abu Gosh, Palestine. Ecole Biblique et Archéologique Française, Etudes Archéologiques, Paris, 1950, pp. 20, 21, 22.

7. Cf. an example from the lower Byzantine level at the Tyropoeon Valley, Crowfoot, J. W. 'Excavations in the Tyropoeon Valley, Jerusalem, 1927', *Palestine Exploration Fund Annual*, V, Plate XIII, No. 35, and p. 74.

8. Cf. Kelso, James L., *op. cit.*, p. 30 and Plate 25, No. A412.

9. Parallels to all of these types of handles are to be found in Murray, M. A. and J. C. Ellis, *A Street in Petra*, Plate X.

10. Cf. Kelso, James L., *op. cit.*, pp. 24 f.

11. Cf. Hammond, P. C., *op. cit.*, Murray, M. A. and J. C. Ellis, *op. cit.*, Plates IX, Nos. 14, 15, 18, 27; X, No. 35; XXVIII, No. 77. Fig. 1, p. 32.

12. Cf. Hammond, P. C. *op. cit.* and 'A Classification of Nabataean Fine Ware', *American Journal of Archaeology*, 66 (1962), pp. 169–180, where a number of parallels in form are noted from Kh. Qumran, N. Wall of Jerusalem, Ophel. Gerasa and 'West Slope Ware', under Class 1.2(b), 2(c), 3(c), the type series of our sherds.

13. Kelso, James L., *op. cit.*, p. 32 and Plate 32, No. Y14.

14. Crowfoot, J. W., *op. cit.*, Plate XIII, No. 21.

15. Cf., de Vaux, R., O.P., *Revue Biblique*, LVII, p. 429; LX, pp. 104, 541, 543, 551, Fig. 4; LXI, pp. 228, 231–234—first century A.D.

16. Horsfield, G. and A., 'Sela-Petra, The Rock, of Edom and Nabatene', *Quarterly of the Department of Antiquities in Palestine.* IX (1941), p. 144, Plate XXI, No. 161.

17. Murray, Margaret and J. C. Ellis. *op. cit.*, Plate XXXVI, No. 16.

18. Stillwell, Richard, Editor. *Antioch-on-the-Orontes III. The Excavations 1937–39*, Princeton, 1941, p. 65.

19. Hamilton, R. W., *op. cit.* Fig. 23, No. 19 and p. 45.

20. Crowfoot, J. W., *op. cit.*, Plate XVII, Nos. 8, 9, 20.

21. Horsefield, G. and A., *op. cit.*, No. 45, p. 122; Plate XI, No. 45.

22. *Idem*, No. 42, p. 122; Plate XI, No. 42.

23. Murray, Margaret A. and J. C. Ellis, *op. cit.*, Plate XXXVI, No. 15.

24. Horsfield, G. and A. *op. cit.*, No. 419, p. 195; Plate XLIV, No. 419.

25. Murray, Margaret A. and J. C. Ellis., *op. cit.*, Plate XXXVI, No. 17.

SELECTED BIBLIOGRAPHY

Abel, M., 'Le Monument Funéraire Peint d'El-Bared', *Revue Biblique* (*RB*), III (1906), pp 587–591.

Allbricci, Anna, 'L'Orchestra Dipinta del Theatro Erodiano di 'Caesarea Maritima''', *Bollettino d'Arte*, IV (October–December 1962).

Amiran, D. H. Kallner—, 'A Revised Earth-Quake Catalogue of Palestine', *Israel Exploration Journal*, I–II (1950–51).

Anderson, William J. and R. P. Spiers, *The Architecture of Greece and Rome* (2nd ed.). New York: Scribners, 1907.

Bailey, Cyril (ed.). *The Legacy of Rome*. Oxford: Clarendon Press, 1923.

Bertou, Comte Jules de, 'Itinéraire de la Mer Morte à Akaba . . . et retour à Hebron par Petra', *Bulletin de la Société de Géographie*, XI (1839).

Bieber, Margarete, *The History of The Greek and Roman Theater*. Princeton: Princeton University Press, 1961.

Blake, Marion E., *Ancient Roman Construction In Italy From The Prehistoric Period To Augustus*. Washington, D.C.: Carnegie Institution, 1947.

——, *Roman Construction In Italy From Tiberius Through The Flavians*. Washington, D.C.: Carnegie Institution, 1959.

Burckhardt, John L., *Travels In Syria and The Holy Land*. London: John Murray, 1822.

Butler, Howard C., *The Publications of An American Archaeological Expedition To Syria in 1899–1900*. New York: Century Co., 1903.

Brünnow, Rudolf E. and A. v. Domaszewski, *Die Provincia Arabia*, I, II, III. Strassburg: K. Trubner, 1904–05–09.

Caskey, L. D., *Catalogue of Greek and Roman Sculpture*. Cambridge: Harvard Press, 1925.

Castlereagh, Viscount, *A Journey To Damascus Through Egypt, Nubia, Arabia Petraea, Palestine and Syria*, I–II. London: H. Colburn, 1847.

Champdor, Albert, *Les Ruines de Palmyre*. Paris: A Guillot, 1953.

Charleston, R. J., *Roman Pottery*. London: Faber and Faber, 1955.

Conder, C. R., *The Survey of Eastern Palestine*. London: PEF, 1899.

Crowfoot, John W., *et al.*, *Samaria-Sebaste I: The Builders*. London: PEF, 1942.

Dalman, Gustaf, *Petra und seine Felsheiligtümer*. Leipzig: J. C. Hinrich, 1908.

——, 'The Khazneh at Petra', *PEF Annual* (1911). London: Harrison and Sons, 1911.

Daremberg, Charles and E. Saglio (ed.), *Dictionnaire des Antiquités Grecques et Romaines* (*DAGR*). Paris: Hachette, 1900.

Debevoise, Neilson, C., 'The Origin of Decorative Stucco', *American Journal of Archaeology* (*AJA*), XLV (1941).

Dorpfeld, William and E. Reisch, *Das Griechische Theater*. Athens: Barth and Von Hirst, 1896.

Ehni, Jacques, 'Souvenirs du Mt. Hor et des ruines de Petra', *Le Globe Journal Géographique*, XXXIII, 5th series, V (1894).

Fiechter, Ernst R., *Die Baugeschichtliche Entwicklung des Antiken Theaters*. Munich: Beck, 1914.

Frézouls, Edmond, 'Recherches sur les Théâtres de l'Orient Syrien. I', *Syria*, XXXVI (1959); II. *Syria*, XXXVIII (1961).

Frova, A., 'Gli Scavi ''Della Missione Archeologica Italiana a Caesarea (Israeli)''', *Annuario della Scuola Archeologica di Atene*, XXXIX–XL, n.s., XXIII–XXIV (1961–62).

Ganneau, Charles Clermont-, *Recueil d'Archéologie Orientale*, IV, Paris: E. Leroux. 1901.

Glueck, Nelson. *The Other Side of The Jordan*. New Haven: ASOR, 1952.

——, 'A Nabataean Mural Painting', *Bulletin of The American Schools of Oriental Research* (*BASOR*), 141 (1956).

Hammond, Philip C., 'The Nabataean Bitumen Industry At The Dead Sea', *The Biblical Archaeologist* (*BA*), XXII (1959).

——, 'Pattern Families in Nabataean Painted Ware', *AJA*, 63 (1959).

——, 'A Classification of Nabataean Fine Ware', *AJA*, 66 (1962).

Harding, G. Lankester, *The Antiquities of Jordan*. London: Lutterworth, 1959.

Harsh, Philip W., *A Handbook of Classical Drama*. Stanford: Stanford University Press, 1944.

Hommel, Peter, *Studien zu den römischen Figurengiebeln der Kaiserzeit*. Berlin: G. Mann, 1954.

Horsfield, G. and A., 'Sela-Petra, The Rock, of Edom and Nabatene', *Quarterly of The Department of Antiquities of Palestine (QDAP)*, VII (1938).

———, '... The Finds', *QDAP*, IX (1941).

Kammerer, A., *Pétra et la Nabaètne*, I–II. Paris: Paul Geuthner, 1929–30.

Kelso, James L. and D. C. Baramki, 'Excavations At New Testament Jericho and Khirbet En-Nitla', *Annual*, *ASOR* XXIX–XXX (1955).

Kennedy, Sir Alexander B. W., *Petra, Its History and Monuments*. London: Country Life, 1925.

Kraeling, Carl H. (ed.), *Gerasa. City of The Decapolis*. New Haven: *ASOR*, 1938.

Kinnear, John, *Cairo, Petra and Damascus in 1839*. London: John Murray, 1841.

Lenoire, Paul, *Le Fayoum, le Sinai et Pétra*. Paris: H. Plon, 1872.

Lepik, Wilhelmina, *Mathematical Planning of Ancient Theatres*. Warsaw: 1949.

Littmann, Enno, *Publications of The Princeton University Archaeological Expeditions To Syria in 1904–1905 and 1909. Div. IV, Sec. A (Nabataean Inscriptions)*. Leyden: E. J. Brill, 1914.

Man, August, *Pompeii*. New York: MacMillan, 1907.

McCown, C. C., 'A New Deity in a Jerash Inscription', *Journal of The American Oriental Society*, 54 (1934).

Middleton, J. Henry, *Ancient Rome in 1885*. Edinburgh: Adam and Charles Black, 1885.

———, *The Remains of Ancient Rome*, I–II. London: Adam and Charles Black, 1892.

———, 'Theater', *Encyclopaedia Britannica (EB)*, XXIII, (9th ed.). New York: Allen 1890.

Millard, Alan, 'A Seal From Petra', *PEQ*, 1961.

Moore, Frank G., *The Roman's World*. New York: Columbia University Press, 1936.

Morris, Edward J., *Notes of a Tour Through Turkey, Greece, Egypt, and Arabia Petraea To The Holy Land*, I–II. London: N. Bruce, 1842–3.

Murray, Margaret A., Petra, *The Rock City of Edom*. London: Blackie and Son, 1939.

——— and J. C. Ellis, *A Street In Petra*. London: British School of Archaeology in Egypt, 1940.

Musil, Alois, *Arabia Petraea*, I, II, III. Vienna: A. Holder, 1907–08.

Nicoll, Allardyce, *The Development of The Theatre* London: Harrup, 1927.

Oikonomides, A. N., 'Notes On Portraits of Alexander The Great.' *Athene*, XXII, 1 (1961).

Parr, Peter J., 'Rock Engravings From Petra.' *PEQ* (1960).

Pauly, A. F. von and Georg Wissowa, (ed.), *Real-Encyclopädie*. Stuttgart: J. B. Metzler (X), 1934.

Robertson, D. S., *A Handbook of Greek and Roman Architecture*. (2nd ed.). Cambridge: Harvard University Press, 1954.

Robinson, Edward, *Biblical Researches In Palestine* ... I–II–III. London: John Murray, 1891.

Savignac, R. and G. Horsfield, 'Le Temple de Rassim', *RB*, XLIV (1935).

Schwarz, H. M., *Sicily*. New York: The Studio Publications, 1956.

Seyrig, Henri, 'Antiquités Syriennes: Heracles-Nergal', *Syria*, XXIV (1944–45).

Sourdel, Dominique, *Les Cultes du Hauran à l'Epoque Romaine*. Paris: Paul Geuthner, 1952.

Starcky, Jean, 'The Nabataeans: A Historical Sketch', *BA*, XVIII (1955).

———, and S. Munajjed, *Palmyra*. Damascus: Directorate General of Antiquities, 1948.

Ward, A. W., 'Drama.' *EB* (9th ed.), VII. New York: Henry Allen, 1890.

Wiegand, Theodor, *et al.*, Petra (*Wissenschaftliche Veröffentlichungen des Deutsch-Türk. Denkmalschutz-Kommandos*, 3). Berlin: 1921.

Wilber, Donald, 'The Theater At Daphne', *Antioch On-The-Orontes*, II. Princeton: Princeton University Press, 1938.

Wilson, Eduard L., *In Scripture Lands* ... London: The Religious Tract Society, 1891.

Wright, G. R. H., 'Structure of the Qasr Bint Far'un, A Preliminary Review', *PEQ* (1961).

Other references are also cited in the text.

PLATES

PLATE I

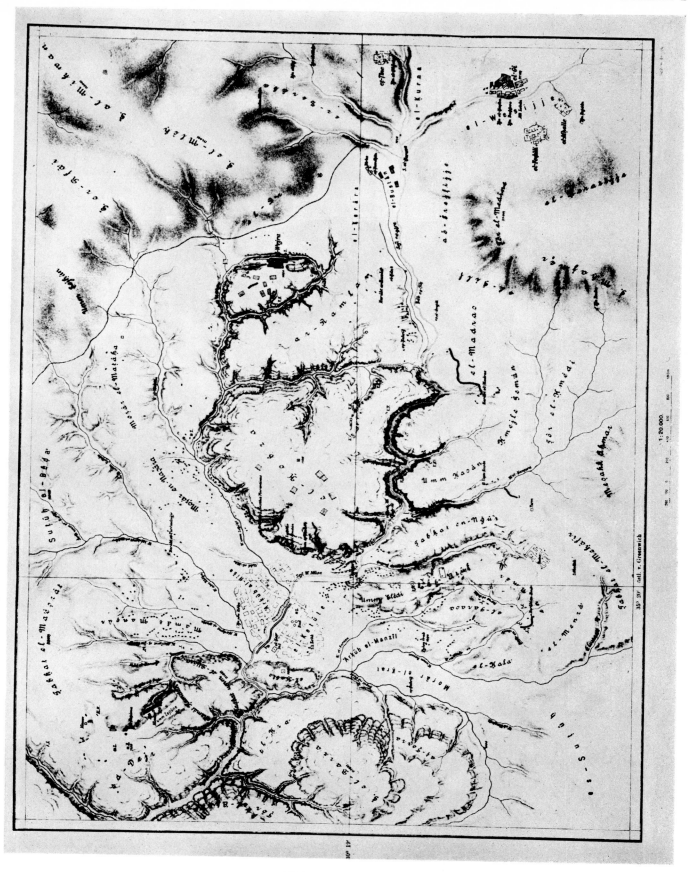

PLAN OF PETRA
Alois Musil, *Arabia Petraea, II, Edom.*

Scale 1:20,000

PLATE II

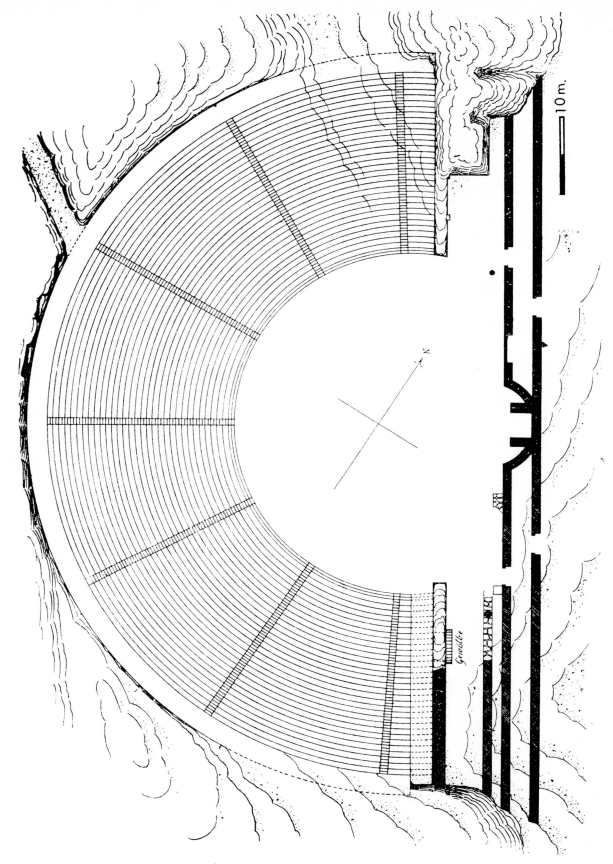

'THE ROMAN THEATER', PETRA

From Theodor Wiegand, *Petra (Wissenschaftliche Veröffentlichungen des Deutsch–*
Türkischen Denkmalschutz–Kommandos, 3).

PLATE III

PETRA: MAIN THEATER 1961-1962

Stratigraphic Analysis

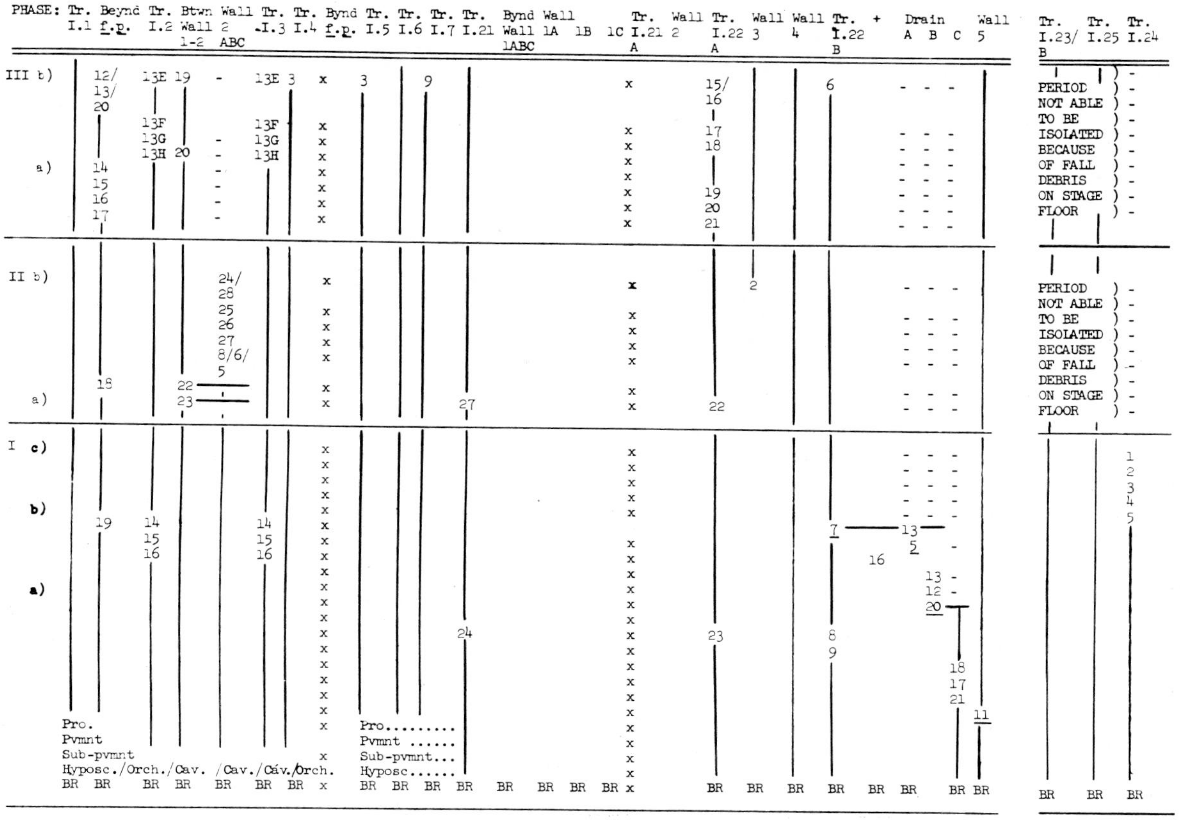

PHASE:	Tr. Beynd I.1 f.p.	Tr. Btwn I.2 Wall 2 1-2 ABC	Wall	Tr. I.3	Tr. Bynd I.4 f.p.	Tr. I.5	Tr. I.6	Tr. I.7	Tr. I.21	Bynd Wall Wall 1A 1B 1C 1ABC	Tr. I.21 A	Wall Tr. 2 I.22 A	Wall Wall Tr. + 3 4 I.22 B	Drain A B C	Wall 5	Tr. Tr. Tr. I.23/ I.25 I.24 B
III b)	12/ 13/ 20	13E 19	-	13E 3	x	3	9				x	15/ 16	6	- - -		PERIOD) - NOT ABLE) -
		13F 13G 13H 20	- - -	13F 13G 13H	x x x						x x x	17 18		- - - - - - - - -		TO BE) - ISOLATED) - BECAUSE) -
a)	14 15 16 17		- - -		x x x x						x x x x	19 20 21		- - - - - - - - -		OF FALL) - DEBRIS) - ON STAGE) - FLOOR) -
II b)			24/ 28 25 26 27 8/6/ 5		x x x x x						x x x x x	2		- - - - - - - - - - - -		PERIOD) - NOT ABLE) - TO BE) - ISOLATED) - BECAUSE) - OF FALL) - DEBRIS) -
a)	18	22 23			x x		27				x x	22		- - - - - -		ON STAGE) - FLOOR) -
I c)					x x x x						x x x x			- - - - - - - - - - - - - - -		1 2 3 4 5
b)	19	14 15 16		14 15 16	x x x x						x x x		7 13 5 16	- - - -		
a)					x x x x		24				x x x x x	23	8 9	13 - 12 - 20 18 17 21	11	
	Pro. Pvmnt Sub-pvmnt Hyposc./Orch./Cav. /Cav./Cav./Orch. BR BR BR BR BR BR BR x				x	Pro......... Pvmnt ...... Sub-pvmnt... Hyposc...... BR BR BR BR		BR BR BR BR x			x x x x x	BR BR BR	BR BR BR	BR BR	BR BR	BR BR

Pro.= Proscenium
Pvmnt = Pavement
Sub-pvmnt = Sub-pavement
Hypos. = Hyposcenium
BR = Bed-Rock

PLATE IV

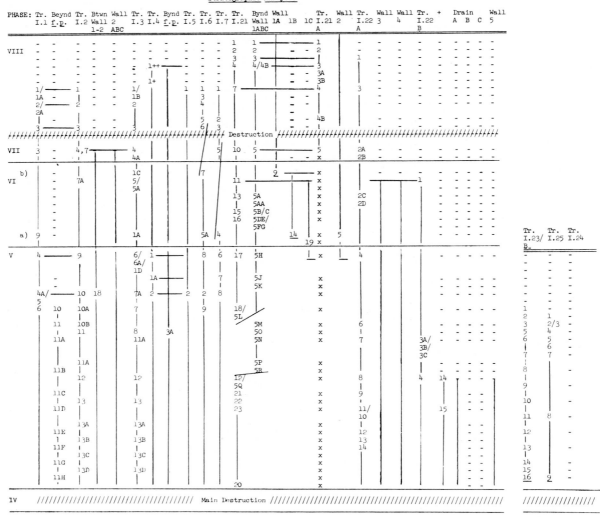

PETRA: MAIN THEATER 1961-1962

Stratigraphic Analysis

PLATE V

1

2

3

PERIOD IIb:
PERIOD OF EARLY RE-USE

1. Triple-faced battered robbery wall, over lower part of *ima cavea*: Wall 2 A–B–C, Trench I.2.

2. Top surface, Wall 2 A–B–C, Trench I.2.

3. Face of Wall 2 A–B–C, Trench I.2, showing rubble build.

4. Face of Wall 2 A–B–C, Trench I.2, from above.

4

PLATE VI

1. Drain in stage pavement, showing also the blocking of Main Door of *scaenae frons*: Period IIb.

2. Drain, showing pavement robbery, with end of drain over exposed *hyposcenium*.

3. *Postscenium* exit, showing rubble blocking (Trench I.22 B (2)).

4. *Postscenium* exit, showing rubble blocking (Trench I.22 B (2)).

PLATE VII

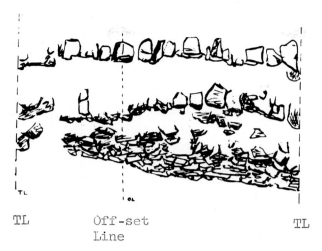

Period IIb: Plan of triple-faced battered robbery wall
(Wall 2 A–B–C, Trench I.2).

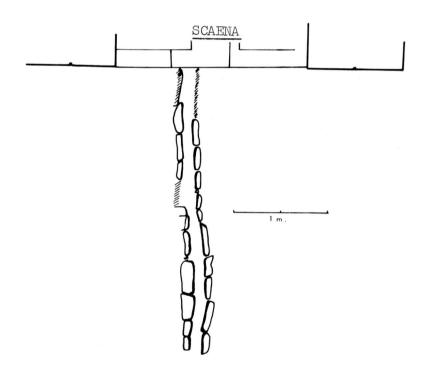

PETRA MAIN THEATER
Trench I.1, Period IIb: stage area intrusive drain cut in pavement.

PLATE VIII

1. Emergence of fall level (Period IV) on stage floor area, looking N.E.
2. Fall level prior to clearance of Period V.
3. Fall level, looking S.

PLATE IX

1. Fall level debris (Period IV), building blocks and architectural pieces.
2. Fall level debris, showing column lines.
3. Fall level debris, column line *in situ*.

PLATE X

1. Period VIb/a: Trench I.1, Wall 1, Main Robbery Wall, showing use of column drums in foundation course, western face.
2. Trench I.21, Wall 1A (VIa) and Wall 1B-C (VIb), western faces.
3. Trench I.3, Main Robbery Wall extension, eastern face (VIa).

PLATE XI

1. Trench I.3, Main Robbery Wall extension, showing line and build, from N; Period VI a/b.
2. Trench I.3, Main Robbery Wall extension, showing build.
3. Trench I.1, Main Robbery Wall extension against eastern face of Wall 1.

PLATE XII

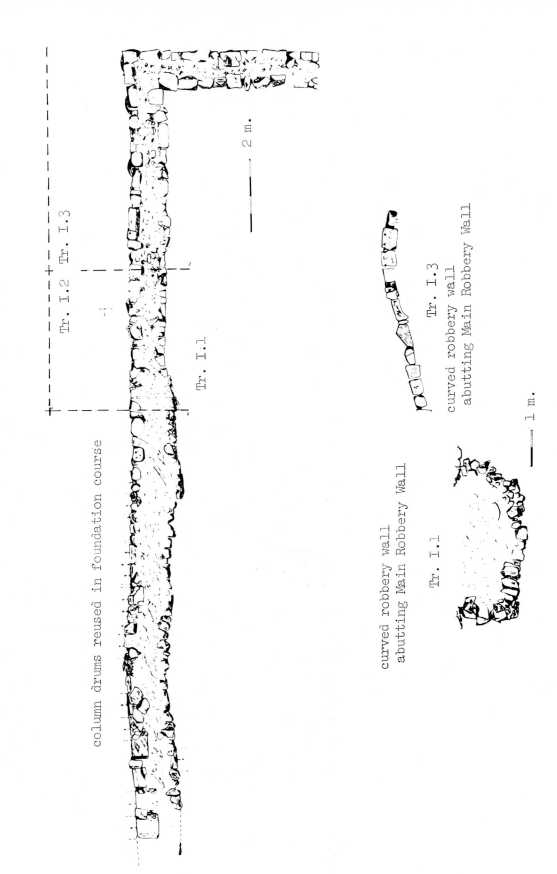

column drums reused in foundation course

Tr. I.2 Tr. I.3

Tr. I.1

2 m.

curved robbery wall
abutting Main Robbery Wall

Tr. I.3

curved robbery wall
abutting Main Robbery Wall

Tr. I.1

1 m.

PERIOD VI a/b : ROBBERY WALLS

PLATE XIII

1. Main theater at Petra, prior to excavations.
2. Theater, following excavations and clearance, 1961.
3. Theater, following excavations and clearance, 1962.

PLATE XIV

1

2

3

4

1. Upper gallery.
2. *Cavea* and stairline.
3. Drain and runnel, gallery of *summa cavea*.
4. *Cavea*, showing natural fissure to NE.

PLATE XV

1. *Cavea*, showing elevation and SW blockade area.
2. *Praecinctio* drain canal, *media cavea*.
3. *Praecinctio* drain canal, with cover for stair, *media cavea*.

PLATE XVI

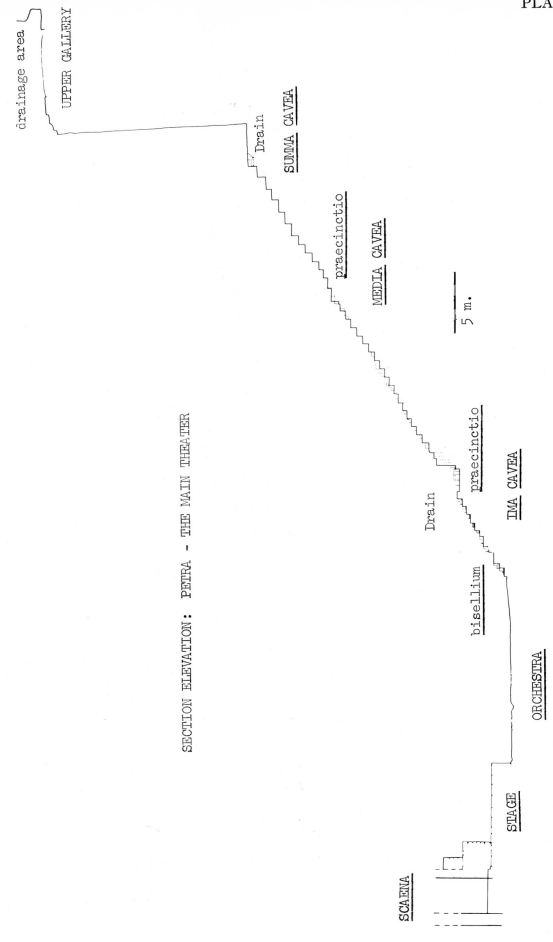

SECTION ELEVATION: PETRA - THE MAIN THEATER

PLATE XVII

1. Blockade walls, NW sector, looking toward SW.
2. Blockade walls, NW sector, looking toward E.
3. *Vomitorium dextrum* and *aditus*, with *tribunalia* platform.
4. *Vomitorium sinistrum*.

PLATE XVIII

1. *Vomitorium dextrum, tribunalia* area.
2. *Aditus* stairway.
3. *Tribunalia* (?) chair, stone cut; *scaena* wall at central door.
4. Tie-davit, *orchestra* floor.

PLATE XIX

1. Wall at central stairway of *cavea, orchestra* (Period 1c), with triple-faced rebuilt wall behind (Period II).
2. Wall after excavation and clearance.
3. Detail, plastered face of wall.
4. Detail, rear of wall.

PLATE XX

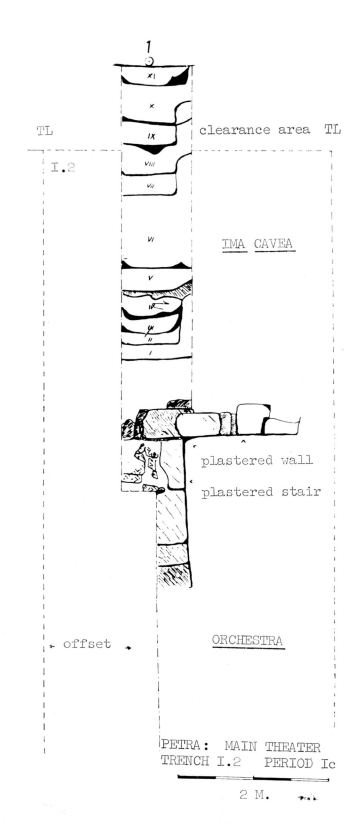

PETRA: MAIN THEATER
TRENCH I.2   PERIOD Ic

2 M.

PLATE XXI

1

2

3

4

1. *Orchestra*-stage area, showing tie-davits.
2. False door, *orchestra* floor.
3. Canal in *orchestra* floor, entering below stage front (Period Ia).
4. Detail of canal.

PLATE XXII

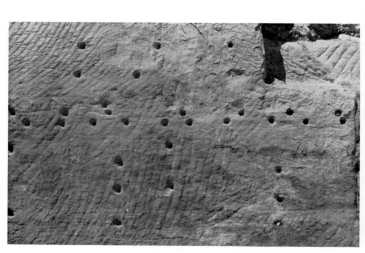

1. *Vomitorium dextrum*, looking SW.
2. *Vomitorium sinistrum*.
3. East wall, *vomitorium dextrum*, showing plugging holes for facing.
4. *Postscenium* exit and exit of *vomitorium sinistrum*.

PLATE XXIII

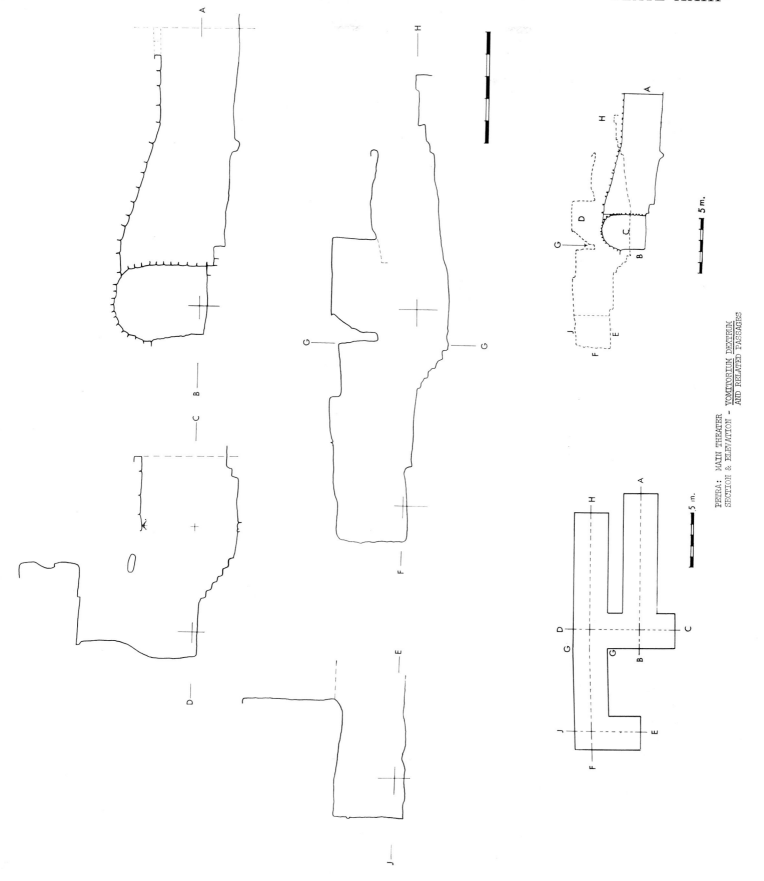

PETRA: MAIN THEATER
SECTION & ELEVATION — VOMITORIUM DEXTRUM
AND RELATED PASSAGES

5 m.

5 m.

PLATE XXIV

1. *Orchestra*-stage area, general view.
2. Sliding door in rear of central niche, stage front (Period Ib), from above.
3. Sliding door from rear; note re-used orthostats used to cover (Period Ic).
4. Stage front, showing curved niche block (Period Ib) and filling (Period Ic).

PLATE XXV

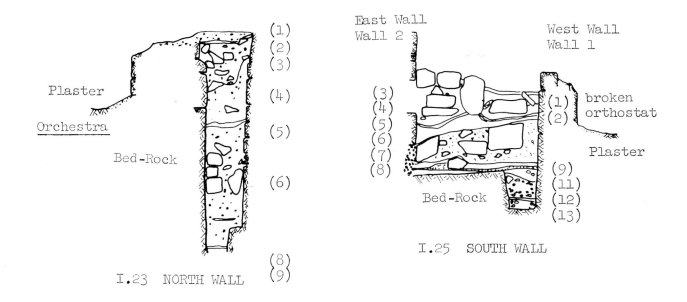

(1)
(2)
(3)

Plaster

(4)

Orchestra

(5)

Bed-Rock

(6)

(8)
(9)

I.23   NORTH WALL

East Wall
Wall 2   West Wall
                               Wall 1

(3)   (1) broken
(4)   (2) orthostat
(5)
(6)
(7)   Plaster
(8)
                                   (9)
Bed-Rock   (11)
                                   (12)
                                   (13)

I.25   SOUTH WALL

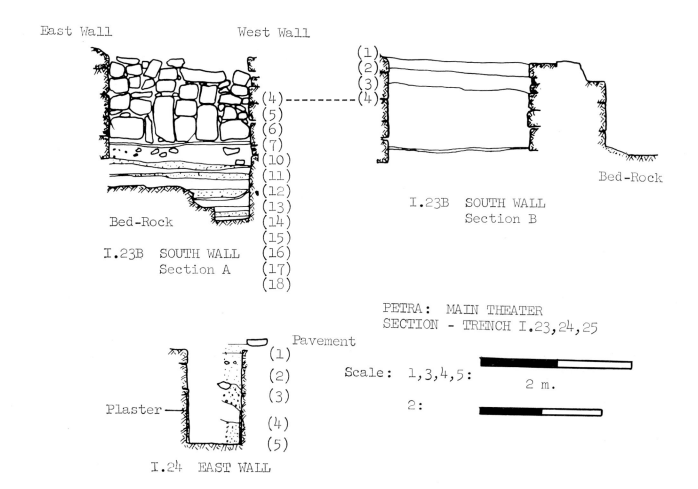

East Wall   West Wall

(1)
(2)
(3)
(4)
(5)
(6)
(7)
(10)
(11)
(12)
Bed-Rock   (13)
                (14)
                (15)
I.23B   SOUTH WALL   (16)
        Section A   (17)
                      (18)

(1)
(2)
(3)
(4)

I.23B   SOUTH WALL
        Section B

Bed-Rock

PETRA: MAIN THEATER
SECTION - TRENCH I.23,24,25

Pavement
(1)

(2)

Plaster   (3)

(4)

(5)

I.24   EAST WALL

Scale: 1,3,4,5:

2 m.

2:

PLATE XXVI

1. Stage front, showing curved niche (Period Ib) and filling (Period Ic), with plaster (Period Ic).
2. Stage front, central niche, showing canal, orthostats (Period Ia) and plastering (Period Ic).
3. Stage front, showing stair additions (Period Ic) and general face.
4. Stair addition, standard support, and fill (Period Ic).

PLATE XXVII

1

2

3

4

1. Side niche, showing original plaster and orthostat (Period Ia).
2. Detail, side niche.
3. Stage front and floor areas.
4. Stage area, showing *hyposcenium* lines and reconstructions.

PLATE XXVIII

1. Detail, stage paving and base facings, south end.
2. South end of stage area, showing paving and *versura* outset.
3. Detail, stage floor make-up, showing bed-rock piers, supporting arches, sub-paving, and paving.
4. Detail, showing bed-rock piers and supporting arches.

PLATE XXIX

1

2

3

4

1. Sub-stage area, showing bed-rock and masonry sub-structure.
2. Bed-rock pier, with impost cuts for supporting arches of paving.
3. Supporting arches, sub-paving, and paving, NE end of stage.
4. General view of stage area, showing curtain slots.

PLATE XXX

1. Curtain slot, NE end of stage area.
2. *Versura*, NE end of stage area.
3. General view, *orchestra*, stage, and *scaena*, after excavation and clearance, showing lines of walls.
4. General view, showing line of *scaena* wall, looking NE.

PLATE XXXI

1. Pavement, *postscenium* exit, NE end.
2. Detail, *postscenium* pavement.
3. *Scaenae frons*, first and second podia, as excavated.
4. General view, *scaena* wall lines from rear.

PLATE XXXII

1

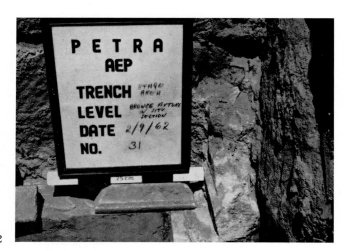

2

3

4

1. Building block from *scaena* wall, with marble plug and fragment of bronze fixture, *in situ*.
2. Detail, method of affixing marble facing (bronze fixture not shown).
3. Detail, base facings *in situ*.
4. *Postscenium* exit, NE, with end of *scaena frons* wall (right).

PLATE XXXIII

1. Stairway to platform of blockade structure, NE end of *scaena*.
2. General view, NE end of *scaenae frons* wall, showing end, *versura*, and *postscenium* exit from *vomitorium sinistrum*.
3. Detail, end of column drum (marl), showing tie-hole and Nabataean mason's marks.
4. Detail, as # 3 above.

9

PLATE XXXIV

1. Columns in fall (Period IV), near Main Door of *scaenae frons*.
2. Column in fall, showing alignment of single column with consecutive mason's marks.
3. Bases, marl.
4. Capital, Nabataean (see also # 3 above).

PLATE XXXV

1. Cornice block, Type 'A'.
2. Cornice block, Type 'B'.
3. Cornice block, Type 'C'.
4. Cornice block, Type 'D'.

PLATE XXXVI

1. Cornice corner block, Type '1'.
2. Cornice corner block, Type '2'; note mason's planning lines.
3. Cornice corner block, Type '3'.
4. Cornice corner block, detail of #2 above, showing mason's correction of planning lines.

PLATE XXXVII

1. Dentil element, corner block.
2. Dentil element, corner block.
3. 'Ionic' type capital, front view.
4. 'Ionic' type capital, side view.

PLATE XXXVIII

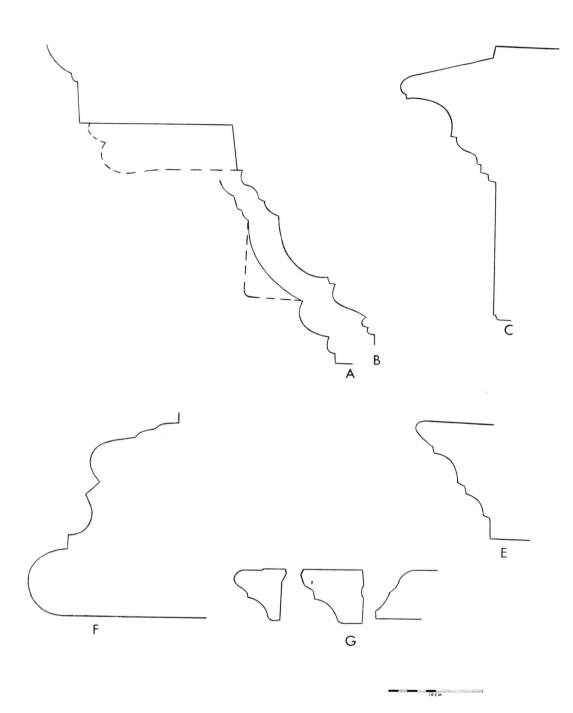

A — Profile, lower cornice, dentil element.
B — Profile, upper cornice, modillion and disc element.
C — Profile, frieze element.
E — Profile, frieze (?) element.
F — Profile, typical column base treatment.
G — Profiles, marble moldings.

PLATE XXXIX

1. Figurine fragment (AEP 61 S, # 27): fragment of female head, hair curled; part of typical female fertility (?) figurine, usually seated on block; back of head; molded red ware.
   So also similar fragment (AEP 62 S, # 246), not shown; back of head of similar figurine; poorly made, molded red ware.
2. Figurine fragment (AEP 61 S, # 22): fragment of horse figurine, front left side, with trappings and rosette ornament; molded red ware; locus–Trench I.3 (6).
   So also similar fragment (AEP 62 S, # 207); left rear half, showing saddle; molded red ware; locus–I.22 B (4).
3. Block with painted plaster, architectural motif; found in fall debris.
4. Molding varieties, all white marble.
5. Tile fragment; crude light red ware.
6. Tile fragments, as # 5 above.

PLATE XL

1. Clearing of torso of Hercules statue (AEP 1961, # 100), *in situ*, curtain slot, NE end of stage area.
2. Torso *in situ*.
3. Torso, showing lion's skin over left arm.
4. Detail, head of draped lion's skin.

PLATE XLI

1

2

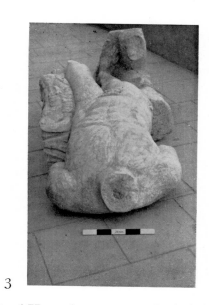

3

4

1. Fragment of Hercules torso, end of club and support, right side of statue (1962), found in curtain slot.
2. Torso, front view.
3. Torso, showing remains of bronze tie-pin for head.
4. Fragment of second Hercules statue (SW end of stage area), discovered in clearance operations of Department of Antiquities prior to 1961 excavations.

PLATE XLII

1. Upper gallery drain area, showing filled drain.
2. *Orchestra* area drain, under *finitio proscenii*.
3. *Postscenium* drain, showing canal type drain (Drain 'A') of Period Ic.
4. *Postscenium* drain, showing canal type drain (Drain 'A') and pressure pipe drain (Drain 'B')
   in situ (Periods Ic and Ib).

PLATE XLIII

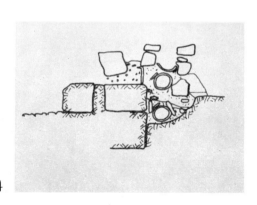

1. Foundation wall: Drain system ('C', 'B', 'A') beyond *postscenium* wall, NE end of theater.
2. Drains 'C', 'B', and 'A' *in situ* in wall section.
3. Pressure pipe section, *in situ*, Drain 'A' (Period Ia).
4. Section Drawing: Trench I.22 B, Drains 'C', 'B', and 'A' (top to bottom).

PLATE XLIV

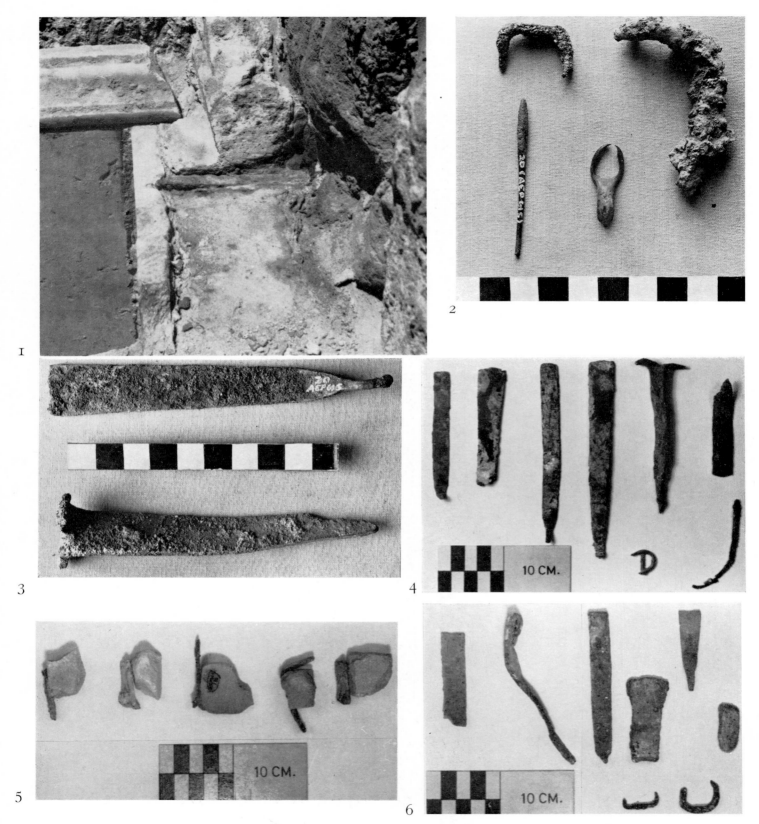

1. Marble molding, plaster backing, bronze fixture, plug, and marble facing, *in situ, scaenae frons*.
2. Miscellaneous metal fixtures and clamps, bronze and iron.
3. Bronze fixtures.
4. Bronze fixtures found in fall and other levels, for affixing marble facings.
5. Marble plugs used to hold bronze fixtures in face of *scaena* and *vomitoria* walls (for affixing marble facings); found in fall and other levels, with fragments of bronze fixtures; indicate method of securing fixtures.
6. Bronze fixture fragments and small bronze clamps found in fall and other levels.

PLATE XLV

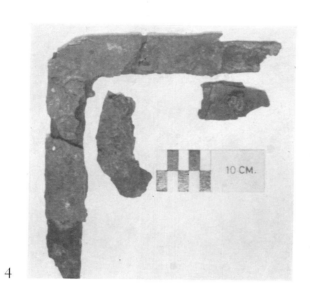

1. Iron nail fragments found in fall and other levels, used for keying plaster.
2. Iron nail fragments, as (1) above.
3. Iron nail.
4. Iron clamp, clamp for architectural pieces (?): AEP # 156.
5. Iron nail.
6. Fragments of iron clamp, note rivets: AEP # 147.

PLATE XLVI

20 CM.

20 CM.

Fragments of Greek inscriptions.

PLATE XLVII

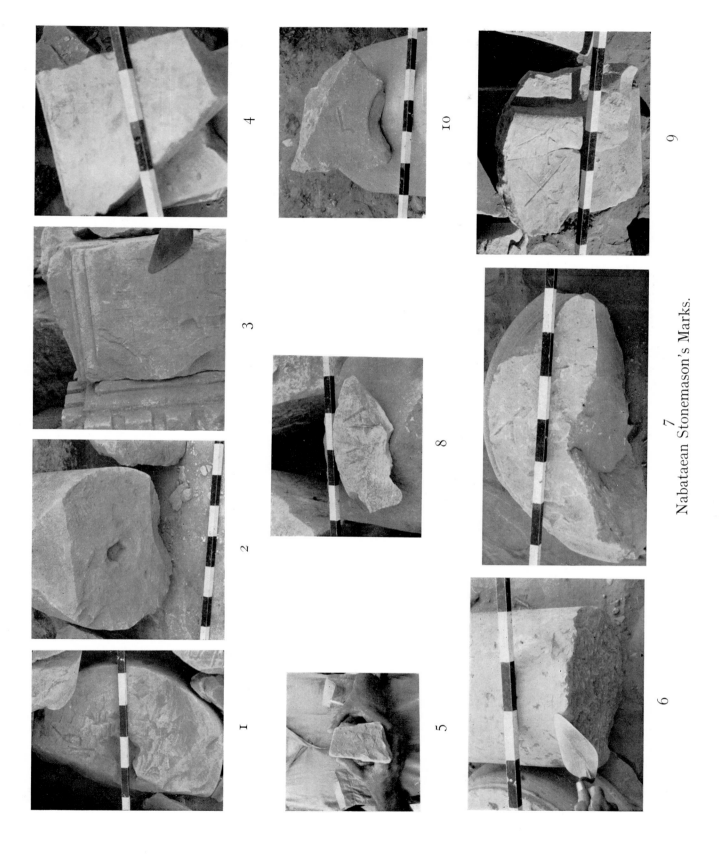

Nabataean Stonemason's Marks.

PLATE XLVIII

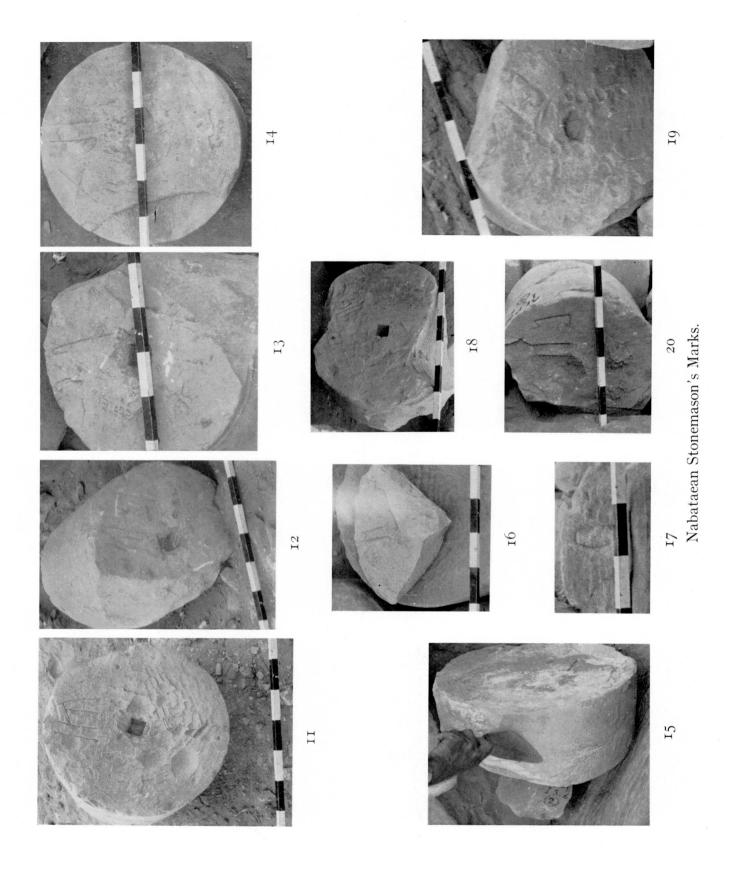

Nabataean Stonemason's Marks.

PLATE XLIX

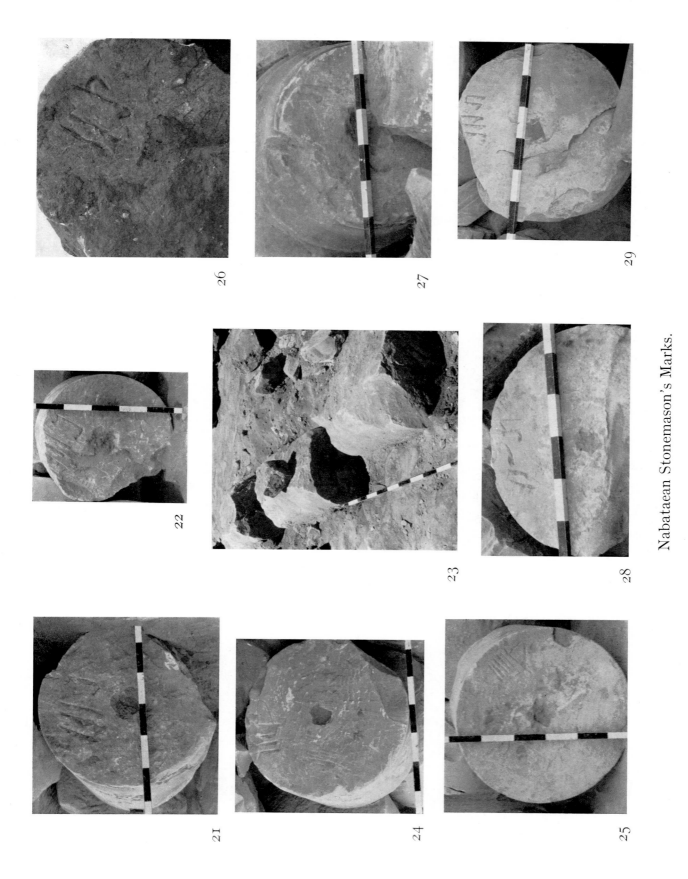

Nabataean Stonemason's Marks.

PLATE L

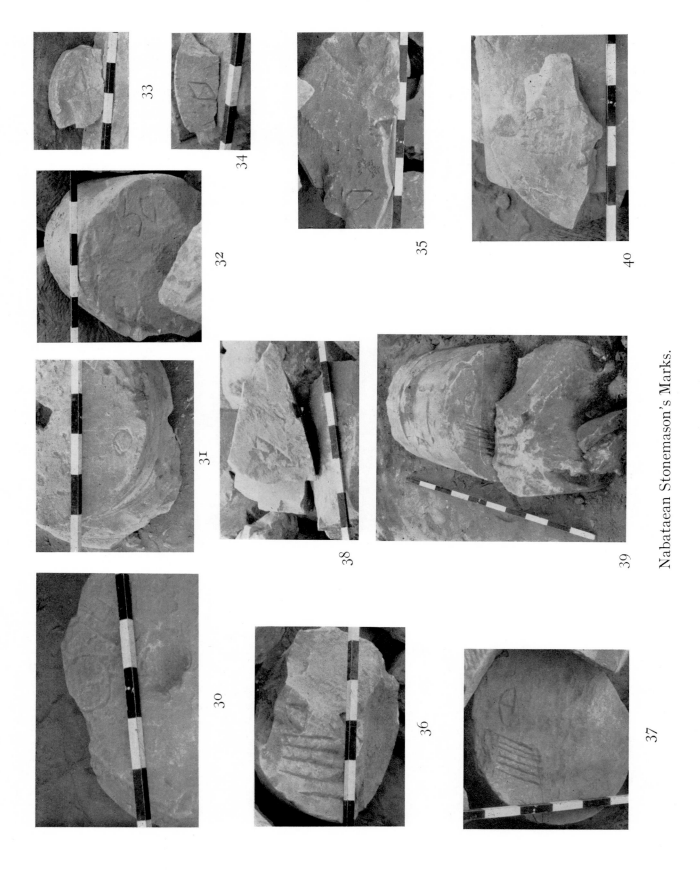

Nabataean Stonemason's Marks.

POTTERY

PLATE LI

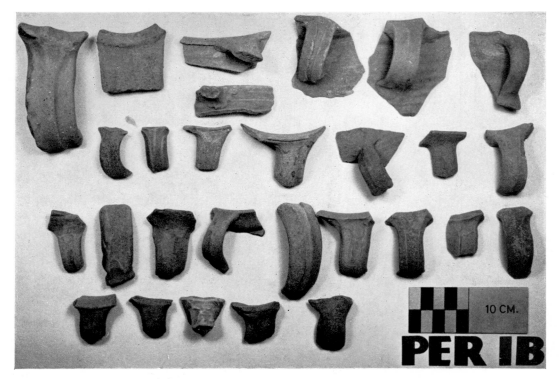

1. Typical handles and rim types; sealed deposit, canal (Trench I.1 (19)); Period Ib.

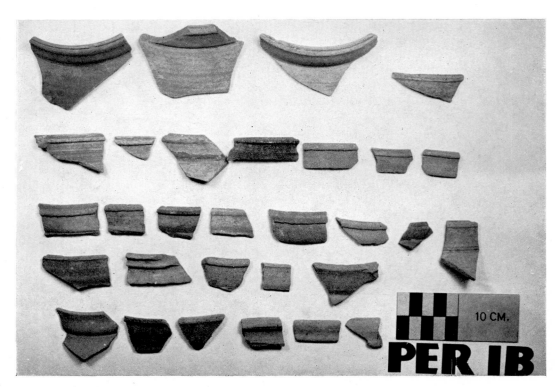

2. Typical rim types; sealed deposit, canal (Trench I.1 (19)); Period Ib.

PLATE LII

2. Typical body and base sherd types; mainly cooking pots; 'marl' combed ware sherd (row 2, right side).

5. Cooking pot rim and handle.

4. Reconstructed cooking pot.

1 Typical handle and rim sherds.

10 CM.

3. Typical rim sherds.

Pottery from sealed deposit, stage front niche (Trench I.24), Period Ic.

PLATE LIII

1. Typical sherds, Period V fall debris and fall cover; cement coated examples represent fill used in original build of Theater (Period Ia); note Nabataean plain wares, ribbed body fragments, bases, and Nabataean lamp fragments; all to be assigned to Period Ia.

2. Typical sherds, Period V fall debris and fall cover; cement coated examples represent fill used in original build of Theater (Period Ia).

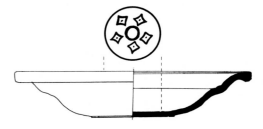

3b. Reconstruction of 5a; c. 1:4.

3a. Late Roman A ware plate; hard fine red ware, red matte finish, incised decoration, interior; Period V.

PLATE LIV

1. Typical sherds, Period V fall debris and fall cover; note Nabataean fine thin ware fragments, painted and plain; later material involved; mixture, Period V and Period Ia.

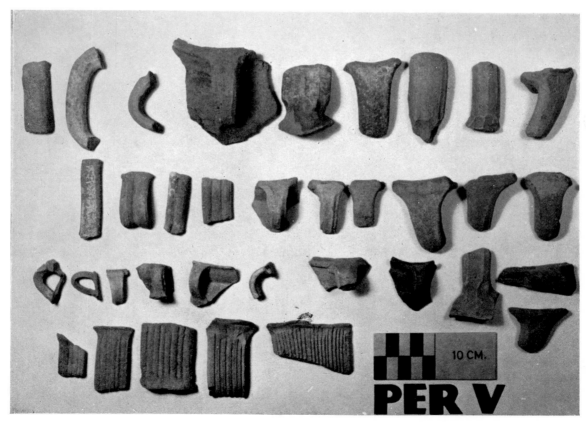

2. Typical handles, fall cover; Period V.

PLATE LV

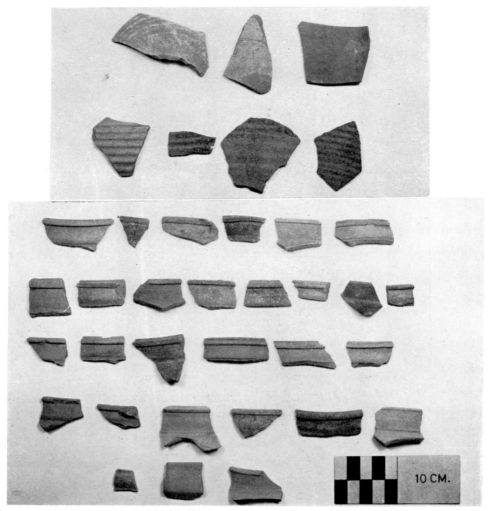

1. Typical body and rim sherds; Period III.

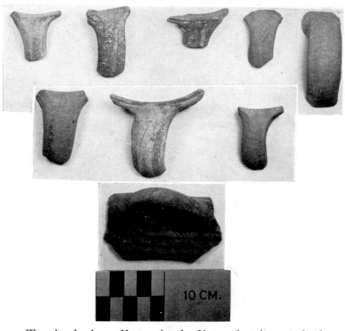

2. Typical handles, including horizontal loop handle; Period III.

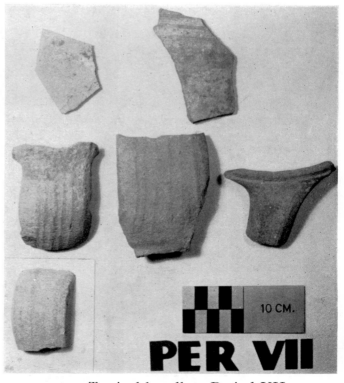

3. Typical handles; Period VII.

PLATE LVI

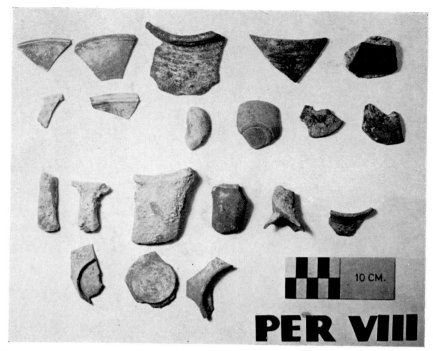

1. Typical sherds; cement coated fragments represent fill from original build, Period Ia, mixed with cover from later fall between Periods VII and VIII; mixture, Periods Ia and VII/VIII.

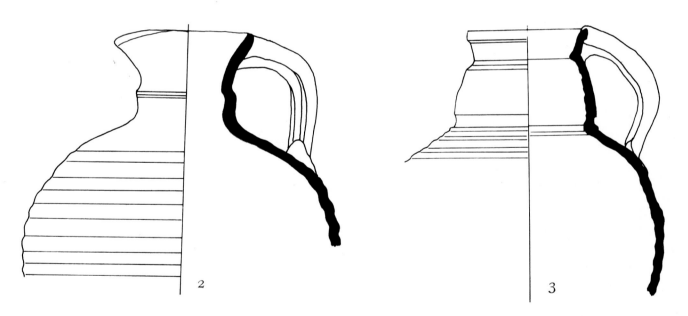

2. Pinched lip pitcher fragment; poorly turned, poorly fired, crude red ware, black slip; worn; ribbed; base missing; found on surface, Trench I.3, level (4/4A); Period VII.

3. Jug fragment; same poor quality of turning and firing as 2 above; crude red ware, poor black slip; slightly ribbed; base missing; same locus as 2; Period VII.

PLATE LVII: Typical Sherds, sealed deposit, canal (Trench I.1 (19)) Period Ib.

1. Cooking pot; red ware; beige slip.
2. Cooking pot; red ware; beige slip.
3. Cooking pot; red ware; tan slip.
4. Cooking pot; red ware.
5. Cooking pot; red ware; beige slip.
6. Cooking pot; red ware; beige slip.
7. Cooking pot; tan ware; tan slip.
8. Cooking pot; red ware.
9. Cooking pot; red ware.
10. Cooking pot; tan ware; beige slip.
11. Cooking pot; tan ware; beige slip.
12. Cooking pot; red ware; beige slip.
13. Cooking pot; red ware; beige slip.
14. Cooking pot; black ware; black slip.
15. Cooking pot; red ware; tan slip.
16. Cooking pot; red ware; black slip.
17. Cooking pot; red ware; dark tan slip (poor).
18. Cooking pot; red ware; black slip.
19. Cooking pot; light tan ware; tan slip.
20. Cooking pot; red ware.
21. Cooking pot; red ware; beige slip.
22. Cooking pot; tan ware; tan slip.
23. Cooking pot; light tan ware.
24. Cooking pot; red ware; beige slip.
25. Cooking pot; red ware; black slip.
26. Bowl; thin red ware; impressed design, exterior.
27. Bowl; thin, coarse Nabataean tan ware.
28. Bowl; coarse, common red ware; shaved rim.
29. Bowl; tan ware; tan slip.

PLATE LVII

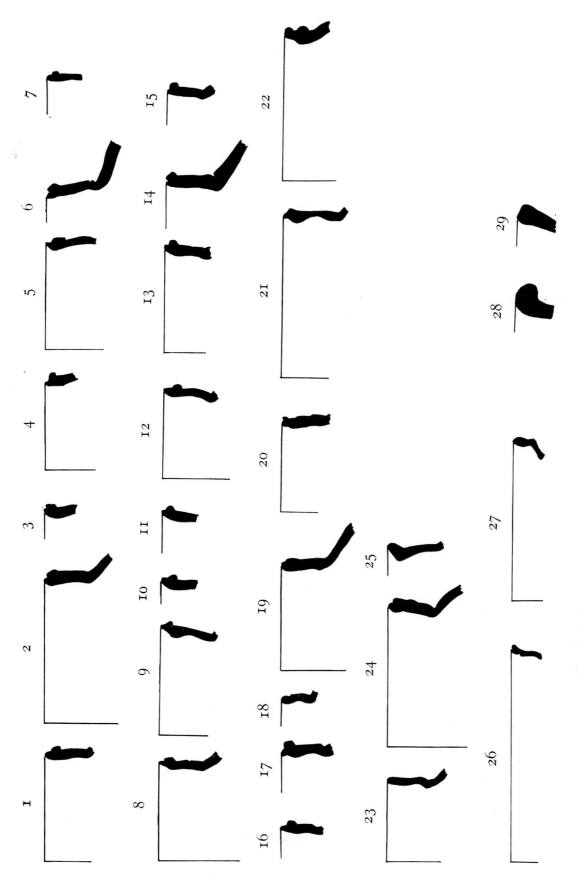

Typical Sherds, sealed deposit, canal (Trench I.1 (19)) Period Ib.

PLATE LVIII: Typical Sherds, sealed deposit, stage niche (Trench I.24); Period Ic.

1. Cooking pot; thin, coarse, light red ware [I.24(3)].
2. Cooking pot; red, coarse, gritty ware; light beige slip.
3. Cooking pot; red, coarse, gritty ware; light beige slip.
4. Cooking pot; red ware; light tan slip.
5. Cooking pot; red, coarse, gritty ware; light beige slip.
6. Cooking pot; red, coarse, gritty ware; light beige slip.
7. Cooking pot; red-tan, coarse, gritty ware; light beige slip.
8. Cooking pot; red, coarse, gritty ware; tan slip.
9. Cooking pot; red, coarse, gritty ware; poor light beige slip.
10. Cooking pot; light red, coarse ware. [I.24(3)]
11. Cooking pot; red, coarse ware; light beige slip.
12. Cooking pot; red, coarse, gritty ware; light beige slip.
13. Cooking pot; red, coarse, gritty ware; light beige slip.
14. Cooking pot; red, coarse, gritty ware; light beige slip.
15. Cooking pot; red, coarse, gritty ware; light beige slip.
16. Cooking pot; red, coarse, gritty ware; light beige slip.
17. Cooking pot; red, coarse, gritty ware; light beige slip.
18. Cooking pot; red, coarse, gritty ware; light beige slip.
19. Cooking pot; red fine ware.
20. Cooking pot; red, coarse, gritty ware; light beige slip.
21. Cooking pot; red coarse ware.
22. Cooking pot; red, coarse, gritty ware; tan slip.
23. Cooking pot; red, coarse, gritty ware; light tan slip.

PLATE LVIII

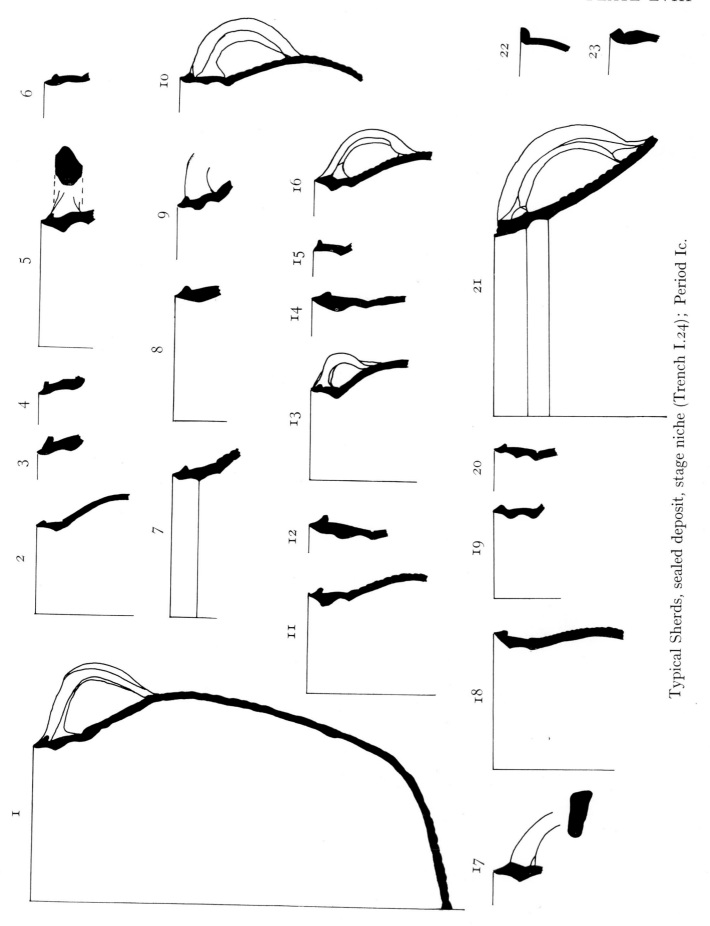

Typical Sherds, sealed deposit, stage niche (Trench I.24); Period Ic.

PLATE LIX: Typical Sherds, sealed deposit, stage niche (Trench I.24); Period Ic.

1. Bowl; coarse, thin, tan ware; tan slip on exterior of rim.
2. Bowl; coarse, thin, red ware; light tan slip on exterior of rim.
3. Bowl; coarse, thin, red ware.
4. Bowl; coarse, thin, red ware; very poor; red (?) slip on exterior.
5. Bowl; coarse, thin, tan-red ware.
6. Bowl; coarse, thin, red ware; light tan slip on exterior rim.
7. Bowl; coarse, thin, red-tan ware.
8. Bowl; coarse, tan, heavier ware.
9. Bowl; coarse, red, heavier ware; red (?) slip.
10. Bowl; coarse, red, heavier ware.
11. Bowl; coarse, black-tan, heavier ware; light tan slip on exterior rim.
12. Bowl; fine, thin, tan ware.
13. Bowl; hard, fine, thin, red, black-painted ware.
14. Bowl; hard, fine, thin, red, black-painted ware.
15. Bowl; hard, fine, thin, red, black-painted ware.
16. Bowl; hard, fine, thin, red, black-painted ware.
17. Bowl; hard, fine, thin, red, black-painted ware.
18. Open bowl; fine, thin, red ware; dark red wash on interior and exterior.
19. Open bowl; fine, thin, red ware; dark red wash on interior and exterior.
20. Open bowl; coarse, red, heavier ware; light tan slip.
21. Open bowl; coarse, red, thin ware; light red slip on interior and exterior; skewed handle.
22. Open bowl; coarse, heavy, red common ware; light tan slip on interior and exterior.
23. Open bowl; coarse, heavy, red common ware; light red-tan slip on interior and exterior.
24. Jug; coarse, red ware; light tan slip; pinched spout.
25. Jug; coarse red ware; pinched spout; combed strap handle.
26. Jug; coarse red ware; light beige slip.

PLATE LIX

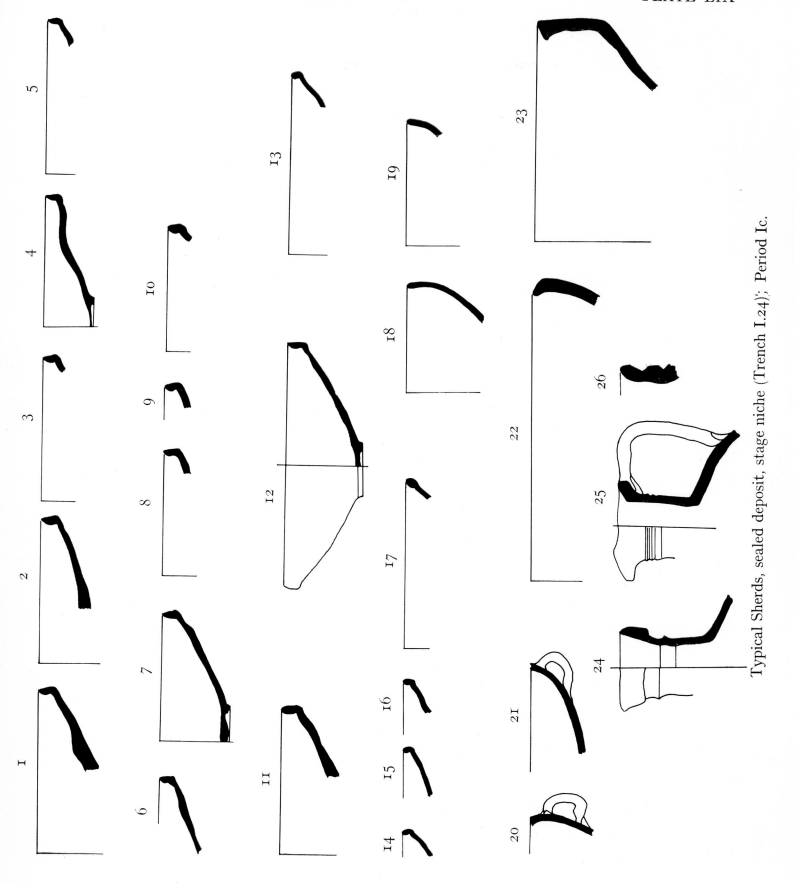

Typical Sherds, sealed deposit, stage niche (Trench I.24); Period Ic.